Maine de Biran's
Of Immediate Apperception

Also Available from Bloomsbury

The Relationship between the Physical and the Moral in Man, Maine de Biran
Bergson: Thinking Beyond the Human Condition, Keith Ansell Pearson
Félix Ravaisson: Selected Essays, Mark Sinclair

Maine de Biran's

Of Immediate Apperception

With an Introduction by Alessandra Aloisi and Marco Piazza
Translated by Mark Sinclair

Edited by Alessandra Aloisi, Marco Piazza
and Mark Sinclair

BLOOMSBURY ACADEMIC
LONDON • NEW YORK • OXFORD • NEW DELHI • SYDNEY

BLOOMSBURY ACADEMIC
Bloomsbury Publishing Plc
50 Bedford Square, London, WC1B 3DP, UK
1385 Broadway, New York, NY 10018, USA
29 Earlsfort Terrace, Dublin 2, Ireland

BLOOMSBURY, BLOOMSBURY ACADEMIC and the Diana logo are trademarks of
Bloomsbury Publishing Plc

First published in Great Britain 2020
This paperback edition published in 2021

Copyright © Alessandra Aloisi, Marco Piazza and Mark Sinclair, 2020

Alessandra Aloisi, Marco Piazza and Mark Sinclair have asserted their right under the
Copyright, Designs and Patents Act, 1988, to be identified as Editors of this work.

Translation by Mark Sinclair 2020

Cover design by Peter Somogyi

All rights reserved. No part of this publication may be reproduced or transmitted
in any form or by any means, electronic or mechanical, including photocopying, recording,
or any information storage or retrieval system, without prior permission in writing
from the publishers.

Bloomsbury Publishing Plc does not have any control over, or responsibility for, any
third-party websites referred to or in this book. All internet addresses given in this
book were correct at the time of going to press. The author and publisher
regret any inconvenience caused if addresses have changed or sites have
ceased to exist, but can accept no responsibility for any such changes.

A catalogue record for this book is available from the British Library.

A catalog record for this book is available from the Library of Congress.

ISBN: HB: 978-1-3500-8619-7
PB: 978-1-3502-6230-0
ePDF: 978-1-3500-8620-3
eBook: 978-1-3500-8621-0

Typeset by RefineCatch Limited, Bungay, Suffolk

To find out more about our authors and books visit www.bloomsbury.com
and sign up for our newsletters.

Contents

Introduction, by Alessandra Aloisi and Marco Piazza — 1

Of Immediate Apperception — 21

First Part
State of the question as considered in various systems of speculative philosophy; discussion of the terms in which it is proposed, and of the means that we have to establish their sense

Introduction — 27
§1 *Examination of Philosophical Doctrines That Take the Terms Proper to the Operations of Intelligence in an Abstract or General Sense, and That Misapprehend the Character of the Primitive Facts of Inner Sense* — 31
§2 *Of a Natural Foundation of the Science of Principles in Locke's Theory; how the Characteristics and Nature of the Primitive Facts can be Distinguished within it* — 44
§3 *Glance at Abstract Metaphysical Systems: How They Indicate the Goal of the Science of Principles in Going Beyond It* — 49
§4 *Our Method in the Search for Primitive Facts of Inner Sense. General Plan and Division of the Work* — 58

Second Part
Of the Grounds of a Real Division of the Primitive Facts of Human Nature

First Section
Division of Affective Sensibility from Voluntary Mobility

Chapter I: Of Elementary Affection, and How its Characteristics and Signs can be Determined in the Mind and Physiology of Man — 71
§1 *Division of Affective Sensibility and Voluntary Motility* — 71
§2 *Diverse Signs Through Which We can Know a Purely Affective state* — 73

1. Immediate Affections Constitutive of Organic Temperament	73
2. Of the Signs of an Affective State During Sleep	75
3. Other Signs of a Purely Affective State in Cases of Mental Alienation	77

Chapter II: On the Power of *Efforts* or *Will*: Origin, Grounds and Primitive Conditions of Immediate Apperception — 83

§1 — 83

1. Systems that Deny the Identity of the Motor and Thinking Principles — 85
2. Systems that Attribute to the Principles of Thought the Movements of all the Organs without Distinction — 87
3. System that Re-establishes the Identity of the Thinking and Motor Principle — 89

§2 *On the Natural System Capable of Determining the Characteristics of Primitive Will as well as the Ground of Personality and Immediate Apperception* — 94

§3 *Hypothesis on the Origin of Personality and Internal Immediate Apperception* — 98

§4 *Responses to a Few Questions Subordinate to the Preceding One on the Origin of Immediate Apperception and the Principle of Causality, etc.* — 101

§5 *On Immediate Apperception in the Relation to the Feeling of the Co-existence of One's Own Body and to the Circumscription or Distinction of its Different Parts* — 106

Second Section

Chapter III: Application of the Preceding to an *Analysis* or Division of the External *Senses* — 117

§1 *Sensory or Passive System* — 119

§2 *Perceptive or Intuitive (mixed) System* — 121

1. Visual Perception — 123
2. Perceptibility of hearing and touch — 127

§3 *Active Apperceptive System* — 129

1. External apperceptions, functions of active touch — 129
2. How Internal, Mediate Apperception is Grounded on the Active Exercise of Hearing and the Voice in Particular — 135

Chapter IV: Of the Relations of Apperception, Intuition and
Feeling with Notions and Ideas   141

§1 *Intellectual Apperceptive System*   144

    1. Relation of Apperception to the Notions and Ideas
Associated to Signs and, first of all, to the Institution
of these Signs Themselves   144

    2. Relation of Apperception to the Sign of Recall or Memory   147

§2 *Intellectual Intuitive System*   152

§3 *Intellectual Sensory System. Relation of Feeling and the
Passions of the Moral Being with Ideas*   157

Notes   165

Index   173

Introduction

Alessandra Aloisi and Marco Piazza[*]

The philosophy of Maine de Biran was appreciated during his life only by a small circle of intellectuals and acquaintances. After his death, however, his thought soon became an inescapable reference for French philosophy during the nineteenth and the twentieth centuries. Victor Cousin had an ambiguous and contradictory relationship to Maine de Biran's philosophy. While reducing him to the role of a pioneer of eclecticism, he nevertheless claims that it is with this philosopher that France, which had not produced a great thinker since Malebranche, returned to metaphysics.[i] Less than a century later, this judgement was echoed by Henri Bergson, who also believed that 'the philosophy from which the whole of French spiritualism derives is the doctrine of Maine de Biran'.[ii] Félix Ravaisson, whose philosophy of habit owes so much to that of Maine de Biran, had previously recognized the 'philosophical regeneration' brought about by his philosophy of the will, seeing it as an essential contribution to the rise of the 'spiritualist positivism' that he promoted.[iii] Much later, French phenomenology, in particular the work of Michel Henry and Paul Ricoeur, would stress the originality of Biran's conception of the body, which, as *le corps propre* [lived body], is placed at the core of the experience of self-apperception.[iv] The essay 'Of Immediate Apperception', written in 1807 but unpublished until 1841, in many ways presents the core of Maine de Biran's philosophy of *effort*, with which he breaks away from Condillac and the Ideological school.

Maine de Biran's life and works

Marie-François-Pierre Gontier already known by his contemporaries as Maine de Biran (a name that he gave to himself), always maintained a strong link with his homeland, the Périgord, where he was born in 1766. He left at nineteen years of age to join Louis XVI's Life Guards, the most aristocratic unit of the Household Cavalry. His life actually took place entirely between the French capital and the chateau of Grateloup, near Bergerac, which he inherited from his maternal family. The philosopher loved to take refuge in this chateau, in search of an alternative to the solicitations of Parisian life, and sometimes in order to escape political upheavals.

As a monarchist and a conservative, Maine de Biran was forced to retreat to his chateau nestled in the French countryside when his unit was dissolved in 1792. Three years later, he went back to his social life in the capital and started an administrative and political career, firstly on a departmental level and then on a national level. He was part of the legislative body until the end of the Empire. After the Restoration, he obtained positions of great prestige, such as that of Deputy of the Dordogne and Councillor of State.

His political career, however, was subject several times to the repercussions of the great upheavals that marked France at the beginning of the nineteenth century. In March 1815, less than a year after the restoration of Louis XVIII, which had given Maine de Biran the coveted position of Quaestor of the Chamber of Deputies, Napoleon's return and the beginning of the Hundred Days forced him to take refuge in Grateloup once again.

For him, the country house was not only a refuge from the possible retaliations of political adversaries. It also represented an antidote to the city's frenetic lifestyle, which distracted him from what he took to be the highest occupation of all: philosophical meditation. In fact, Maine de Biran's whole existence is marked by a schism between the social and the private dimensions of his life, between the space of the *dehors* (the 'outside') and that of the *dedans* (the 'inside'), between the external man and the inner one.[v]

His life was restless, divided between the ambition of the politician and that of the philosopher. As a philosopher, his aspiration was to found a 'science of man' capable of accounting for our inner life and our nature as active subjects who have to face bodily resistance. This science could not be conducted with the abstract and imprecise instruments of Condillac's 'sensationism', which represented man as essentially passive in considering ideas and therefore our own volitions as mere transformations of sensations.

Precisely because he lived the everyday tension between the power of thought and concentration, on the one hand, and external resistance and habits, on the other, Maine de Biran elaborated a philosophy of *effort* that was intended to define an individuality that resists the passions and finds its propulsive centre in the will.[vi] That resistance coming from the body and over which the self –

apperceiving itself as an *a priori* fact of consciousness, and therefore precisely as effort – tries to have power, is the same resistance which Maine de Biran experienced in his life and that he never stopped fighting, often in vain, passing from states of quasi-mystical exaltation to moments of despair and depression.

Biran's somewhat unstable and emotionally fragile character did not prevent him from leading serious and in-depth philosophical studies. As Jules Gérard wrote in the second half of the nineteenth century, Maine de Biran was a philosopher not only by vocation, but 'above all by temperament, or better, almost by necessity of nature'.[vii] During his life, Maine de Biran published very little,[viii] but obsessively returned to what he had already written in order to improve it. According to some critics, over the years he did nothing but work on the same book, which can be considered the work of a lifetime, recasting parts of his previous works. Maine de Biran, in the words of Henri Gouhier, is 'the author of a single book' which, however, 'he never wrote'.[ix] However, the assiduous correspondence with well-known scientists and philosophers of the period (such as Ampère and Destutt de Tracy),[x] as well as a series of prize-winning essays, stand as a proof of his intense philosophical activity.[xi]

The essay on 'immediate apperception'

The occasion for writing the essay entitled *De l'aperception immédiate* came to Maine de Biran in the form of a competition announced in October 1805 by the Académie des Sciences et Belles-Lettres of Berlin. The announcement called for participants to deepen the study of the 'primitive facts of the inner sense', which the academy considered not to have been sufficiently examined in studies on the origin and reality of human knowledge, and posed the following questions: Are there internal immediate apperceptions? In what way does internal apperception differ from intuition? What differences are there between intuition, sensation and feeling? What are the relations of these acts or states of mind with notions and ideas?

Reading the announcement, Maine de Biran could not help but immediately feel a deep affinity between these questions and the problems at the centre of his philosophical interests at the time. As he recalled years later, in the *Nouveaux essais d'anthropologie*, the announcement published by the Academy of Berlin had almost seemed to be addressed directly to him.[xii] He had already written essays that had been awarded prizes in 1802 and 1805 by the Institut de France and were devoted, respectively, to the *Influence of Habit on the Faculty of Thinking* and to the correct analysis or 'decomposition' of thinking (*Mémoire sur la décomposition de la pensée*). The 1805 essay, which marked the emergence of Biran's own philosophy and his break with the Ideological school, already contained all the answers to the questions raised by the Berlin Academy. Maine de Biran rewrote and reformulated his thoughts in March 1807, and he wrote a new essay for the Berlin competition. The essay won only second prize (the first prize went to a follower of Schelling, David Theodor August Suabedissen), but this was accompanied by a medal and an offer to publish the work, which Maine de Biran did not accept. Like most of his work, the essay on immediate apperception, the themes of which he never stopped returning to, was not published until after his death.[xiii]

The main problem that Maine de Biran addressed in this essay was, in accordance with the terms of the announcement, to demonstrate the existence of immediate internal apperception and to explain what it consists of. This also gave him the opportunity to clarify the meaning of a few terms – such as 'apperception', 'intuition', 'sensation', 'perception' and 'feeling' – which, although indicating clearly defined states of the soul, had been, in his view, confused by philosophers or considered only in the abstract.

After situating his work in relation to the main philosophical systems – Condillac and *Idéologie*, on the one hand, Locke and the metaphysical systems of Descartes, Leibniz and Kant, on the other[xiv] – Maine de Biran laid out the plan of his work and described his chosen method, founded on a real, not abstract, analysis of sensation. His point of departure was to distance himself from the French followers of Condillac's sensationism, and to clarify, first, that sensation *is not* simple. On the contrary, it is made up of two elements: the personal form, which derives from the *self* (unique, indivisible and always identical to itself), and the matter, provided by what is called *affection* (constantly variable and multiple). These two elements, the nature of each of which is examined more closely later in the essay, are always present in a 'complete sensation'. Their relationship, however, can change in an inversely proportional way, according to an infinity of degrees and different gradations, on the basis of which the affective component can increase or decrease while the feeling of the self is correspondingly obscured or revitalized. Indeed, the self is not always associated in the same way with the various modifications of sensibility; it does not always adhere to it with the same 'intimacy'. There are sensible and affective modes that the self is not a part of at all, or is a part of in only an obscure way.

According to Maine de Biran, in order to demonstrate the existence of immediate internal apperception, one needs to start from a study of these simple affections, which can be traced solely to matter. Indeed, if immediate internal apperception, as he proves later in the essay, is original from the perspective of conscious acts, there is, nevertheless, inside and outside of us, a purely sensible life that temporally precedes the appearance of the self and continues to exist, for example, during sleep:

> The human being begins, indeed, to live, to feel, before being capable of knowing his life or of apperceiving his sensation (*vivit et est vitae nescius ipse suae*) [still lives and knows not that he lives]. Even in the full development of all his faculties, when a wholly affective sensibility is carried to the highest tone, the human being feels and lives without apperception of himself or of the impressions that he undergoes; and it is in this sense that his existence can be brought back to the state of native simplicity [...], prior to the birth of the conscious *self*, and which would seem to be the result of all the organic forces that 'conspire and consent' in a common life.[xv]

This form of impersonal and unconscious life, which includes the organic and animal level of existence, necessarily escapes us, but can be studied in its fleeting points of contact with consciousness. Here, Maine de Biran makes a parallel with an astronomic image: the obscure affections situate themselves, so to speak, at the limit of the line that separates the illuminated part of a celestial body from the part in shadow. In order to determine where the circle of light represented by the self and by consciousness begins, one first needs to study the boundary of the shadow zone where the simple affections are found. It will involve, in other words, tracing the 'contours of the shadow in order to know the point at which the light begins' (80).

According to Maine de Biran, an excellent model for understanding the simple affections, stripped of all personal spatial and temporal form, can be found in Condillac. In the *Traité des sensations*, Condillac provides a particularly effective representation of the simple affections. He describes the state in which an animated statue, still lacking a sense of self, is identified with all of its modifications without perceiving them, to the point of becoming one with them.[xvi] Condillac's error, however, was in thinking that repetition and memory were in themselves all that was needed for the statue to learn how to distinguish itself from, as an example of such a modification, the scent of roses. In other words, Condillac did not grasp that the self is something active, and that between *perceiving* and *perceiving of perceiving* there is a jump that any merely repeated experience cannot explain.

All of the appetites, inclinations, determinations and automatisms that we can attribute to the sphere of instinct and habit can be traced to this purely sensible and passive form of existence, which corresponds to Condillac's rose-scented statue. Characteristic of the newborn, this unconscious and impersonal life, of which we have no memory, never leaves us. It is not only observable in cases of somnambulism and mental alienation, or predominant during sleep, when it is manifested through dreams, but it is like a form of background noise that constantly interferes, without our realizing it, in conscious life, determining the emotional undertone of specific objects, places and situations:

> The fugitive modes of such an existence, now happy, now baneful, succeed each other, push each other like mobile waves in the torrent of life. We thereby become, without any other cause than the simple affective dispositions to which any return is forbidden to us, alternatively sad or cheerful, agitated or calm, cold or ardent, timid or courageous, fearful or full of hope. Each age of life, each season of the year, sometimes each of the hours of the day sees the contrast of these intimate modes of our sensory being. 74

This phenomenon, which Maine de Biran calls 'organic refraction' and which in many ways recalls Rousseau's *morale sensitive*, is the reason, without any apparent cause, nature appears to us 'now with a gay and graceful aspect, now covered with a funeral veil' (74). It is also the origin of what we call 'character', which, liberally reformulating Bichat, Biran defines as the 'physiognomy' [*physionomie*] of the organic 'temperament' distinctive to each of us.[xvii] To glean the importance that he attributed to this affective foundation of our existence, determined by corporeity, it is enough to look through the pages of his *Journal*.[xviii]

Once he has thus traced the 'contours of the shadow', Biran moves on to study 'the point at which the light begins'. Alongside the purely affective life, man also knows a life of relation and awareness, founded on perception of the self and one's own existence. The origin of this perception, which coincides with immediate internal apperception, needs to be sought – and this is the great insight that Biran began formulating in 1804 – in the *will*, which is none other than the *felt effort* of muscular contraction. This effort or voluntary movement, which I produce and always feel I can produce not only in relation to external objects but also in regard to my own body, whose organic resistance I perceive, is 'the result of the same effort, which is always available for as long as the state of wakefulness or the individual feeling of my existence remains' (96). This felt effort is the expression of a 'hyperorganic', non-locatable effort that provides us with evidence of the self.

Introduction

In a single move, Maine de Biran re-founds the concept of will (which, as an active, operative, conscious force, needs to be distinguished from desire) and rehabilitates the notion of causality, which derives not from habit and repeated experience (here, the confrontation with Hume is decisive), but from the very perception of effort, with each one of us feeling ourselves to be the cause of our own voluntary movements. In addition to this, Biran brings into focus all of the ambiguity of our relationship with the body, which we can experience in a mediated way, as one object among others, as well as immediately experience in an intimate, direct way, as interior space, as our 'own body', an integral part of the experience of self.

Having revealed the origin of immediate internal apperception and defined its nature, Biran next clarifies the meaning of the other terms highlighted in the announcement: sensation, intuition and feeling. While the sensible and affective life, 'carried forward in the perpetual flux of the impressions that compose it' (117), is never interrupted (it only stops with death) and never repeats itself, the feeling of effort, upon which the perception of the self and individual personality is founded, re-emerges always identical to itself, although periodically suspended during sleep. It has already been noted that, 'as long as this invariable mode persists, for as long as the wakefulness of the *self* endures, sensory and accidental impressions [...] can participate according to diverse laws or conditions in its reproductive activity and in the light of consciousness that springs from this source' (118). Biran is now in a position to look more closely at these 'diverse laws or conditions' through which the self associates itself with impressions, showing how they originate three fundamental systems, which he called 'sensitive', 'perceptive' and 'apperceptive'.

While the 'sensitive', or 'passive', system includes all of the affections (internal and external) of sensibility that do not in any way entail the active participation of the self or will (this is the case for the above-mentioned phenomena of 'organic refraction'), the 'perceptive' system has instead a 'mixed' nature and includes all of the modifications that, originating from the initial action of some external or internal cause extraneous to the will, require a consecutive reaction from the latter. This second system is that of 'composite sensations', which Biran can now more clearly define as 'every mode composed of an immediate, variable affection together with the unitary, identical feeling of personality, in so far as the impression is related to an organic seat that is therefore in some way separate from personality' (122). Unlike simple affections, sensations are always localized and locatable. Within this system, Biran introduced a further distinction, according to the external senses that participate in the various sensations. While the passive part prevails in the sensations that come from smell, taste and passive touch spread throughout the whole body, the active, or 'perceptive', part dominates in the sensations connected to sight, hearing and active touch. The latter senses, unlike the others, 'do not always wait for objects to seek them out', but rather 'have their own force that makes them fly above those objects' (123). Intuition, which is in particular proper to sight and includes 'all that the soul sees or perceives *spontaneously*, in itself or beyond itself, without any *effort* on its part or without any apprehended activity' (128) is distinguished from perception in so far as the latter requires voluntary attention or effort.

Finally, the third system, called the 'active apperceptive' system, includes all of the modes or acts produced by the will. It includes the external apperceptions, which are produced by active touch and originate our objective life, and mediated internal apperceptions, which can be observed, for example, in cases of the active or simultaneous use of voice and hearing, when the subject discovers him- or herself to be 'the modifying force or cause' and, at the same time, 'the modified product'. 'The voice joined to hearing', according to Biran, 'provides to the individual the sole means of modifying himself sensibly by the successive acts of his will without any external cause' (138).

These three systems are next analysed in terms of intellectual organization, in relation to notions and ideas, with Biran distinguishing between an 'intellectual apperceptive system' that includes the memory or evocative faculty and is based on the use of signs, an 'intellectual intuitive system', which is where the creative and spontaneous imagination of artistic and scientific genius is located, and an 'intellectual sensory system', which includes feelings (for example, of beauty, goodness, truth, etc.). In the last part of the essay, the theory of knowledge digresses into a study of the passions and the foundations of moral and social life, to which Biran will later return in the *Fragments relatifs aux fondements de la morale et de la religion* of 1818.[xix]

Maine de Biran and his main philosophical interlocutors

Maine de Biran's definitive break with the *Idéologues* came, as we have noted, at the end of 1804 and coincided with the *Mémoire sur la décomposition de la pensée*. It is here that, formulating his philosophy of effort for the first time, Maine de Biran became a philosopher in his own right and completed what Henri Gouhier called his first 'conversion'.[xx] The development of this progressive and irreversible deviation from *Idéologie* can be traced in his correspondence with Destutt de Tracy, dating to the same period during which he wrote the *Mémoire* of 1804.[xxi] Maine de Biran saw Tracy as one of the precursors of his philosophy of effort who, developing Condillac's analysis of touch, was the first to reveal the key role of voluntary motility and the sensation of resistance in intellectual life and in knowledge of the external world. However, this insight, which Biran later developed in the direction of immediate intimate experience of the self, coincident with will and effort, was limited in Tracy's thought to the simple understanding of objective knowledge; what interested him, in the impression of resistance, was simply the object that resists.

Maine de Biran's main charge against the *Idéologues*, Tracy included, was precisely the fact that they had neglected the study of the interior dimension of internal sense. This is why he felt it necessary to correct and integrate the philosophy of his French predecessors, the heirs of Condillac, adding 'subjective ideology' to 'objective ideology', the latter having been the only one taken into consideration by the *Idéologues*. While, as we read in the Berlin essay, 'objective ideology' is solely concerned with the relationships that 'a passive or purely sensory being' has with 'the external objects on which it depends', 'subjective ideology' (which he himself sought to establish) must consider 'the interior of the thinking *subject*, aiming to reach the facts of consciousness or right to the heart of the internal, constant and necessary relations that this *subject* holds with itself' (30). The addition of this new point of view would, however, require scrapping the analysis of human knowledge carried out previously by sensationism and *Idéologie*, starting over from scratch. Their analyses would need to be entirely re-done because, as noted above, they ignored the active element of sensation, considering the latter to be something simple and passive:

> Just as the omission on the part of the old chemists, in taking no account of the influence of the air or of a part of the air on the phenomena of combustion and the acidification of bodies, meant that all the analyses had to be remade or checked by our modern *pneumatists*, who discovered in the analysed air the true principle of these phenomena, so too the distinction of a new sense that can be united with all the others without being confused with any one of them, having been absolutely neglected or misrecognized by the author of the *Treatise of Sensations*, would impose today the task of recommencing all the analyses, or of producing a new verification for them. This is the work that I would have in view.

According to Maine de Biran, although the Ideologists had made an enormous contribution to the study of sensibility (in particular Cabanis, for his consideration of internal sensations, and Tracy, for the identification of the 'sensation of movement'), they had become tangled up in Condillac's 'metaphysical abstraction'. The latter, starting from the 'common, unique and, as it were, sacramental term *sensation*' (42), had believed that it was possible to explain everything through the 'system of transformed sensations' (43), in which he had seen the mechanism at the origin of thought and all of the intellectual faculties. But, according to Maine de Biran, this meant carrying out a purely logical analysis of knowledge, based on recourse to general and abstract terms that lack all real meaning, and comprehension of which is simplified in direct proportion to their extension. The imagination can use these terms arbitrarily and however it likes, and they serve solely to feed what Biran called 'systematic illusions'. These illusions, to which Condillac and his followers fell victim, are produced when language, originally modelled on thought, turns back on and cages it, substituting 'conventional order and the logical forms of our signs for the real order of the facts of nature or of the primitive ideas of the understanding' (31). Systematic illusions are in substance the ones through which automatism of calculation replaces vitality of thought, in a dynamic that Biran had already examined in the essay on habit.

This is why Maine de Biran had no difficulty in throwing back the accusations launched by sensationism and *Idéologie* at metaphysics, which they thought they had freed themselves from by establishing that all of our knowledge and higher faculties derive from experience, through the mechanism of 'transformed sensations'. Biran demonstrates that, in so doing, Condillac and his followers ended up instead reintegrating precisely the same metaphysics that they thought they had banished, since they were advancing, through recourse to general terms, a merely abstract and logical analysis of knowledge. Maine de Biran's aim was, on the contrary, to carry out a 'real' or 'concrete' analysis, one that was founded not on 'classification' but on 'observation' and that, for this reason, could not ignore, alongside experience of sensible and exterior things (the only experience considered by sensationism and *Idéologie*), interior experience. That was the type of experience that should be the concern of metaphysics, which Biran in turn tried to rehabilitate by putting it in a new light and understanding it no longer in terms of the traditional sense, criticized by his French predecessors, of a discipline concerned with the study of spiritual or abstract entities (substance, the soul, ideas, etc.), but instead as a science of the considered faculties of the thinking being – and so as synonymous with psychology. As defined by Biran,

Introduction 11

metaphysics was no longer concerned with that which is situated beyond experience, instead reflecting on the interior, 'hyperorganic' reality that can be experienced only by the internal sense.

According to Maine de Biran, before Condillac and the *Idéologues*, Locke had already correctly distinguished between 'simple ideas of sensation', deriving from passive modifications of sensibility (whether internal or external), and 'simple ideas of reflection' or free acts of intelligence and will, which are accompanied by internal feeling or self-apperception.[xxii]

In Maine de Biran's view, Locke is right to differentiate between external senses and internal sense, but he failed to recognize the active character of reflection. This latter is marked, like sensation, by receptivity and not yet by the spirit's activity. Maine de Biran identifies three obstacles preventing Locke from formulating a science of principles able to relate the reflexive faculty to the real source of every idea, that is, to the will: a) the supposition that the ideas of sensation arrive in the intellect from the outside and do not contain in themselves any reflective element, while the idea of sensation – as an idea – must contain reflective elements that derive from the activity of the thinking subject;[xxiii] b) the identification of all the passive modifications expressed by the generic term of sensation, whereas it is necessary to distinguish between the modifications deriving from the motor activity of the subject, and those caused directly by the outside and received passively;[xxiv] c) the transfer of the whole activity of the thinking subject to the will in a narrow sense, and the explanation of the passive receptivity of the intellect according to the Aristotelian principle *nihil est in intellectu quod non prius fuerit in sensu*, whereas there are simple ideas which are purely reflective and arise from the inner sense.[xxv]

The silencing of the intimate sense is the precise meeting point between the empiricists like Locke and the 'pure metaphysicians'. The latter are innatists like Descartes or Leibniz, who eventually gather in a common 'abstract region' where the categories no longer engage with the real facts that underlie our thinking power. It is a backward journey from the original facts of the internal sense to theological or cosmological 'general ideas' (such as substance, power, force or cause). In this journey, the 'original activity' is lost and the universal ideas become the causes of particular facts, whose existence is ultimately made to depend on 'laws' and 'possible forms', in a total reversal of the order of facts.[xxvi] Descartes, by conceiving thought as an immaterial activity depending on 'innate ideas' which 'are associated or composed in sensible experience' with impressions and material images, excludes any 'active power or efficient virtue'.[xxvii] On the other hand, Leibniz considers the higher faculties as 'intellectual forms' of the monad awaiting the matter supplied by the senses as a function of the generation of ideas.[xxviii] He elaborates a conception of the 'human soul' as 'essentially an agent', but traversed by a force that is independent of the conscience or immediate apperception.[xxix] Leibniz thus intends that the soul arbitrarily distances itself from the experience of the internal sense, that is from that primitive datum or fact of the effort. According to Maine de Biran, that effort constitutes the principle from which that real and positive science must move – a science able to overcome the problem of the dualism between body and soul and to found psychology without falling into the extreme of idealism or that of materialism.

Maine de Biran is interested in Kant's philosophy because of its attempt to develop a pure psychology able to avoid any logicism unhooked from the plane of experience. However, he knew it only in an indirect way, apart from the *De mundi sensibilis atque intelligibilis forma et principiis dissertatio*, which he had read. It is a matter of distinguishing the plane of objective experience and that of subjective experience, and of separating, among the perceptive compounds offered by experience, formal elements from material ones. For Maine de Biran, we need to implement a reflexive abstraction allowing us to identify the simple ideas which are inseparable from the primitive fact of consciousness. In other words, we need to put in place the proper modes of development of voluntary actions that serve as a necessary basis for the work of reason. These ideas correspond to the 'reflective abstractions' to which Maine de Biran refers in the essay on immediate apperception and which constitute what he himself calls the formal 'mould' that gives its 'stamp' to the matter of perception.[xxx] Thus, in the immediate internal apperception, the ego apperceives itself as a pure phenomenal self in the fact that it feels itself as an immanent effort. Taking up the same terms as the Kantian *Dissertation* of 1770, which he quotes in a footnote, Biran states that 'the *self*, constituted as such in internal and immediate apperception can really be said to be *abstrahens* (or *abstrahens* itself) rather than *abstractus*' (38).

Around 1805, Kant's philosophy must have constituted an important stimulus for Maine de Biran. However, he considered that Kant had not realized the sort of revolution in the theory of knowledge that he had within political philosophy. This idea was widely shared by the *Idéologues*. The debate on Kant had been lively in France, in the context of a particularly early reception. In 1800 to 1804, this reception went through a very intense and contrasting phase.[xxxi] The

Idéologues looked with interest and curiosity to Kantian criticism, but they misunderstood some of its fundamental moves. They believed that the solution it adopted in order to emancipate itself from metaphysics ran the risk of a dangerous relapse in that very abstractionism that Kant wanted to escape. Maine de Biran repeatedly quotes Kant in his essay on immediate apperception. The reason might be that he wanted to prove, to his Berlin colleagues, his ability to enter into dialogue with German philosophy, while avoiding at the same time any pedestrian imitation of the great systems of thought of the era. Moreover, he must have been aware that the Berlin Academy was divided about Kant: within the Academy, Kant was opposed by several, including Ludwig Friedrich (Louis Frédéric) Ancillon,[xxxii] who considered the consequences of the Kantian system to be literally fatal, as he had already written in 1796.[xxxiii] However, the overlaps between pure Biranian psychology and Kantian criticism are striking. The reflexive ideas or abstraction mentioned by Maine de Biran may appear to be really close to the categories, since in *De l'aperception immédiate* they are presented as functions of unification of sensory multiplicity. However, on closer inspection, Maine de Biran does not make those ideas the object of deduction, since they are immediately readable in the primitive fact of the intimate sense. Such ideas are inseparable from the subject of effort and, on the side of the ego (purely phenomenal), they correspond to the qualities with which it conceives itself as one, simple, identical, permanent, and as the cause of its own acts. The difference between Kant and Maine de Biran – who will be called the 'French Kant' – lies in the fact that for the former the spontaneity of the subject is a transcendental function, while for the latter it corresponds to an empirical activity of the psychological subject.[xxxiv] And conversely, while Kant suggests that one cannot have any empirical knowledge of the 'I think', Maine de Biran claims that immediate apperception is in itself a perfect knowledge which is far from being empty. This because the ego is not known as an external object, but rather knows itself from within, in a *sui generis* manner that is not the way in which it knows the world.[xxxv] This is possible as long as one of the reflexive ideas through which the self apperceives itself has a primacy. Maine de Biran also sees it as the essence of ego, namely the idea of cause. In other words, it is as a cause that the self apperceives itself as one, simple and identical. Two orders of resistance correspond to this cause: the 'organic resistance' inherent in 'one's own body', which we perceive through muscular resistance; and the external resistance produced by a 'foreign body'.[xxxvi] On this theme too, Maine de Biran shows that he uses criticism of conceptual devices in an original way. As he will clarify in the *Essai sur les fondements de la psychologie*, he differentiates between two things.

On the one hand, there is the essence of the bodies *in se*, a so-called *noumenal* plan, in which the body is one among other foreign bodies. On the other hand, there is the essence of our body *for us*, since what matters, on this *phenomenal* plane, is the way we perceive it, which is absolutely different from that with which we perceive foreign bodies.[xxxvii] The primitive fact of consciousness is thus confused with the *croyance* in the subject–object dialectic. The latter, in the case of the pure phenomenal self and of one's 'own body' – perceived internally as *effort* and *resistance* – are described by Biran with the allusive and slightly vague terms of 'substances or noumena'. However, for those who have conceived it, it is evident that the primitive fact of effort provides, through the organic resistance opposing it, the theory of knowledge, with an anchor in reality that is neither transcendental nor substantialist. Maine de Biran here distances himself from his German colleague. In his conception, the will – understood as a real force, the object of psychology – underlines the role played by tactility (for Condillac), and motility (for Destutt de Tracy).[xxxviii]

Maine de Biran's legacy

The history of Maine de Biran's reception is closely linked to the editorial story of his works, which were published posthumously, the majority from the 1830s. Around the end of the nineteenth century, when readers could have access to the texts that form the essential corpus of his work, his philosophy extended beyond France and chimed with a general rejection of the limits of positivism and experimental psychology. Among the works that stand out, it is worth mentioning the pioneering works of Nathan E. Truman (1904)[xxxix] and of Susan Stebbing (1914) in the English-speaking world,[xl] those of Alfred Kuehtmann and Albert Lang in Germany, both dating back to 1901,[xli] and, in Italy, the lectures of Giovanni Amendola, published in 1911,[xlii] and the 1915 monograph by Luigi Ventura.[xliii] Readers now have access to the monumental edition of Maine de Biran's works, edited by François Azouvi,[xliv] which provides a precious tool allowing an accurate reconstruction of the existential and philosophical path of Maine de Biran. The complexity and originality of his philosophy are today widely recognized,[xlv] and its essential features have already been identified by Henri Gouhier, in his remarkable 1948 monograph.[xlvi] Moreover, Aldous Huxley's exquisite and engaged essay allowed English-speaking readers to approach the philosophy of Maine de Biran.[xlvii] In the mid-1950s, thanks to the critical edition of his *Journal*[xlviii] – with which Maine de Biran

Introduction

inaugurates, although not deliberately, a new literary genre called the 'metaphysical diary'[xlix] – it was possible to complete his portrait, also on a biographical level.

Maine de Biran's influence on later philosophy, at least throughout most of the nineteenth century, was heavily conditioned by the delay of the publication of his works until after his death. The main person responsible for this delay was an ambitious leading figure in French philosophy, to whom the executor of his will had entrusted Maine de Biran's writings in 1825, one year after his death, for their publication. This individual was Victor Cousin, who had been a member of Maine de Biran's philosophical society since 1816. Other members of the society included Royer-Collard, Ampère, de Gérando and the Cuvier brothers.[l] Cousin is known for having dominated French philosophy with his eclecticism for a few decades, but also for having heavily influenced state policy with regard to the teaching of philosophy as well as to recruitment of university-level philosophy professors. As has been amply demonstrated – and as was denounced at the time by Pierre Leroux (1797–1871) – the father of eclecticism not only delayed publication of the works of the man he himself described as one of his three philosophical references (the others were Laromiguière and Royer-Collard), but, in the preface to the first of the three volumes of those works (volume one was published in 1834 and the others in 1841 under pressure from Biran's friends and relatives), he also penned an ambiguous presentation of Maine de Biran, recognizing the value of some of his philosophical insights but at the same time denying his absolute originality, out of the unacknowledgeable but clear fear that the establishment of a Biranian spiritualism could have challenged the hegemony of eclecticism.[li] Cousin wrote that Maine de Biran and his work had the merit of having rehabilitated Leibniz as a metaphysician, the Leibniz who was the true precursor of eclecticism, since the version of Leibniz's philosophy provided by Maine de Biran was only partial, having excluded the non-I, nature with its immutable laws, object of impersonal reason, which was obfuscated, if not ignored, by the primacy of will with which Maine de Biran had – and this was something he had to be given credit for – overturned the domination of sensation that had been imposed by Condillac's materialism.[lii] This was a partial reading that, among other things, left in shadow the vital dimension of the Biranian self, which he maintains in connection with physiology and that serves as a check for the metaphysical, if not mystical, tendencies of his own thought, but that above all prevents the temptation to oppose sensationist materialism with a metaphysics incapable of dialoguing with the science of man. The ten years of delays that preceded the publication of a volume that contained only a small part of the works left nearly ready for publication by his teacher thus gave Cousin the opportunity to establish himself in French philosophy as the one with the philosophical system able to demolish the dangerous edifice constructed on the basis of Condillac's sensationism thanks to a philosophy that brought metaphysics back to psychology, creating space for the subjective and active dimension of the self, in a way that was in reality far weaker than that in Biran's corpus.[liii]

It was a brilliant student of Cousin, Félix Ravaisson, who recognized the depth and richness of Biran's thought, presenting it as the true precursor of spiritualism, through a metaphysical reading of his work that fed his doctoral thesis on habit[liv] and that was soon after expounded upon in an article on the philosophy of Hamilton and later in the survey *La philosophie en France au XIXe siècle* that he wrote in 1867. For Ravaisson, Maine de Biran was, therefore, the one who 'had drawn from sensationism the new theory' that separates activity from passivity, perception from sensation, elevating it 'to the rank of first principle' through the doctrine of the self understood as effort, thanks to which philosophy becomes 'the science of inner Mind [Esprit] in its living Causality',[lv] a path not fully followed by eclecticism. The latter had refused to conceive of voluntary effort as the sole source of our first awareness of ourselves, claiming to arrive at the metaphysical notions of cause and substance through psychological observation, and therefore misreading the nature of internal apperception, which cannot be isolated from the phenomenon, being instead a metaphysical experience related to corporeity and sensation.[lvi] In Ravaisson's view, therefore, Maine de Biran was the first true 'spiritualist positivist', even if, in the effort to establish the independence of man from sensation, he defined the self solely through will.[lvii]

At the beginning of the twentieth century, Henri Bergson affirmed that Maine de Biran was 'the most metaphysical of the psychologists of the previous century'.[lviii] It is clear that Bergson himself took that path in the development of his own thought, which derives the idea of the driving action of the soul on the body from Biran's principle of effort. Bergson uses this term to indicate the state of tension of the self, present to itself and to the world, that is not reduced to either attention paid to a specific object or the state dominated by an automatism in which the self is absent. It is a union of the soul and the body that does not re-introduce a form of monism and that, in its dual physiological-psychological reference, locates itself beyond both materialism and idealism.[lix] Then again, not even psycho-physical parallelism exhausts the relationship between the two terms, since, on the one hand, there is an unconscious sphere that operates unbeknownst to the self – Maine de Biran's animal life – and, on the other hand, there is a conscious dimension lacking all spatiality that goes beyond the limits of the brain and imitates some of the features of the self understood as hyperorganic force by Maine de Biran.[lx] Bergson, unlike Maine de Biran, does not conceive effort as a primitive fact, since, according to him, one cannot understand the causality of the will without relating it to that which gives to it the impulse, that is, to the 'vital impulse', which presupposes anticipation and the gap between present and future.[lxi]

The path traced by Ravaisson and Bergson was later also followed by Louis Lavelle, who, until the end of the 1940s, centred his spiritualistic philosophy on the idea of the self as activity – and so as act – traceable to the primary experience of effort understood as the site of suppression of the opposition between being and knowledge, since *ratio essendi* and *ratio cognoscendi* come to coincide in the original action.[lxii] An act that cannot become image without obliterating itself, since if the self looks at itself, it stops being that primordial activity and becomes an object lacking life; it immediately shifts from present to become past.[lxiii] Internal immediate apperception is made possible by the same light that accompanies every act of our interior life. Consciousness is not a light that illuminates our interiority as if it were an object, but is 'the very act that produces this light'.[lxiv] In Biranian terms, it is concentrated, not specular light.[lxv]

According to Anne Devarieux, Michel Henry should be placed in the same spiritualist lineage. On the basis of a phenomenological reading of Maine de Biran made by Maurice Merleau-Ponty in the late 1940s, Henry elaborated an 'unintended phenomenology' in which the individual must be understood as 'interiority or absolute Ipseity',[lxvi] and in which it is capable of freeing itself from the limits of the determined ego, to which the Biranian effort would still be imprisoned.[lxvii] In Henry's view, Maine de Biran is indeed 'the first and actually the only philosopher who, in the long history of human reflection, saw the necessity for originally determining our body as *a subjective body*'.[lxviii] In the procedural experience described by Maine de Biran regarding immediate internal apperception, the resistant corporeity is neither configured as an inner extension separate from the I, nor something that the I possesses, but rather as something that the I is: something that is one with the self.[lxix] In this way, the notion of 'one's own body' – first introduced into philosophical vocabulary by Maine de Biran[lxx] – would challenge the Cartesian dualism between soul and body.[lxxi] However, Michel Henry claims that one cannot distinguish, in Maine de Biran, between one's own body, intended as an 'original body', and the resistant 'organic body'. The latter is indivisible, is not the objective body of science, and 'it has neither autonomy nor ontological sufficiency'.[lxxii] The same Biranian doctrine would nonetheless open the way to a simpler relationship than that which binds the ego to the body proper, which is at the same time an organic body. In other terms, this body is what connotes the 'internal transcendental experience' of movement in terms of a subjectivity that 'reveals itself immediately to itself' as the original body, that is, as a subjective body that makes one with the ego.[lxxiii] For Claude Bruaire, however, the 'primitive duality' that connotes voluntary effort must be reconfigured in a 'triplicity' that makes room for the 'neutral energy of living desire' or 'appetite', in full harmony with the reading made by Ravaisson of this principle.[lxxiv] Only then can one remedy the aporia that marks 'the sole philosophy of the subject' capable of being 'inextricably a philosophy of the body'.[lxxv] Maine de Biran outlines a subjectivity, simultaneously 'absolute' and 'finite',[lxxvi] that is centred on the government of one's own body by the will. The latter is nothing but the expression of a *subject who unconditionally performs the action*',[lxxvii] which is a metaphor for the very 'Absolute' that Maine de Biran will pursue in the transition to the 'Life of the Spirit' and which becomes a place of conjunction with the divine.[lxxviii]

The premises of both these phenomenological readings are all contained in the course on 'The union of the soul and body in Malebranche, Maine de Biran and Bergson' that Maurice Merleau-Ponty held in 1947 to 1948 at the École Normale Supérieure of Lyon and Paris. The three philosophers were on the programme for the *agrégation* in philosophy in that year. Although in the corpus of Merleau-Ponty's works, the name of Maine de Biran does not appear, that course reveals the extent to which he had meditated on Biran's philosophy, and how much this had contributed to strengthening his conception of the relationship between the individual and the world. Merleau-Ponty recognizes, indeed, that Maine de Biran has taken 'the experience of the body and its motility' as a 'point of departure',[lxxix] whose individual and interior evidence 'cannot be communicated directly'.[lxxx] Biran, in describing this experience, 'did not reduce consciousness to motility but he identified motility and consciousness. The primitive fact is consciousness of an irreducible relationship between two terms irreducible themselves'.[lxxxi] According to Merleau-Ponty, Biran opened a path that he nevertheless hesitated to take decisively, limiting himself to a simple psychological description, even though he tried to avoid any reductionist solution. When, at the core of the experience of effort, we do not have 'a consciousness becoming movement, but a consciousness reverberating in movements', then we are not actually facing either an 'interior fact' or an 'exterior' one, but rather the 'consciousness of self as relationship of the I to another term'.[lxxxii] We are thus facing 'a philosophy which recognizes as fundamental a certain antithesis, the antithesis of the subject and of the term which bears its initiatives'.[lxxxiii] The site of phenomenology seems therefore prepared: 'what is hence forth embedded at the heart of philosophy is no longer the recognition of the I by the I, but the relationship of the I to what is not itself'.[lxxxiv] At this point, it is a question of giving a more robust ontological foundation to the intuition of the primitive duality apprehended by Maine de Biran. This latter has the great merit of having tried 'to show that the presence of the body was necessary for thought itself',[lxxxv] sketching an 'at once concrete and reflective'[lxxxvi] philosophy and 'anticipating phenomenology' itself.[lxxxvii]

The search for an ontological foundation for the psychology of the primitive fact runs underneath Michel Henry's *Philosophie et phénoménologie du corps*, whose subtitle from this point of view is very telling: *Essai sur l'ontologie biranienne*. Studying the nature of the apperception of oneself as an immediate relationship between the ego and the body means to define the being of our absolute subjectivity. The path of Maine de Biran's ontology had already been travelled by Vancourt in the mid-1940s, in the framework of Neo-Thomism. It is run again in the early 1980s by Bernard Baertschi, whose doctoral thesis on *L'Ontologie de Maine de Biran* states that while it is undeniable that Maine de Biran has 'never written a treatise on ontology',[lxxxviii] his psychology provides nevertheless an ontological foundation. Although it is a 'subjective science of the subject', as it is based on 'immediate internal apperception', Biranian psychology captures 'the essence of the ego' and can – using the terms of Maine de Biran's vocabulary – mingle with the 'objective science of the subject' in a 'mixed science' that gathers both.[lxxxix] Such a psychology is in Baertschi's view to all intents and purposes an 'implicit ontology', that contains useful elements for relating subjectivity to the 'absolute'.[xc] If immediate internal apperception represents phenomenal self-knowledge (just as external mediated apperception represents the phenomenal knowledge of the non-ego to the ego), the need to suppose the human being's permanence beyond the discontinuity of its appearance to itself, refers to the soul as a substance, that is the 'noumenon' or absolute to which that ego/apperception is the 'fundamental way'.[xci] As a cause, the ego is an 'absolute duration' and it cannot be identified in its entirety with its own body, because the will is hyperorganic while the body is organic. Thus, there is an ontological difference between the ego and the body, even if the latter can be defined as the 'incarnation of the subject', namely the 'point of contact between the ego and the world', and is therefore a 'mixed reality'.[xcii] If Maine de Biran insists on their unity, he does so to distinguish the internal structure of the subject from the external one, which puts the subject in relation to objects in the world, and yet the body and the I can be distinguished even though one cannot exist without the other. Baertschi, at the end of his thesis, inscribes his work in the same 'movement' of thought as did Michel Henry, who recognized in Maine de Biran 'one of the true founders of a phenomenological science of human reality'.[xciii] According to Baertschi, the merit of this 'movement' has been, among other things, to show 'that history was wrong in seeing in our philosopher nothing but the origin of the French spiritualistic school that will end with Bergson'.[xciv] After more than thirty-five years, post-Bergsonian spiritualism, the phenomenological school, and the French ontological school show important areas of intersection, to the point that according to some, the history of French spiritualism would still have to be written. What is certain is that the great initiator of a metaphysical psychology which has been one of the main pillars of spiritualism was Maine de Biran, who used the tools elaborated in works such as the essay on immediate apperception.

***

The text provides the English translation of all the phrasings and passages in French and in Latin. Either in the body of the text or in footnotes, the translations of French and Latin always appear in square brackets. All the works cited by Maine de Biran are provided with full bibliographical references, which are also presented in square brackets. Some additional editorial endnotes appear at the end of the book and are designated with roman numerals. All the other footnotes are to be ascribed to Maine de Biran. For this edition of Biran's text, we have consulted manuscript 2130 of the library of the Institut de France and checked our work against two existing French editions: that of Ives Radrizzani (*Oeuvres*, Vrin, vol. IV, 1995) and the more recent one by Anne Dévarieux (Le livre de poche, 2005).

Our thanks are due to Conal Grealis, for his advice on Latin and Greek and for the English translation of some passages in Latin, and to Catherine Dromelet. This research was funded by the European Union's Horizon 2020 research and innovation programme under the Marie Sklodowska-Curie grant agreement No. 660528.

Of Immediate Apperception

Si phaenomena principia sint cognoscendi caetera,
sensionem cognoscendi ipsa principia principium esse,
scientiamque omnem ab ea derivari dicendum est.
Hobbes, *Physica sive naturae phaenomena*, pars quarta, chap. XXV

Berlin Academy Programme

(Extract from the Moniteur français,
31 October 1805)

The Berlin Academy has noticed that in research concerning the origin and the reality of human knowledge philosophers had neglected, or at least had not carefully observed, distinguished and elaborated the primitive facts of inner sense that ground *the science of principles* and that form the sole basis of the work of reason. Philosophers had been as demanding with the objects of experience as they had been quick to admit the certainty of particular forms of our knowledge. Consequently, the Academy thought that more precision in the examination and statement of primitive facts would contribute to the progress of science. The branch of speculative philosophy thus proposes the following question to European science:

Are there internal immediate apperceptions?
In what way does internal apperception differ from intuition?
What difference is there between intuition, sensation and feeling?
What are the relations of these acts or states of mind with notions and ideas?

Essay

First Part

State of the question as considered in various systems of speculative philosophy; discussion of the terms in which it is proposed, and of the means that we have to establish their sense

Introduction

If the excellence of a method is determined by the extent and the precision of the results to which it has led, by the number and the importance of the practical truths that arise from its repeated application, and, above all, by the useful direction it imparts on the human faculties, by the development and capacity that it grants to the exercise and to the play of these faculties, then it is impossible to contest the advantages proper to the method of *experience*, proclaimed and promoted with so much success by the illustrious restorer of the natural sciences.

If one follows its conquests since Bacon, it is evident that its progressive influence extends to ever more diverse studies, and ends up by embracing in its sphere the whole system of human knowledge, the *metaphysics* of mind as well as the *physics* of body, the science of *abstracta* as well as that of *concreta*.

In the present period of progress that is due to it, if we contested the pre-eminence of this method in the hands of its most faithful and exclusive partisans, they would surely invoke all the dissipated chimeras, all the vague and obscure ideas now clarified, all the mysterious procedures of our intelligence removed from darkness by means of a wise and rigorous analysis, one always applied so as to delimit and circumscribe sharply the simple and primitive *facts* of sensory nature, and this before postulating *a priori* laws or before rising to the action of primary causes. They could also invoke a logic purified and rid of all the empty forms that for so long hindered the march of the human spirit, the discovery of the true technique of reasoning and its submission to more simple laws, modelled on the essential relations of our ideas with the signs that express them, establish them and often give them being.

To justify further the general employment of this same method, applied to the most diverse systems of ideas, they would cite perhaps, together with the *language* of calculation – analysed down to its roots and lending, by fortunate convergences, some of its light to the more common procedures by which all our ideas are formed in the understanding, expressed externally, arranged and co-ordinated in the regular forms of discourse – they would cite, I say, the language of our modern chemistry, in which the genius of Lavoisier meets so happily the genius of Condillac.[1]

But without weakening the recognition due to such advances, without undermining the *place* that a philosophy of experience can occupy in the primary *science* of the human mind, and without rejecting the evidence or evident utility of its greatest results, one can attempt to rise above them, for within the limits of sense-experience some minds can find themselves all too confined. Following the progressive incline that leads unceasingly from the results to the principles, as from effects to causes, we are led to search after a less mobile basis on which the thinking subject can depend in order to reflect on himself, to know the principle of his inner operations, to assign the real and primitive source of his ideas, to know how – with what justification and by which collection or network of conditions and circumstances – he finds himself constituted as an individual and intelligent *person*, capable of knowing, of representing to himself external existences and of apperceiving his own existence.

Without rejecting the validity of that same method, but with regard to a sort of wholly internal experience, different to that which has constantly guided Bacon's *disciples*,[2] it would be possible to ask whether metaphysics, considered as

---

[1] See the preface to Lavoisier's *Elements of Chemistry* [A.-L. de Lavoisier, *Traité élémentaire de chimie* (Paris: Cuchet, 1789), trans. R. Kerr, *Elements of Chemistry* (New York: Dover Publications, 1965)].

[2] *Mens humana, si agat in materiam (naturam rerum et opera Dei contemplando) pro modo materiae operatur, atque ab eadem determinatur. Sin ipsa in se versatur (tanquam aranea texens telam), tum demum interminata est; et parit certe telas quasdam doctrinae tenuitate fili operisque admirabiles, sed quoad usum frivolas et inanes* (Bacon, *De Augm. Scient.*). [F. Bacon, *De Dignitate et Augmentis Scientiarum*, trans. *The Advancement of Learning*, M. Kiernan (ed.) (Oxford: Clarendon Press, 2000),

State of the question *as considered in various systems of speculative philosophy* 29

a science of the faculties proper to the thinking subject, does not constitute a science distinct from that of the practical employment of these faculties, and, above all, from a science of the object of these faculties, as developed and applied to external objects – distinct, that is, from logic and physics, and also from any system of knowledge that the modern French mind might be familiar with under the all too general heading of Ideology. In this case, it would also be possible to ask whether this science of the faculties or primary operations of the understanding can or must be exclusively subject to the procedures of the other experimental sciences, and constrained to find, like they, its primary facts in the sensory appearances of the phenomenal world.

It would also be possible to ask whether the doctrines thus focused on the sphere of sensory objects do not abandon, as if it were hidden behind them, another, in some way *hypersensible*, world, whose reality, if it is real, is manifest only to a particular inner sense and verifiable only by its testimony. One would thereby be led to wonder whether Bacon's method, recommended by so much success in the physical sciences, can reach even the outer limits of a genuinely first philosophy, and whether, in following the procedures of the analysis practised by Locke, Condillac and their disciples, it would ever be possible to reach even the first link of the chain that envelops, from the ground up, all knowledge, all the diverse operations and ideas of the human understanding.

The question posed by the illustrious Academy, and above all the terms of the programme that precede it, authorize and motivate these doubts, but also furnish the opportunity and perhaps even the means to dissipate them. This question is taken, indeed, according to all the depths of the thinking subject, since it points back to the original of the faculties or primary modifications that constitute the subject as such. Enjoying a point of view higher than all known systems, the question wards off their seductions, since it prevents us from beginning with one of these theoretical systems set out in advance, and in bringing us back to the real and primitive facts of the inner sense, it warns us that it is from this source that we should draw the veritable facts [*données*] of the science of principles.

---

book I, p. 24: 'For the wit and minde of man, if it worke vpon matter, which is the contemplation of the creatures of God worketh according to the stuffe, and is limited thereby; but if it worke vpon itself, as the Spider worketh his webbe, then it is endless, and brings forth indeed Cobwebs of learning, admirable for the finesse of thread and worke, but of no substance or profite']. This passage thus proves the exclusive value that Bacon attached to the experimental method of the physical sciences; we see clearly that any metaphysics, even any ideology, finds its condemnation in it.

If these primitive facts had been distinguished or circumscribed with sufficient precision, if they had been attached to univocal fixed signs, and, in a word, if the proper sense of the terms entering into the enunciation of the problem had been determined, and thus its exact solution realized wholly or in part, then perhaps the trial to which metaphysics has for a long time been subject would be brought to a close. We could add to the balance certain decisions that exclude it from the realm of the sciences as well as the qualifications that its powerful advocates present in favour of its reality. We would come to know if the moderns, who have replaced a perhaps too vague and audacious title with one more modest and more appropriate to our means of knowing (that of the analysis of ideas and sensations, and, more recently, of ideology), are not themselves compelled to recognize a sort of ideology that could be called *subjective*, quite distinct from the *objective* ideology to which they have limited themselves; the former, focused on the interior of the thinking *subject*, aiming to reach the facts of consciousness and right to the heart of the internal, constant and necessary relations that this *subject* holds with itself in the exercise of the acts that it determines or of the modes that it *apperceives*, while the latter, concerning the affective impressions it receives or the images that it forms of them, seems to be wholly grounded on the relations with the external objects to which a passive or purely sensory being is subject.

It would thus be possible to judge which of the two sorts of ideological analysis comes closer to the true elements of our ideas or of our knowledge, and which of the two, above all, deserves the title of 'science of principles'. But to discern better the difference between these two doctrines, and to judge the reality of the one founded entirely on inner sense whose primitive facts it attempts to distinguish and to recognize, it will not be unhelpful to evaluate the terms of the question posed, in adopting alternately the two diverse points of view, of which one is attached more to the ground of the *subject* and the other to the form or to the matter of the *object* of thought. It seems necessary, above all, to examine, from each of these points of view, the nature of the ideas of these acts or states of mind that are signified by the verbs *apperceive, perceive, feel* and *see* (with the mind's eye) (*intueri*), or by the corresponding abstract substantives: *apperception, perception, intuition, sensation* or *feeling*. Are these terms common and general, or *particular* and *individual*? Does each correspond to a general and composite idea, in its extension or comprehension, like, for example, those placed at the head of a chain of physical facts, summarizing in a certain number of circumstances common to the particular phenomena that are directly subject to observation or experience? Or else, do they each express a *singular* idea, one

State of the question *as considered in various systems of speculative philosophy*   31

that is *particular* and necessarily individual by the very nature of the act or of the simple mode corresponding to it in the mind, when the latter turns back onto itself in order to account for its own operations and to get to know itself?

In a word, do such terms express only *categories*, pure products of the understanding working to classify the materials given to it? Or do they signify realities, primitive facts given in a world of wholly internal phenomena that have to be studied, observed in their *native* simplicity, without it being permitted to transform, compose or decompose them, as if they were like the artificial ideas that we use or the inert things given in objective experience?

The choice of one or the other of these two meanings, which seems to interest only *logic*, can decide the fate of the question posed. Depending on whether we are led to adopt one meaning at the expense of the other, we will understand differently the *science of principles*. These principles will either be abstract elements or primitive facts; and these facts themselves will have an external or internal, logical or real basis; consequently, we will be led either to recognize that there is an *immediate internal apperception*, distinct from *intuition* and *feeling*, or to deny the real ground of these distinctions, accepting them perhaps only as genres or categories that reason establishes to co-ordinate the system of diverse ideas on which it operates, but without consequences for the reality of the things or facts to which these ideas are related.

In seeking, first of all, what might be inexact or incomplete in either point of view compared to the other, we will learn to bring into focus the one suitable for treating our subject, in order to arrive, if possible, at a real solution.

§1

Examination of Philosophical Doctrines That Take the Terms Proper to the Operations of Intelligence in an Abstract or General Sense, and That Misapprehend the Character of the Primitive Facts of Inner Sense

The artificial forms of our languages, perhaps originally modelled on the natural forms of thought, lend to it something of their stamp, as if by a sort of reaction, and serve to motivate the systematic illusions substituting a conventional order and the logical forms of our signs for the real order of the facts of nature or of the primitive ideas of the understanding.

It is, I think, by an abuse of language and a lack of propriety in the forms (or in the regularity of forms) of metaphysical language in particular, that passive modes or states, which cannot be taken as having their own *existence* or as capable of any *action*, are expressed by *verbs*, which essentially denote *existence* and *action*.

It is as a result of such abuses that the representative terms of the permanent or accidental properties under which the imagination presents things, *objects* of external knowledge, have passed, in language, from a natural *adjectival* form, expressing their *addition* or their necessary inherence in a concrete whole, to a conventional substantive form, in which these abstract properties become new artificial wholes and thereby *subjects* of verbal propositions and purely *logical* affirmations, becoming thus misleadingly assimilated to other substantive terms of a different nature, which properly express the transitory acts or the phenomenal results of *causes* or *forces* necessarily conceived as individual and substantial. Unable to represent these effects in the form of images or to find, in a language originally modelled on sensory analogies, singular terms that express them, these purely logical affirmations have borrowed the signs of the effects by which their action is externally manifest on the outside, and remain thus identified with these effects in the substantial form of those same signs, though they are, at bottom, distinct from them in thought.

Let us determine, as a first example, the sense of the following abstract (verbal) substantives in the language of the physicists: *attraction, gravitation, magnetism, vegetation*, etc. These doubtless express in a real way the effects themselves, generalized on the basis of analogies or propositions observed in diverse circumstances of time and place; but they also include, though in a more hidden manner, the claims of the causes or forces that produce these classes of phenomena. Certainly, these causes hardly enter into the calculation of the facts, and it is legitimate for physicists to abstract from their real value and even, without any apparent abuse, to neglect their names; but we will see that this example is a dangerous one to follow in other systems of knowledge.

The double sense of the same general terms is still more remarkable in the language of the physiologists, who have too often abused it when they confused under the same abstract titles – such as *organization, vitality, sensibility* – both the apparent properties of organized bodies with the unity of the functions which work together to produce a life common to them, and the internal cause or force that animates and brings into play these living springs, with or without awareness of the results of its impulsion.

We thereby arrive at the most dangerous abuses in the language of the metaphysicians, those faithful disciples of Bacon, who have attempted to introduce into the wholly internal science of the operations or proper

State of the question *as considered in various systems of speculative philosophy* 33

modifications of the thinking subject, a method apt for the study of represented bodies or phenomena. Following the example of the physical observers in classifying effects in abstraction from their productive causes, these metaphysicians have indistinctly included under the same generic terms and sometimes under the simple sign of the broadest classification, the various specific modifications, essential or accidental, of the thinking and feeling being, together with the unity of the successive acts that gather for consciousness passive impressions not perceived in themselves, as well as the constitutive attributes or properties through which the *self* exists in apperceiving its self-identical existence, and this while always neglecting, following the example of the physicists, the essential individual force that is productive of this order of quite particular phenomena whose stage is consciousness.

This imitation in method and language entailed that the partisans of a philosophy of experience, studying all thought solely according to the modifications of a passive sensibility, with which they wholly identify the subject, had to abstract from the substantial subject as well as from the cause that can realize within it the phenomena of the perceptibility of the movement of thought. Consequently, they had to focus solely on ordering the latter into certain classes expressed by a common or abstract term, like objective properties separated from their subject of inherence and compared between themselves following certain analogies or external resemblances.

In this way, the terms *sensation, perception* or *apperception* have taken on, in Ideological language, the form of abstract substantives, not of the sort that, deriving immediately from *verbs*, indicate the real existence and action of a cause producing, within it or beyond it, certain effects that manifest it and from which its idea is inseparable, but of the sort that, by indicating the qualities inherent to complete wholes in which the imagination grasps them, can be separated in thought from those wholes or be grouped by means of artificial signs on which the understanding operates, without any consequence for the absolute truth or reality of the things signified.

When the famous author of the *Treatise of Sensations*,[3] aiming to separate from the object of his researches the obscure notions of *substance* and *force*, excludes any foundation for the subjective ideas and facts of *personality*, of *causality* or of interior *activity*, sensed or apperceived – when, beginning with the adventurous hypothesis that the individual subject of sensation, or the *soul*

---

[3]   [E. B. de Condillac, *Traité des sensations* (Paris: Chez de Bure l'aîné, 1754), trans. G. Carr, *Treatise on the Sensations* (Los Angeles: University of Southern California School of Philosophy, 1930)].

of the *statue* lacking immediate apperception, is *identified* absolutely with each of its modifications and can be nothing else, for itself no more than for the ingenious architect who made it, he seems to me to see a world of indeterminate phantoms, formed of modifications and mobile images without external support and without a fixed subject of inherence, that continually change in the eye of the imagination that creates it, or rather in the eye of the systematic spirit that raises, on this mobile basis, a chain of logical propositions, linked to each other perhaps more by the expression than by the ideas, but foreign to the absolute truth and reality of what exists.

Like extension and quantity, when abstracted into their own signs, having become the artificial subjects of a multitude of attributions of properties and relations that the geometer's understanding conceives in seeming to create them, and from which he grounds a science whose fecundity will never be exhausted, so too sensation, realized first as a particular modification that the statue *becomes*, but then abstracted into the general sign as well as into the chain of *transformed* characteristics, becomes the artificial subject of a logical theory in which everything is reduced to the mechanism of a language in which it is only ever a matter of *transforming*, deducing or substituting these terms, following the initially posited conventions and suppositions.

We can judge whether such a system of ideological classification nears, indeed, a veritable science of principles, and whether it serves, above all, to distinguish and recognize the nature and real characteristics of the primitive facts of inner sense.

Every general or complex idea – whether the mind receives it as such or forms it, *without a model* or without a *real archetype*, by its characteristic activity – can be resolved into its elements or become capable of analysis. This entails that if we come to hold, as with the system that we are now considering, that the signs that express ideas or the facts of our sensory and thinking nature are general names, classificatory headings, categories, then these ideas or these terms will appear always to have to furnish material for analysis – a *logical* rather than real analysis, whose final term and elements, its principle as well as its end, will be difficult to assign.

If these elements of analysis are considered only *in abstracto* or in general terms, they will have to be of the same abstract order. It follows that it will be possible to multiply the divisions and subdivisions, *to do metaphysics on the basis of a metaphysics*, without finding a ground on which to stop and without ever attaining the real limits of the science of principles. One could even find oneself becoming further removed from these principles, if it is true that the principles of any science of realities cannot be drawn from *abstractions*, from *pure products of the understanding.*

It is easy to see that, for example, *sensation*, and the original *faculty of sensing*, that Condillac takes to be the final term of *decomposition* or analysis (see his *Logic*), cannot be for him a primitive and real fact of inner sense, and that it is rather a principle of the abstract order, a general idea, a pure category. To prove this, I need only invoke the way in which he proposes to decompose sensation, a general term that he applies to the operations of the understanding as well as to the sensory impressions that are its materials.

How, indeed, does he execute this decomposition? Will it be in contenting himself with enumerating the diverse accessory characteristics or modes that the same sensation can adopt, taken, so to speak, as a single aggregation, without a real, intrinsic division? For, although it is said to be transformed, it remains, *ex hypothesi*, fundamentally identical to itself, since it is always ready to receive the same name. But such an enumeration of characteristics is not a decomposition. For example, the present sensation that, in acquiring by some *cause* a higher degree of vivacity, becomes *exclusive of any other*, will be said to adopt the particular characteristic expressed by the term *attention*; but is this anything other, so to speak, than a mode modified in a certain way, just as a colour or sound can, in conserving the same fundamental tone, pass without decomposition through several nuances or successive degrees? Does the same sensation persist when the object no longer acts on the organ? It will become *ex hypothesi memory* or *remembrance* and will merely adopt a new form without changing fundamentally. Can two sensations, or a sensation and a memory, work together without being confused? The resulting composed modification will be called *judgement* or *comparison*, etc.

In the successive enumeration of these diverse characteristics or properties that the same fundamental mode receives one after the other, I see only a logical analysis, or a definition of a general term whose sense is determined successively in being limited to each step or each particular characteristic that it embraces in its extension; but here I find no more decomposition than real gold can be found in the definition of the complex idea attached to this metal, if someone brought to mind all the physical qualities recognized in this substance, such as *colour, ductility, malleability, solubility in royal water*, etc. All the ideas are united under the same gold, but with this difference that, in the complex idea of a physical substance, it is a matter of properties constitutive of a fixed and determinate object whose complexion it is not in our power to change or alter, while in the case of the metaphysical idea taken as an archetype, we can amplify, reduce, unite or divide the elements available to us in some way, without having an external *criterion*, nor rules or a model inside ourselves, if we do not begin with the facts of inner sense or the real facts drawn without alteration in this primitive source.

It is, therefore, understandable that celebrated disciples of Condillac, unsatisfied with the logical analysis of sensation, have attempted to re-establish it on a new basis, and have found that these abstract elements have to be either augmented or restricted, but without appearing to notice that they are merely changing the system of classification, developing or reducing the terms of a sort of logical equation, without introducing any fact, any new truth, into the real field of the science.

Less importance, it seems to me, would have been attached to these artificial divisions of *faculties* supposed to enter as *elements into the general faculty of sensing,*[4] by observing that, if there is a *science of principles* based on a certain number of truly primitive facts, then the ideas corresponding to the latter can be only simple, and, consequently, the words expressing them in metaphysical language, being *particular* and *singular* and no longer general or common, will not be able to offer the material for any sort of real decomposition, and will not lend themselves even to logical analysis. They will have to be the last terms of analysis – analysis that will find in them fixed and necessary limits when it resolves our diverse ideas and knowledge into their real elements – like the first starting points of the synthesis aiming to recompose all of the materials or products of human understanding.

But if these two methods which help to establish on a principled basis all our deductive knowledge have no direct purchase on the primitive facts, and if, moreover, these facts themselves, or the ideas that express their reality, cannot have an external archetype or model, it can only be a question of assigning, in inner sense or in the reflection of certain acts and constitutive states of the thinking subject, the particular or singular characteristics by which these principal facts can be known, of determining their status and original conditions, of studying their liaison or linkage with ideas or facts of another order, and this by a method different to physical analysis applied to the objects of our external knowledge, or to logic confined within the field of categories.

---

[4] See Condillac's *Logic* [E. B. de Condilliac, *La logique ou les premiers développements de l'art de penser* (Paris, 1780; *Logic, or the First Developments of the Art of Thinking* in *Philosophical Writings of Etienne Bonnot, Abbé de Condillac*, vol. 1, trans. F. Philip (Hillsdale, NJ: Lawrence Erlbaum, 1982)] and de Tracy's *Elements of Ideology* [A.-L.-C., Destutt de Tracy, *Eléments d'Idéologie*, I-III parties (Paris: Courcier, 1801–5)].

State of the question *as considered in various systems of speculative philosophy* 37

But in order to justify these reflections and to apprehend better how much the method we are combatting is inappropriate for the science of principles as well as for the discovery of the primitive facts, let us observe again the difference that separates a genuinely reflective analysis from that which we will continue to call *logical*, and let us gauge this difference by means of their elementary products, which are all too generally confused under the heading of abstractions, which have at least two species.

The abstractions produced by the logical method are bound to a common sign with a capacity for extension that is proportionate to the very *simplicity*, to the small number of elements that it encompasses.

This term becomes complex in its *extension*, on the one hand, at the same time as it is simplified, and, on the other hand, in its *comprehension*; which entails that if the imagination comes to grasp such a sign in order to objectify its value, it will find a vast and indeterminate field of its application, and will remain master of the choice of the *sensory complements* that have to be added in order to grasp it.

Thus, for example, in employing the sign of a broad class such as that designated by the term *animal*, I have in mind either merely a simple denomination or the reflective idea of the operations of mind that have determined the formation of this genus; but if my imagination grasps this general idea in order to individualize its sign, it could indifferently join to it whatever sensory complement it pleases, so as to make of it the specific idea of a *man*, a *lion*, etc.

It is the same for all the general ideas of classes, of genera or families, of objects or phenomena, along which each branch of physical knowledge develops. It follows that when these sciences are instituted and erected as bodies of doctrine, one can and one must *analyse their principles* – these being taken only as the most general effects that have always to be resolved into particular cases and elaborated in all their detail right down to the last elementary fact – if one wants to obtain all the precision and exactitude of which these sciences are capable.

It is not the same for the veritable *science of principles*, stated in the Academy programme and into which the principles (improperly speaking) of all the practical sciences have to resolve themselves in order to find a more profound and more stable basis.

Will the primitive facts composing such a science be taken for abstractions,[5] because they can be separated, indeed, from such perceptible composites given in

---

[5] I relate here a passage from one of Kant's Latin dissertations entitled *De mundi sensibilis atque intelligibilis forma et principiis* [(Königsberg: Regiomonti, 1770)] which seems to have been his first work and the prelude to his *Critique of Pure Reason*: '*Necesse autem hic est, maximan ambiguitatem vocis* abstracti *notare, quam, ne nostrum de intellectualibus disquisitionem maculet, ante abstergendam*

objective experience? But if they enter into these composites, it is not as integral parts or elements of composition, but rather as sorts of formal elements that serve to link the parts of the whole and impress on it the form in which it exists in the mind as a sensory image, as objects of new elaborations. It is in this way that the mould is not a part of the matter that adopts its form or receives its imprint.

These *reflective* abstractions have therefore a quite different character to the ones just discussed. First of all, while the latter become increasingly distant from a real and individual character the more they are abstracted or *simplified*, the latter, on the contrary, come increasingly close to the characteristic of individuality or of truth the more that they are *purified*, so to speak, in being extracted from the material composites with which they are intimately associated and, as it were, fused in a purely sensory experience. Thus extracted, they acquire the eminent characteristic of immediate evidence, appropriate to the facts of inner sense, the real and unique source of all evidence, while the logical abstractions either remain deprived of all the light proper to the mind or acquire from the latter only a false illumination by means of the imagination that applies them indeterminately,[6] and thus participate only in the sort of certainty or evidence that is a product of *reason*,

---

esse satius duco. Nempe proprie dicendum esset: ab aliquibus abstrah*e*re, *not* aliquid abstrahere. *Prius denotat: quod in conceptu quodam ad alia quomodocumque ipsi nexa non attendamus, posterius autem, quod non detur, nisi in concreto et ita, ut a conjunctis separetur. Hinc conceptus intellectualis* abstrahit *ab omni sensitivio,* non abstsrahitur *a sensitivis et forsitan rectius diceretur* abstrahens, *quam* abstractus.' ['It is, however, necessary to notice here the extreme ambiguity of the word '*abstract*', and I think that it would be better to eliminate this ambiguity beforehand lest it spoil our investigation into that which belongs to the understanding. Properly speaking, we ought, namely, to say: *to abstract from some things*, but not: *to abstract something.* The former expression indicates that in a certain concept we should not attend the other things which are connected with it in some way or other, while the latter expression indicates that it would be given only concretely, and only in such a way that it is separated from the things which are joined to it. Hence, a concept of the understanding *abstracts* from everything sensitive, but it is *not abstracted* from what is sensitive. Perhaps a concept of the understanding would more rightly be called *abstracting* rather than *abstracted*', I. Kant, *On the Form and Principles of the Sensible and Intelligible World*, in *The Cambridge Edition of the Works of Immanuel Kant. Theoretical Philosophy, 1755–1770*, ed. D. Walford and R. Meerbote (Cambridge: Cambridge University Press, 1992), pp. 377–416, section II, § 6, p. 386]. I adopt entirely this distinction in applying it to the primitive facts and to the manner in which they are manifest to our inner sense when consulted well. We will see, indeed, that the existing *self*, as *one, simple, identical, substantial* is not *abstracted from sensations* as what would be most general or universal in them, but that it abstracts itself or separates itself from material impressions as well as the sensory objects that cause them. This in such a way that the *self*, constituted as such in internal and immediate apperception can really be said to be *abstrahens* (or *abstrahens* itself) rather than *abstractus*. What can fool metaphysicians here is that they almost always speak of the general ideas of *substance*, *existence* and *unity*, already erected as categories, without wanting to go back to the source of these ideas or to the facts that serve as their natural foundations in inner sense and impress on them the characteristic of evidence and necessity, which, as real in the primitive source, can next become purely logical in the continual combinations or applications that the understanding makes of these mother-ideas or of their signs erected as categories.

6   It in this way that the imagination will apply the general or abstract term *sensation* to a particular *odour*, a particular *colour* or a particular *sound*, and never to the *individual act* that it can also express in the sense of reflection.

State of the question *as considered in various systems of speculative philosophy* 39

which is a function of the repose of the mind when it apperceives clearly that its own conventions are met by the use of signs whose value it has determined without leaving the sphere of its own ideas. In the end, while these logical abstractions have an indeterminate power of application and unlimited extension, which varies according to the circumstances and often according to a mobile imagination, the reflective abstractions drawn from the primitive facts of inner sense are fixed, invariable, univocal and always identical, since they do not have to be untangled from the imagination, which can only alter and denature them.

The philosophers who, reducing all the elements of science to logical or physical abstractions, have thought it possible to obtain the principles of our knowledge from a decomposition or artificial resolution of the impressions or sensory images provided by experience, in believing it also possible and even necessary to analyse and decompose the real principles, have, in fact, abandoned themselves to the torrent of the habits of the imagination.

It is perhaps also this illusion and this theoretical error, which a few practical successes cannot justify or legitimate, that has determined the direction taken in France, since Condillac above all, by the philosophy of the human mind. The same illusion explains everything incomplete, restricted and excessive in the most modern doctrines, in its language as in the things of which it speaks.

I will also add, as a final reflection on the abuses and errors of method, that the limits at which what is called the physiologists' *analogy* should stop are determined by the very nature of the means that it can employ, and above all, by the nature of the object to which it is appropriate. These means, indeed, can be borrowed only from the external senses, and from the imagination or representative faculty. Its sole object consists in the appearances or phenomena represented beyond the *self.* It can have no purchase, therefore, on the species of primitive facts that fall under the inner sense; and if there is a sort of observation or sense particularly appropriate to the elementary facts of this order, the analogies or phenomenal resemblances that offer themselves to an external or physical point of view cannot return into the internal sphere in which the thinking being is present, as a reflective witness, to its finest operations, to its most inner modifications. Here, everything is simplified and individualized; there, on the contrary, everything is generalized and composite. *Classifications* and *laws* that are, after the observation of effects, the two great motors of the natural sciences,[7] will hardly find useful employment in the

---

[7] A very judicious philosopher presents precisely the successive operations of science in the discovery of factual truths: *Observe, classify, draw the laws, find the causes* (see Prévost of Geneva's *Philosophy Essays* [P. Prévost, *Essais de philosophie, ou Étude de l'esprit humain* (Genève: J. J. Paschoud, 1804)]).

knowledge of primitive facts or of the truths of feeling that can be deduced from them in the most immediate way.

But it is above all in the search for causes – which is the fourth and final progress indicated by the method of the experimental sciences – it is, I say, above all in the general and necessary application of the *principle of causality* that the experimental method seems to us to have to distance itself from the method appropriate to a veritable science of principles.

Indeed, we have already sensed that, in the object of the physical sciences, the sensory phenomena represented in isolation can always be analysed, compared each to the other and classed according to the order of their succession or their analogies, in abstraction from the real or productive *cause* or *force*. Since the proper and necessary idea corresponding to the latter does not fall under the senses or the imagination, and does not enter into experimental calculations, its true value remains hidden in the sensory form of the effect, itself generalized.

But in the reflective science of the acts or states of the thinking subject – themselves presented as facts of the inner sense – none of these acts can be conceived or immediately apperceived in its production without the consciousness or the inner feeling of its principle or of its productive cause, this cause being nothing other than the *subject* or *self*, which exists *for itself* only in so far as it knows itself, and knows itself only in so far as it *acts*.

This is a truth or fact of inner sense, which ought not to require proof, but which will, at the right moments, gain all the necessary elucidations. In anticipating a little the analyses that will follow, as an example able to confirm the principle just laid down, let us take one of the active modes in which the subject can be manifest to itself as an *agent* or cause of its act: the effort that the will determines in making the body move as a whole or just in some of its particular organs that are directly subject to its influence. Now, I say that the inner feeling of the cause or productive force of the movement – which is the *self*, identified with its effort – and the particular sensation (*sui generis*) that corresponds, in the natural order, to the contraction of the muscular organ can be considered as two elements of a total mode in which the *cause* and the effect (the *effort apperceived* and the contraction felt as a *result*) are bound together in the same consciousness, in such an indivisible way and according to a causal relation that is so necessary[8] that one cannot abstract from the force or *cause*

---

[8]   *The principle of causality* (as one philosopher whom I take the liberty to cite here says, a philosopher who may perhaps be one of my judges) is the father of metaphysics; the way of considering or deducing it is of interest to the fate of the whole science; on it depends the question of knowing if it is really a science or a chimera; the means of saving it from shipwreck is to prove that the principle

State of the question *as considered in various systems of speculative philosophy* 41

without changing or denaturing entirely the idea of its effect. And, in truth, the muscular sensation, when no longer accompanied by effort or caused by the will (*self*), would be only a purely organic affection, or would remain obscure and unnoticed [*inaperçue*], like the vital movements that take place within the body, beyond the limits of will and, consequently, beyond the *apperception* that depends on the latter (as we will see in what follows). In the end, it would be only a completely passive impression, like the beating of the heart or convulsive movements that we feel without producing them.

I conclude from this simple example, whose consequences cannot be developed here, that in the analysis of internal phenomena it is not permitted, or even possible, to abstract from the cause, and that this cause itself, far from being something *unknown*, enjoys all the evidence of a fact of feeling, since it derives from the very character of its product, which becomes perception only in it and by it.

From this it also follows that, in the science of principles, we will not be authorized to dissimulate the real title of the cause under that of the generalized effect; nor will we be able to content ourselves with giving it a name. We will also have to determine its idea, to conceive it precisely and to draw it back to its primitive, individual and real source.

It will also not be permitted, in the analysis of ideas or the science of human faculties, to alter the proper value of the terms signifying the operations of the thinking subject, the most constant modes of the exercise of its activity, such as *attention, recollection, comparison*, etc., by generalizing them in an arbitrary manner in order to bind their abstract sense to the characteristics that a passive impression is supposed to possess (either in the impression's excluding any other, by its predominance, independently of the activity of the subject that makes it predominant, or in the impression's spontaneous self-reproduction) in the absence of its external cause and without taking into account the internal force of production, etc.

For it is clear that substituting logical abstractions for real facts, artificial and conventional values for natural and precise acceptations, would be to denature the sense of the ideas and words. It would also amount to taking away from the understanding any further power it may have, and any real foundation from a

---

of causality is not a simple form, a simple category, a general idea (see the collection of Berlin Essays for the year 1801). In drawing this principle back to the primitive facts of inner sense and to the very phenomenon of the *self*, realized in immediate apperception, I believe I have come to agree with this philosopher, to whom I was close before having met him [Maine de Biran refers to: L. F. Ancillon, 'Mémoire sur l'analyse des principes dans les sciences', in *Mémoires de l'Académie royale des Sciences et des Belles-Lettres depuis l'avènement de Frédéric Guillaume III au trône* (1801) (Berlin: Decker, 1804)].

science of principles. Consequently also, in renouncing its status and abdicating its most positive rights over the system of ideas that constitutes its privilege, metaphysics would either become a chimera or find itself entirely under the aegis either of physics, whose principles it has to clarify, or of logic, the forms of which it has to ground.

I thought it important to announce the reality of certain primitive facts of inner sense, facts distinct from the phenomena of external nature, before ascertaining what these facts consist of, and what are their signs and characteristics. I wanted to establish in this way the necessity of an inner observation as well as a method appropriate for these facts, a method distinct, in its principle and results, from the one that has been taught by Bacon and practised with so much success in the natural sciences.

It seemed to me that the transformation of the ideas of *cause, forces, faculties* in the method and language proper to the natural sciences could be applied to the science of principles only at the cost of grave abuses that denatured the real object of that science, made us wholly pass over its foundations, and dissimulated both its means and its end.

I had all the more need to make these remarks given that when – from the perspective that I present in what follows, according to which the immediate *apperception* of the thinking subject (*self*) is in no way different to the internal feeling of the cause or productive force of certain movements of the body as well as of certain operations of the mind – the objective cause is confused, in its sign as in its idea, with its objective effect, or, prior to that, effort with its product, the act with its result, the question posed, that I regard as fundamental to metaphysics, presents almost as many *nonsensical* ideas as there are words, and would find itself rebutted in advance by those to whom the common, unique and, as it were, sacramental term *sensation* is sufficient to explain everything in the science of human faculties.

I would have wanted to attempt to show, before entering into the depths of the question, that it is almost solely in virtue of an erroneous application of, or fictive value given to, the *principle of causality* that the analysis of the operations of intelligence, identified with the modifications of sensibility, has been reduced to the alternatives of: a purely physiological theory of functions or results of functions, analysed or materially decomposed in their instruments or organic seats;[9] a logical method of classification of the transformed modes of a passive sensibility, whose

---

[9]   See the work of the doctor Cabanis on the *Relations of the Physical and the Moral in Man* [P.J.G. Cabanis, *Rapports du physique et du moral de l'homme* (Paris: Crapart, Caille et Ravier, 1802)] and, in particular, the 'Physiological History of Sensations' ['Histoire physiologique des sensations'].

State of the question *as considered in various systems of speculative philosophy* 43

abstract characteristics are supposed to be derivations or transformations of a unique, fundamental sensory mode, in abstraction from the cause or real force that transforms; and, finally, supernatural, mysterious notions of this *subjective* cause, realized in an order of absolutes, beyond all products brought about in real existence, and as if reduced to certain *innate* forms with which it is supposed to clothe, in time, the phenomena of sensory experience. These are three points of view equally distant, to my eyes, from a true science of principles.

We have just shown this for the system of transformed sensations. This system presented itself for our examination first when we wanted to account for the facts of the matter and discuss the proper sense of the terms in which the question is posed. It is this system which first struck us, as much by the proximity of the links and its close relations to, as much as by the contrasts it seemed to offer with, a doctrine grounded on the testimony of inner sense and with a method of observation and language appropriate to the discovery and to the distinction of the primitive facts of consciousness.

We are now going to examine, with the same goal, the original instantiation of this doctrine, which we will see come closer than what derives from it to a real science of principles; we will see it return close to the source, but stopping at its edges and without drawing from its depths. From there, we will take another look at other systems of first philosophy, whose authors, after having partially seen and even touched, in passing, the truly fundamental point, were led beyond it by an audacious drive towards the mysterious region of essences in which *virtualities, forms, categories* and *ontological laws*, realized independently of existent things, come to be placed before the latter in a logical order of *application* (rather than of generation) of the human faculties. We will be able to judge the foundation of these ideal doctrines in which the human being, positing itself in an *a priori* fashion as a wholly spiritual being, seems only to communicate with wholly pure intelligences, and finds itself separated from material nature by reflection, just as the physical observer found himself unified and almost identified with sensation.

In this way, we will imitate in our inquiries the march of the human mind, which does not advance progressively towards its goal, in always following a straight line, but sometimes comes closer to the goal without touching it, sometimes moves away from the goal in overshooting it, thus proceeding according to an irregular curve, full of points of inflection and reversal that it is interesting to note and important to recognize, in order to arrive at or to remain in the mid-point which must be the closest to the truth as well as to the real origin from which all the variables of the curve depart in diverging from it.

§2

Of a Natural Foundation of the Science of Principles in Locke's Theory; how the Characteristics and Nature of the Primitive Facts can be Distinguished within it

The terms employed in our languages to express *acts* of will or the *operations* of the intelligence – the *verbs* indicative of existence and action, indivisible from a real subject, such as *apperceive, will, judge, feel,* and the corresponding *abstract* substantives, their natural derivations – terms that are constantly and necessarily employed in the forms of discourse, doubtless do not represent nonsense or purely conceptual entities. Unless the testimony of inner sense is rejected absolutely, it cannot be denied that they correspond in the mind, if not to sensory images, then at least to intellectual and positive ideas. But it cannot be admitted that these ideas, however they are established in the understanding, are introduced within it like the immediate impressions of objects, by the same direct *senses* and by the same absolute way. Far from resembling sensations or images, these most intimate ideas or modes disappear before them, like the pale light of the stars disappears in the light of the sun. They are also separated from it by a remarkable contrast of the characteristics of composition and variety, on the one hand, which are quite opposed to constancy and simplicity, which indicate, on the other hand, a different source or origin.

But if these first ideas do not come from the senses, and if they are not *innate*, to what can their origin be assigned? And do we not have to search for it in the primitive exercise or the development of a particular internal sense by means of which the individual, or the *subject* constituted as such, would find itself in relation with itself, in the exercise of its proper acts or most internal modes, as it is in relation to a nature foreign to it by means of the external senses? In this way, we arrive at the natural foundation of a science of primitive facts of inner sense, considered as *principles*, and at the sort of observation that is appropriate to it.

This is the fundamental point of view of Locke's doctrine. This philosopher, beginning with a double origin assigned to all the modifications and ideas of the human understanding, was able to propose as a goal the separation or analysis of two sorts of elements or two orders of primitive facts that, though combined in experience remain distinct by certain characteristics deriving from their respective sources. Thereby, indeed, it became possible to distinguish and to recognize the elementary facts, in making them emerge from the composites in experience by a sort of decomposition, that is not *logical*, as was Condillac's, but real, in the manner of the chemists.

State of the question *as considered in various systems of speculative philosophy*   45

When Locke points out, first of all, an essential distinction between *simple ideas of reflection* and the *simple ideas of sensation*,[10] between the inner feeling that accompanies the operations of the will or the free acts of the intelligence and the wholly passive modifications of external and internal sensibility, depending respectively on the action of the material objects or the imagination's own projections, this wise philosopher seems to me to be on the way towards an exact and real analysis of the primitive facts, and ready to establish the science of principles.

But in signalling *reflection* as a source of ideas, was it not necessary to draw this faculty back to a more immediate source, one closer to the common origin of *all ideas*, of *all known existence*, of any conceivable primitive fact?

Three principal reasons seem to me to have prevented Locke from making this return to the source and from taking to its conclusion an analysis that perhaps would have produced a happy simplification in the science of human faculties.

The first relates to the supposition, admitted without sufficient examination by the author of *Essay on Human Understanding*, that all the ideas of *sensation* come from outside into the understanding, and are formed from scratch, so to speak, without the aid of the activity proper to the subject. Consequently, this philosopher had to consider the two origins as absolutely separate from each other, without communication, without reciprocal influence, the superior *source* (reflection) never mixing with the inferior (*sensation*), which cannot, for its part, raise itself to the height of the former.

Thus, as the external senses are naturally endowed with a purely receptive capacity of sensations, with simple ideas of sensation, the soul or the thinking subject *innate to itself* will be supposed endowed by its nature with a faculty or power of *reflection* (*also innate*, perhaps), which, being applied exclusively to the

---

[10]   Leibniz objected to the supposed *simplicity* of the ideas of sensation established by Locke: 'They seem simple to us', he says, 'only because they are confused, and the more we penetrate into one of our sensations, the more elements we will discover in it' [approximate quotation from G. W. Leibniz, *Nouveaux essais sur l'entendement humain*, Amsterdam et Leipzig: Rudolf Erich Raspe, 1765, trans. P. Remnant and J. Bennett, *New Essays on Human Understanding* (Cambridge: Cambridge University Press, 1996), book II, chap. II]. What Leibniz means here by *sensation* is not what the author of the *Essay on the Understanding* named an *idea of sensation*. The former considers sensation outside of, so to speak, the feeling subject, while the latter takes it in its actual relation to consciousness or to the immediate apperception of the individual subject which feels itself modified in a simple and uniform way, whatever the number may be of the elementary and constitutive impressions; here, as in most metaphysical discussions, the misunderstanding belongs principally to the expression, and nothing will be more common, indeed, than these sorts of misunderstandings when there is often only a single word to express the external cause of the impression together with the play of the organ, and the effective result with the apperception of the *self*, etc.

subsequent operations of a developed intelligence, will have its own sphere of activity beyond the realm of sensations and images.

But do not the first simple ideas – already complete, *ex hypothesi*, when they arrive from the outside – suppose the active participation of the subject that perceives them? Are they not in its consciousness? But what is this consciousness, if not an act designated by Locke himself as *apperception*, an act that must necessarily be bound to the sensory impression for it to rise to the rank of *idea*?

We should add that, according to the same doctrine, the soul cannot *feel, act* or *think* in general without immediately apperceiving that it feels, acts or thinks. It is here, as is said, the sole characteristic of the operations or modes that can be attributed to the soul as a thinking subject.[11]

But in this case, I ask how and in what this immediate apperception differs from the *superior* act named *reflection*, if not by the difference in the objects or in the modes of application, or in the degree of depth and distance from a source that can be really *one*.

If these difficulties were clearly presented to the author of the *Essay on Understanding*, he would doubtless have understood that the *idea of sensation*, which is apparently the most simple, must already admit, as an idea, the reflective element that should not be sought on the outside, but rather within an activity inherent to the thinking subject.

The second reason that prevented Locke from finding in the idea of sensation everything that is to be found within it, and which made him assign to it a more distant source in reflection, is the equality or the perfect analogy of properties, of characteristics and nature, that he supposed to exist (again without adequate examination) between all the species of passive modifications expressed by the generic term: sensation. This celerity in generalizing and concluding by analogy, the source of so many abuses in all the sciences and in metaphysics in particular, made him, I think, grant too much and too little influence to the functions of the external senses on the origin of our knowledge and ideas, when he attributed to all, on the one hand, the same perceptive or representative faculty, and, on the other hand, a complete and general *passivity*.

If this philosopher had studied more profoundly these primary sensations that he considered so casually, he would have doubtless pointed out the species of those, deriving their characteristics and forms from the motive activity of the subject participating in them, that involve a sort of interior *redoubling* that would already suit the name *reflection*, and, distinguishing them from those that,

---

[11] See Book I of *Essays on Human Understanding*.

directly and passively received from the outside, without any active participation, are limited to affecting immediately the soul, are not repeated in its consciousness, and exclude, on the contrary, any return of the individual onto what he experiences or feels in his organization.

Thus, and after having observed these very notable differences in each specific and individual sensation, Locke would have been able to discover, in some if not all of them, a higher faculty contributing to them, a faculty that he supposed foreign to them. And here reflection would have found itself brought together with the original sensation, which would no longer be regarded as simple, but would have presented itself as a sort of composite of two elements that had to be pointed out and recognized according to the real order of their primacy.

A third cause that distanced Locke from the veritable source of primitive facts and from a *science of principles* was that – perhaps too astute to settle for the division, generally accepted by philosophers, of all the faculties of the soul into *understanding* and *will* – he transported, like the Cartesians, all the activity of the thinking subject to the system of will, as if that of the understanding could be absolutely separate from it. He circumscribes, in my opinion, the extension and the limits of a power of *willing*, in attributing it exclusively to the movements or acts available to the *self*; but when he subsequently excludes this power from the primary formation of ideas, he had to, as a necessary consequence, remove from its empire the whole domain of the understanding, including the reflection that is part of it. This reflective faculty will now be considered only as a sort of wholly internal sense without an *organ*, whose exercise is posterior to that of the physical or external senses, receiving like them and for them, in an equally passive manner, the secondary materials that are elaborated there and spontaneously transformed there... Here we see how Locke's doctrine prepared for that of his most important disciple, whose principles we have already examined.

In beginning with the famous principle: *nihil est in intellectu quod non prius fuerit in sensu* [there is nothing in the intellect that was not first in the senses], Locke was thus determined by all the preceding causes to distinguish a proximate and immediate origin from another, more distant and mediate origin. But since this restriction was not able to meet the approval, after him, of those *enlightened minds* who prefer, above all, *simplicity* and *unity of principles*, one came even to ignore inner sense in denying the reality, the primacy of the facts or of the ideas that are originally related to it in order to save the rigour and the general applicability of Aristotle's *maxim*. Was there not a means to reconcile this principle with a testimony stronger than it (since all the principles depend on it)? Could one not admit purely reflective simple ideas, without denying that these ideas themselves could come from sensation, not from *sensation in general*, but from a certain mode of exercise of certain senses in particular? This conciliatory point of view has not presented itself, I think, to any philosopher; we will see in what follows whether it is possible to find a basis for it.

The English philosopher, having as a principal goal that of analysing and gaining knowledge of human understanding as it is actually constituted, did not feel the need to go back to the origin of his moving forces, to the truly primary and constitutive operations or acts of reflection and apperception itself. It was enough for him to have signalled the respective sources of the two sorts of ideas that he found generally established in the understanding, to have classed these diverse ideas and to have analysed their composites, to have shown in the end their use, their extent and their limits in the different species of knowledge. He did not see the necessity of going deeper into the sources and of putting what he took to be the elements themselves to the test of analysis.

In helping himself to all that the science of ideas offered that was accessible to our means of knowing and most immediately practically applicable, he had only to occupy himself with the *objects* or *results* of our intellectual operations, without wanting to work, in the science of inner sense in particular, on the very nature of these acts in order to know the distinctive characteristics of the diverse faculties to which they can be related.

Also, when he speaks of the system of purely reflective ideas that have their proper names in our ordinary languages, this is solely to remark on the character of simplicity that essentially belongs to them, but not to distinguish them from each other and to try to determine their number, not to assign the primitive conditions and the circumstances in which they might arise (in the subject capable of originally acquiring the *immediate apperception* of them), and not to seek how they are combined in experience with impressions or sensible images, in the face of which they disappear in giving them a form.

The result of these omissions was that the system of reflective ideas, which more than any other was crying out for the regulatory hand of a philosopher sufficiently wise and capable to co-ordinate it, remained in the same state of confusion and inexactitude in which he had found it, and, having fallen into complete discredit among many of his disciples, was then forgotten.

I will observe, in concluding this section, that the same philosopher who traces out the elements of a theory wholly of reflection was hardly led by it in the science of intellectual operations, or in the precise determination of the individual ideas that were to be connected to the terms signifying these diverse faculties. When it is

State of the question *as considered in various systems of speculative philosophy* 49

a matter of recognizing their nature, of determining their number, of fixing their limits, or, in a word, of circumscribing the proper domain of these facts of inner sense, the products of a true or reflective analysis are almost always confused in his theory with arbitrary generalizations. Beginning with a classification of ideas, or from an arbitrary or logical *category*, he often links the term of this class to the artificial idea of a faculty that is purely nominal. When he distinguishes, for example, a *faculty of abstracting* and another of *composing*, is this not uniquely because, with the goal of classifying ideas, he distinguished the abstract from the composite? And why not link a faculty of this nominal or hypothetical order to every class of ideas? How and why is their number to be limited? Why place so much importance on determining it, when it is no longer a matter of real and primitive facts, witnessed by inner sense or by the reflection of our acts, but of simple *abstract possibilities* or pure *categories* that can be extended or shrunk at will, and of which ample materials are to be found in the general signs of language and the logical analysis of their forms? Was it not in this way, indeed, that the scholastics made the *entities* and *occult faculties* almost equal to the number of qualities or abstract properties substantiated in language?... Is it not in this way that the sectarians of experience, who took *exclusive sensation* as the basis of an ideological doctrine, as well as the *pure* metaphysicians, who began with the *bare* existence of the thinking subject, have ended up meeting each other in an abstract region whose empire is disputed by categories, after having excluded the primitive facts and reduced the inner sense to silence?

We have seen the nature of the motives and the results of this singular direction imparted to a philosophy that, forming its primary elements from sensations, consequently finds itself composed only of classes, genera or logical categories that it erected for itself. We are going to find very similar results in another philosophy, opposed to the former in its principles and starting point, but which, after having drawn its real elements from pure reflection, is going to err far from real facts in an abstract world of its own creation.

§3

Glance at Abstract Metaphysical Systems:
How They Indicate the Goal of the Science of Principles in Going Beyond It

When Locke undertook to combat and to overturn the system of *innate* ideas, he did not examine as much as he should have the martial knowledge or the capabilities of those that defended it. In renewing Aristotle's principle, it seems that he did not examine sufficiently the motives that, for a long time, had made eminently meditative minds abandon it; and the comparison of the *blank slate* left, and will leave for a long time perhaps, many difficulties that it was necessary to resolve, and many objections that it was necessary to counter.

The objections, indeed, reappear with renewed force as soon as one makes the observation noted above: that the first ideas of sensation (whose spontaneous formation as well as simplicity and original unity the English philosopher presupposes) necessarily presuppose some consciousness or inner sense and an active co-operation of the thinking subject, who joins to the sensory or organic impression elements drawn from his own source, the indivisible elements of personality or of the *self*, which exists as one, simple and identical, and apperceives itself precisely as the same under diverse internal modifications that are successive in *time*, just as it perceives or represents to itself, beyond itself, other external modifications, co-ordinated in *space*. Can these elements, I say, or these essential and properly subjective conditions of the *first idea of sensation*, be considered as occurring outside of time or as being able to emerge from the outside into the understanding? Or is it possible to bind them by some relation of immediate *causation* to a material cause or to the action of the phenomenal objects whose presupposed real existence is perhaps itself only a result of subjective laws of thought, a judgement or an act of *belief*, whose ground and value cannot be assigned to anything beyond inner sense? But if these personal elements, these first forms of the idea of sensation that seem to strike us as simple, are somehow essential attributes of the existence of the sensing and apperceiving subject, do we not have to consider them as *innate*, in the same way as the subject who apperceives or senses is innate to itself?[12]

That is not all! Secondary *simple* ideas, whose origin Locke attributed to reflection or to the inner feeling of certain intellectual acts, can be considered to be as different from the faculties themselves, or from the powers on which these acts depend, as the copy differs from the original, or as the *image* differs from the object that it represents. However, although according to this wise philosopher, the whole science of the faculties of mind comes down to the collection of simple ideas, acquired by inner reflection on its acts – just as the science of phenomena or of the properties of bodies comes down to the whole of the composite or mixed *ideas* that it is possible for us to acquire from the senses initially – it is no less true that, in his anti-idealist doctrine, corporeal things, comparable in this

---

[12] This is also what Leibniz objects to Locke in his *New Essays on the Human Understanding*.

State of the question *as considered in various systems of speculative philosophy* 51

regard to the faculties or essential attributes of the thinking soul, are always supposed to enjoy a truly *noumenal* existence, the one outside of the present sensation representing them, the others outside of the reflection that translates them, so to speak, into ideas or into immediate facts of inner sense.

If there is an essential distinction to note between these two species of ideas or of knowledge – of which one effectively takes the place of natural signs in the mind, as representative of the things or objects whose existence they attest to and whose presence outside of *the self* they announce, while the other are their own signs or their own objects without announcing anything beyond them – and if such a distinction is the fundamental point and the most important issue in philosophy (in order to protect oneself from both the gross illusions of materialism and from the impotent doubts of a sceptical idealism that destroys, in one fell swoop, the origin, the ground and the reality of all knowledge), it is simply not the case that Locke established it. The way in which he expresses the *simple ideas* of certain faculties currently in exercise announces clearly enough that he considers these noumenal powers as pre-existing in the human mind, innate in it or with it.[13] Thus Condillac reproaches him (in the *Summary* of the *Treatise of Sensations*)[14] for having established the doctrine of *innate faculties* when seeking to overturn that of the actually *innate* positive ideas that nobody really defended.

Whatever the case may be, as soon as one admits – as a supposition and perhaps solely by virtue of a *realized* abstraction – really pre-existing faculties or powers in the soul[15] that are prior to the original simple ideas and acquired in experience by an inner sense of their acts, it is quite natural to ask what these

---

[13] *'Conceptus in metapysica obvii non quarendi sunt in sensibus, sed in ipsa natura intellectus puri, non tanquam conceptus connati sed e legibus menti insitis (attendendo ad ejus actiones occasione experientiae) abstracti, adeoque* acquisiti' (Kant, *Dissertatio praecitata*, §8) ['Since, then, the empirical principles are not found in metaphysics, the concepts met with in metaphysics are not to be sought in the senses but in the very nature of pure understanding, and that not as *innate* concepts but as concepts abstracted from the laws inherent in the mind (by attending to its actions on the occasion of an experience), and therefore as acquired concepts', Kant, *On the Form and Principles of the Sensible and Intelligible World*, § 8, p. 387]. This view does not seem to me to differ from Locke's. It even seems to me to establish in a more precise manner the real foundation of a science of principles, deduced from these primitive facts that the mind comes to know in fixing its attention on its own acts in experience. But how and on what basis can the mind pass from the immediate apperception of these individual primitive facts to the general concepts of the permanent faculties of *possibility, existence, necessity, substance, cause,* etc., erected as categories, and even, at bottom, realized in the absolute, beyond the thinking subject and prior to any fact of existence? What grounds does he have to erect such categories as principles and thus to displace the real foundation of science? This is what has not yet, I think, been sufficiently examined.

[14] [E. Bonnot de Condillac, *Extrait raisonné du 'Traité des Sensations'*, in *Oeuvres philosophiques de Condillac*, G. Le Roy (ed.), *Corpus général des philosophes français* (Paris: PUF, 1947–1951), t. I].

[15] The interior noumenon, to which the phenomenal *self* [*moi*] in experience corresponds.

powers or forces can be, considered in themselves, as waiting to act without yet having acted. Do they not then depend on the still inactive inner sense, or can they not be said *to exist* under the heading, if not of innate ideas, then at least of *virtualities, dispositions, pure forms*, etc.? Can we not consider the soul as essentially endowed with active forces[16] that, although they may be undeveloped and unable to manifest themselves in the total absence of causes or means of sensation, are no less constantly disposed to act and exist prior to sensory impressions, since they communicate to the latter the form necessary to rise to the height of the *idea* of sensation, just as they produce the primary fact of inner sense or reflective experience, since they alone can *actualize* it and constitute its laws?

Let us examine these questions which, soon, will no longer belong to dogmatic metaphysics, and let us observe the retroactive movement of the human mind. It can rise to the theological or cosmological ideas of *substance, power, force* or *cause* of existence in general, etc., but only in starting from certain primitive facts that immediately make manifest to inner sense the reality and the permanent existence of the same *self* [*moi*], its substantiality, its constitutive force, its power or its causality in the modes and acts that it attributes to itself. These truly primitive facts of inner sense are therefore the roots and the veritable archetypes of the general ideas, which are deduced from them afterwards by virtue of a principle that seems to be inherent to the very nature of the human mind and that led it to imitate or to repeat indefinitely outside of itself copies whose unique original it carries within itself. Nevertheless, a synthetic method (that belongs exclusively to the sciences that have conditional truth as their object), reversing the natural order of the formation of ideas, tends always to displace the principles and the origin of science in putting the universal ideas before the particular facts from which they have been deduced, and in making the real existence of these facts depend on the laws or the possible forms to which these facts alone were able to serve as a model.

If this inverted progress follows the same procedure as that of *pure reason* in the logical linking of acquired elements of knowledge, it belongs no less to the essential and natural order of their progressive acquisition.

---

[16] 'Vis activa actum quemdam sive Entelekeiam *continet, atque inter facultatem agendi actionemque ipsam media est*'(Leibniz) ['Active force, in contrast, contains a certain act or entelechy and is thus midway between the faculty of acting and the act itself', G. W. Leibniz, *De primae philosophiae emendatione et de notione substantiae*, in *Opera Omnia*, ed. L. Dutens (Genevae: Tournes, 1768), t. II, part I, p. 20; *On the Correction of Metaphysics and the Concept of Substance*, in *Philosophical Papers and Letters*, ed. L. E. Loemker (Dordrecht-Holland: D. Reidel Publishing Company, 1969), p. 433].

State of the question *as considered in various systems of speculative philosophy*   53

From these attempts – made perhaps with a too presumptuous confidence in the capacities of the human mind, and before making a sufficiently exact survey of the natural means that it has in order to know both things and itself – to penetrate into the essence of the faculties of the soul or to know what they are in themselves, outside of their primitive exercise or of the reflective sense of their acts, two principal systems of metaphysics emerge.

The first, having Descartes at its head, does not distinguish the faculties from the ideas corresponding to them. He considers them in this way under the heading of *innate* ideas, as infused in the human soul at the moment of its creation, inseparable from it, forming its essential attributes or its very essence, independently from its union with the body and, consequently, of all commerce with a material nature.

The second, having at its head the honourable leader of an in many ways illustrious school, Leibniz, conceives these very faculties or *noumenal* forces only as simple *dispositions*, *virtualities* or intellectual *forms*, attributes of the human monad, residing or pre-existing there as if in a *germinal* state, until the senses developed according to pre-established laws come to furnish them with the required matter able to constitute with it complete perceptions or genuine ideas.

These two systems, which have both split off into so many branches, and which are apparently opposed to Locke's doctrine on the relation of principles and the real origin of knowledge, return to it for all that, just as it remains close to them on certain fundamental points. Like that doctrine, and even better than it, they signal the nature and character of the truly simple ideas resulting from simple reflection.

They present, first of all, an essential and primitive distinction between two sorts of elements that work together to form complete sensation, or the *idea of sensation*, which Locke thought was simple, namely a *material* or *passive* element that comes from the object or resides in the organization, and a *formal* element, inherent in the subject or produced by it in time.

Whence the possibility, already presumed, of a sort of analysis or decomposition that could lead us to the source of the elementary ideas or of the primitive facts of inner sense, by a sort of resolution of the sensible composites of experience, where they would be intimately combined. But could there not be, beforehand, some means of signalling the existence, nature and characteristics of each order of elements, prior to their combination in experience? Could one not know what is, in itself, this formal or subjective part of a perception or complete idea, before its intimate union with the material part? To say how it resides in the soul or the subject of thought, prior to the experience that sets it to work? Whether it is *infused* in it as an attribute or essential property of a passive substance, or as the constant product of a force essentially endowed with activity? We find here the principal difficulties as well as the issue on which these diverse systems diverge.

In conceiving the internal and formal thought to be outside of matter and believing that it can be separate from the soul no more than an attribute can be separate from the substance in which and by which it is conceived, Descartes consequently could not attribute to this soul any faculty that was not already there as a positive *innate idea*. But these innate ideas that in sensory experience are associated or composed with impressions, images or material *species* are received by the soul just as it received its own existence, without any active power or efficacious virtue that it does not have in its nature being able to contribute to its production.

In contrast, following Leibniz, the *innate* virtualities or dispositions do not consist in simple receptive capacities. The human soul, essentially *force* or *monad*, is essentially active,[17] and it is its products, originally bare and obscure, but developed and clarified in time by their harmonic union with sensory matter, which alone can effectuate clear representations, veritable perceptions or, as Locke says, the *ideas* of sensation.[18]

Kant came to situate himself between these two perspectives: the forms that he attributes to the thinking subject outside of experience and prior to any sensory impression are supposed to reside in it as essential attributes of a passive substance, and, in this sense, these pre-existing forms resemble Descartes' innate ideas. However, since he attributes to them the full value or title of perception only in their union with a sort of matter furnished by sensory objects, he approaches Leibniz's point of view.

We can observe in this latter system in particular that the active faculties or operations of intelligence seem to be merged, in their signs, with their results, or classified in the same way and under the same headings. It does not seem that there is any real exercise or deployment of reflective activity. The

---

[17] This force is, indeed, always at work, but its acts are far from coming to consciousness; they remain, for the most part, in the lowest and most obscure degree of perfection, which excludes apperception and consciousness.

[18] Descartes' and Leibniz's differing points of view on the matter and the form of which they suppose our first ideas are composed can be compared to the respective systems of Aristotle and Plato on the same elements of composition considered in the very objects of the real or phenomenal world. Plato completely realizes the forms as pre-existing ideas in the divine understanding, beyond matter with which they come to be joined in time. Aristotle considers the forms only as virtually or logically distinct, but not as really separate. There are many other parallels between Leibniz and Plato, but there is an even stronger parallel between Plato and our own Descartes, as justified by his disciple Malebranche.

State of the question *as considered in various systems of speculative philosophy* 55

understanding, like sensibility, is reduced to a certain number of passive *forms* under which the impressions and ideas come spontaneously to be arranged and *moulded*. Consequently, the same forms, abstracted from the subject in which they appear, substantiated in their general terms, will be distinguished, enumerated and ordered symmetrically between themselves only as categories or as cases still empty of facts and ideas. Thus, the science of principles would proceed wholly as a sort of logical analysis in which it will not be possible to apprehend the individual idea of a particular intellectual act, confused in the class of modes or abstract properties, summarized under a general term, in which the positive facts of inner sense would always be identified with abstractions, the sensory signs of a living force with the dumb signs of a dead language... And here we discover a certain similarity between two systems of philosophy that one might have thought to be quite separate: the one reducing all the faculties of the understanding to the abstract characters of the same transformed sensation, while the other shows us faculties within it only in the artificial forms in which it has clothed them as categories, before having distinguished or observed them as facts of inner sense.

The two systems in question (preoccupied, it seems, with certain logical results) do not take into account the real power that can *form* as well as *transform* sensation. Both seem to confuse the producer with his product, the product with the matter employed; they strip the former of its force, and the latter of its reality.

It is not that force is lacking in the original doctrine, that of Leibniz, but it is realized without consciousness or immediate apperception that constitutes the *worker* or the acting subject. It follows that this force, existing and operating without consciousness, is assimilated in the depth of its essence or the primacy of its origin to the other forces of the phenomenal world. It is not essentially reflective in its nature, but it is still in some way calculable in its effects. It is thus that the metaphysical laws of the thinking being come to be unified with those of a *transcendent dynamics*, in a region of the possible, foreign to the natural and real order of the facts of inner sense.

From here, we can draw another parallel between the philosophies of Leibniz and Condillac, which is quite far from such an elevated view: do not both of them suppose that metaphysical analysis can be subject to the procedures of the method of the geometers in the resolution of unknown quantities?[19]

---

[19] See Condillac's *Logic* and Leibniz, *Works*, vol. 2 (*Logic and Metaphysics*), which contains this remarkable passage: '*In metaphysicis plus quam in ipsis mathematicis, luce et certitudine opus videtur, quia res mathematicae sua examina et comprobationes secum ferunt, quae causa est potissima successus; sed in metaphysicis hoc commodo caremus. Itaque peculiaris quaedam proponendi ratio*

Without going any further into the examination and comparison of these metaphysical systems – neither time, nor my capacities, nor the sense of the question posed allow me to do this – I will observe in summarizing what I have said that the analyses, the distinctions or clarifications established in the preceding views of a *pure* metaphysics relate only, indeed, to an abstract world of *possibles* in which the foundations of the science come to be transported beyond that of existence, a world in which *unity, identity, substance, causality* are considered (*in abstracto*) before and outside of the subject constituted as *one, simple, identical,* as substantial or permanent, as the cause or productive force of the acts it attributes to itself, etc. – constituted thus, I say, for itself and in the very facts of inner sense that provide the source of individual and purely reflective ideas before they are generalized and transposed to all existences. The abstract doctrines of which we are speaking go in the opposite direction, and thus as soon as one wants to bring them back to the real and positive facts of inner sense, they find themselves without any application there, and lead us, along the path that has been cleared, blindly down the slope formed by the habits of the imagination that from the beginning present mere composites instead of what is simple, which they veil from our eyes with variable illusions instead of permanent realities.

A wholly *pure* metaphysics, far from dissipating these tricks of the external senses, often only replaces them with others of a different nature. In arrogating to itself the right to judge experience and to give laws to it, it has often received its own laws in subjecting itself to blind habits, and has sanctioned them by precipitate decision instead of rectifying them by reflective examination.

Notice, indeed, the vast empire of the habits of the imagination that everywhere seeks and creates analogies, false or true, in order to compose its pictures and to enclose the greatest number of objects in the one frame, and the most varied perspectives within it. Notice, I say, this same empire in the *pure* doctrines just as much as in those of *sensory* experience. See how, everywhere, an equal simplicity or ... of composition, identity of *forms*, similitude of character, is supposed in all the most diverse modes summarized by the unique term

---

necessaria est, et velut filum in Labyrintho, cujus ope non minus quam methodo ad calculi instar quaestiones resolvantur, etc.' [G. W. Leibniz, *De primae philosophiae emendatione et de notione substantiae*, Dutens (ed.), in *Opera Omnia*, t. II, part I, p. 19 (quotation slightly modified); *On the Correction of Metaphysics and the Concept of Substance*, p. 433: 'Yet it seems to me that light and certainty are more needed in metaphysics than in mathematics itself, because mathematical matters carry their own tests and verification with them, this being the strongest reason for success in mathematics. But in metaphysics we lack this advantage entirely. And so a certain distinctive order of procedure is necessary, which, like a thread in a labyrinth, will serve us, no less than the method of Euclid, to analyse our questions in the form of calculus, yet nonetheless preserve the clarity which should never be lacking from popular speech.'].

sensation, by virtue of an arbitrary generalization! With an over-hasty examination, it is supposed that all these phenomenal modes of sensibility and perceptibility (greatly diversified by the play of the instruments that co-operate within it, by the way the external cause acts, and above all the part played by an internal force essentially endowed with activity, etc.) contain the same elements, enjoy the same properties, are *formed* or *transformed* in the same way. This solely because in attributing them to the same subject of inherence, one believed it to be justified, once and for all, to attribute to them the same *appellation*, to order them under the same category. It would not be difficult, I think, to demonstrate that most of the abuses and of the oppositions to be found in the different metaphysical doctrines, and above all the principal cause that makes almost all of these doctrines proceed on the basis of a system of conditional truths without making any definite steps towards the absolute truth or real knowledge, derive from this generalization from such primitive particular phenomena of internal or external sensibility, a generalization made much too quickly, without study or reflection, according to analogies that are supposed rather than observed.

Thus, for example, and as we will see later, there is a species of sensations that are purely *affective* without being *representative*, whereas some are representative without having any affective character in their nature. What is more, such a species of modes, or rather such individual modes, include personality or the feeling of the *self*, which is hardly essential to other purely sensitive impressions. One order of sensations admits the form of *space* as a common element, or as the *unum* and the *commune* of all. Another admits *time*; and some admit both forms at once. There are perhaps some admitting neither the one nor the other and that never rise to the rank of clear perceptions, or even to that of confused perceptions. Once these differences are established (and we will show that they have a natural foundation), what is signified by general affirmations such as these: everything that is in the understanding comes from *sensation* or is merely *sensation*. Or else: in the soul there are only representations? Or again: the forms inherent to sensibility are *space* and *time*; it clothes all phenomena in them, etc.? About which type of sensation is one speaking? For surely, what is true of the one is not true of the other; all these affirmations are true in a particular sense, and all false, perhaps, in the general intention, and when considered as absolute principles. Their authors are all right when they criticize each other; they are all wrong when they become dogmatic in the views that they hope to establish exclusively, etc. Perhaps the nearest to the truth and to a science of principles would be the one that, situated between them all, would take as much care in distinguishing and separating as they spend in generalizing and composing.

It is in this way, indeed, beginning with a hypothetical classification and proceeding always on the same path, from generalization to generalization, poorly or inappropriately formed, that the most diverse doctrines become sciences that base themselves only on logical analyses, consult only *verbal* forms, and lead to a system of merely conditional truths in which the reality of the things or facts of inner sense are no longer *involved*.

In highlighting, frankly and as we see it, gaps in the philosophies aiming to erect a science of principles on foundations that are foreign to the fact of inner sense, we have committed ourselves to avoiding these traps that we have pointed out in advance. We have thus said enough to give an idea of our manner of viewing the proposed question, as well as of the most fitting means to answer it. It is time to present our own thoughts and to address the question.

§4

Our Method in the Search for Primitive Facts of Inner Sense.
General Plan and Division of the Work

The philosophers who have distinguished in primitive sensation two sorts of elements – one composed by *matter* and the other constituting *form* – have considered this *matter* and this *form* as being equally unified, equally indivisible, in all the species or classes of sensory impressions. Consequently, if the link between the two is indissoluble, their intimate, constant and inalterable association never varies, never increases or diminishes in the sensory modifications. Reflective experience has no means to consider them as separate, and so the distinction between them rests on no fact of feeling. The analysis is thus not real, but purely logical. The supposed distinction between the matter and form of sensation would thus be grounded merely on a preconception that considers one and the same indivisible mode of our sensory being under the two relations that it can have: to the *object* that causes it or the organ that receives it, and to the subject that attributes that object to itself. But the relations that the mind establishes between the objects or the modes that it apperceives do not enter into the latter as elements of their composition, and do not alter their simplicity, if they are simple in their nature. There exists perhaps a natural and more real foundation for the same distinction or for a true analysis of *sensation*, one able to bring to light the primacy of the facts of inner sense.

Take the form of *sensation* in the *unitary*, indivisible and self-identical *self*, and *matter* in what we will call *affection* (*physical* pleasure or pain), which is always multiple and variable. If it is true that there are affective sensory impressions or modes to which the *self*, constituted in its own individual form, does not belong, or belongs only in the most obscure manner, if everything in passive sensibility is not really in *consciousness* and *apperception*, if there are a multitude of degrees according to which the organic or sensory impression can increase or diminish, while the feeling of the *self* or the forms of causality, identity, of individual duration that are granted to it become obscured or, contrastingly, more lively – if the laws of these differences or these developments can emerge in observation, and from our inner experience, applied to diverse states, diverse circumstances and the conditions of human sensibility and perceptibility. . ., then, perhaps, and in having regard for all these differences, we are closer than the doctrines of pure metaphysics to a way to assign, in the real order of facts, the two elements that must necessarily belong to any complete sensation or perception. The first of these, which we can now characterize as a primitive fact of inner sense, cannot be absolutely identified with the second, which emerges in its material simplicity when it is considered from the right perspective and in the right way.

Indeed, I think that in observing human nature according to the two sorts of relations that constitute it, it is not impossible to prove that the variable sensory matter and the *unitary* personal form do not belong in the same way, according to the same mode of combination or the same intimacy of association, to these diverse modifications to which it is customary to apply the common and general term *sensation*. This would entail that no one of these modifications, nor even sensation in general, can be taken as a type or basis of all the subsequent deductions with which one might hope to compose a *science of principles*, and this is a result conforming to what we have already observed about the dangers of over-hasty generalization from particular ideas or facts.

I say, first of all, that there is an individual mode, quite distinct from all the other species of sensations, and which can be considered as *formal* in so far as it has its unique ground in the subject of perception, in the *self*, which is, perhaps, constituted only in it and by it.[20] This active mode is one that I call *effort*, which,

[20] I announce here my opinion in the form of a doubt until I am able to clarify it or justify it by the whole of the considerations that will be exposed in the course of this essay. I must signal in advance that this fundamental mode or primitive act designated here under the individual sign of *effort* is quite distinct from sensation of movement, taken also by other philosophers as fundamental or as originating consciousness (see in particular de Tracy's *Elements of Ideology*). I must say in anticipation that it is not enough that the movement is simply felt for it to have the characteristic of the immediate apperception that I tie to effort; it is also necessary that this movement be produced and *initiated* by this hyperorganic force, properly termed *will*, as we will see in what follows.

freely occurring and following certain conditions that we will have to determine later, includes in the immediate apperception of the living force that continuously produces it the correlative feeling of an organic or material resistance, which is necessarily and originally perceived outside of the force as its term of application, beyond the *self* as its object.

I say, secondly, that this effort, and this resistance thus conceived as indivisible and, correlatively, essential, already constitutes a complete mode, under the individual heading of apperception (it cannot be classed under the general heading *sensation* without confusing everything), independently of all matter furnished by the objects of the external, phenomenal world. It is essential to note this straight away.

Furthermore (or from another perspective), I say that there are or can be simple, absolute affections, reduced to *matter*, in so far as they all have their ground in the living organization or in some kind of wholly passive impression. The affections stripped of all form of personality – and consequently of those of *unity, identity, substance,* perhaps even those of *space* and *time* – can be considered only as incomplete sensations, which cannot ground, and from which no particular operation of the intelligence can be deduced as a *transformation* (as Condillac attempts to do with the first absolute affection of his statue) .

On this basis, it emerges that effort, the fundamental, uniform and identical mode determined by the active force continuously producing it, comes to unite itself with the diverse passive impressions of a *living* rather than *thinking* organized machine, and joins itself with it in diverse ways: partly by intimate combination, partly by a simple relation of co-existence. Together, these two elements could constitute all the classes or species of sensation, perception or of the composite modes of our existence, regardless of how they are designated.

This opens different avenues for the analysis of sensation, diverse ways of recognizing the primitive facts and reaching them, either in beginning with the composite in order to discover what is *simple*, or in beginning with the latter in order to reconstitute the composite.

In adopting this manner of synthesis, we would still have to choose, in the order of primacy, between the element constituting the *matter* of sensation and that which gives it its form. In the latter case, one would depart from a true principle, or from a really primitive fact of inner sense. It would be here also that one would find the most direct solution to the first part of the question: *is there an immediate internal apperception?*

But it is necessary to consider that light arises from contrasts, and that in subjects where knowledge is more often negative than positive we learn of what

State of the question *as considered in various systems of speculative philosophy* 61

an object is after being assured of what it is not and of how it was merely thought to be.

A more direct consideration must perhaps determine a change in the proposed order of our enquiries concerning primitive facts.

The essential fundamental mode of personality or of the individual *self,* truly primary in the order of the facts of consciousness, may well not belong to the phenomena of a purely sensory life that we can observe as external to us and grasp, so to speak, in its points of contact with the life of consciousness.

The human being begins, indeed, to live, to feel, before being capable of knowing his life or of apperceiving his sensation (*vivit et est vitae nescius ipse suae*) [Still lives and knows not that he lives].[i] Even in the full development of all his faculties, when a wholly affective sensibility is carried to the highest tone, the human being feels and lives without apperception of himself or of the impressions that he undergoes; and it is in this sense that his existence can be brought back to the state of native simplicity signalled with so much energy by a famous philosopher (*homo simplex in vitalitate, duplex in humanitate* [*the human being is simple in its vitality, dual in its humanity*], Boerhaave, *De morbis nervorum*[ii]), a state anterior in the order of time, prior to the birth of the conscious *self,* and which would seem to be the result of all the organic forces that 'conspire and consent' in a common life (*conspiratio una consentientia omnia* [Conspiration one, all things in sympathy], Hippocrates).[iii]

Here is the first link of the chain to which a complete analysis of sensations and a genuinely first philosophy (or science of our feeling and thinking being) has to attach itself, if it is true that the principles grounding a science cannot be taken from the ideas or facts of which it is composed.

But everything that in the living or feeling being is or could be, from the simple fact of organization, subject to the laws of vitality and foreign to the laws of inner thought, ought to return into the domain of physiology. This experimental science should therefore provide essential data for the science of human faculties.

It is physiology that could distinguish and recognize the characteristics of the affections or, as Leibniz said, of these *obscure perceptions* which, having preceded in time consciousness and apperception,[21] still remain in the absence of the latter. It could relate them to their respective sources or seats, assign their causes and their effects in the natural or perverted order of the functions that fall under

---

[21] *Apperceptio est perception cum reflectione conjuncta,* Leibniz, *op. cit.* vol. II [G.W. Leibniz, *Commentatio de anima brutorum,* in *Opera Omnia,* t. II, part I, § XIII, p. 233: 'Cogitatio autem est perceptio cum ratione conjuncta' ('But consciousness is perception with reason conjoined')].

them, and determine their influence on the physical and moral aspects of the human being.

Exploring the most secret details of physical sensibility, it would come to circumscribe its own limits: in making us know better man as simple in *vitality*, man under the blind and unique impulsion of the organism, it would lead us to the exclusive source of the free and reflective determinations that constitute, outside of its sphere, *the human being double in humanity*.

In beginning the proposed synthesis of the first material element of sensation, we would begin, perhaps, like nature itself, which one never knows better than when imitating its products. This would be to reunite the advantages of a method of composition that grasps one by one the elements of a composite to the advantages of another method of co-ordination, which aims to know and to order these elements according to the natural relations of their filiation or reciprocal generation.

But whatever the methodical order of our inquiries may be, and regardless of whether we begin either from one or the other element of sensation in order to reconstitute each of its composites, or from its diverse composites in order to rediscover something simple, our method and means can only differ from those that have been employed heretofore in order to arrive at knowledge of primitive facts.

While, on the one hand, the doctrines grounded on originary sensation generalise *ex abrupto* these still incomplete facts, hurry to *form classes* and to pose arbitrary laws before observing the individual, specific phenomena, we will be concerned, on the contrary, to divide and distinguish the facts, so as to be able to study them in their most simple state.[22] Before generalizing the term *sensation*, we will assign the specific real characteristics of the modifications corresponding to the exercise of each sense considered in isolation, and, furthermore, to both of the active and passive functions that co-operate in this exercise, for it is here and not in general ideas or categories that the principles or primitive facts are to be found.

While, on the other hand, the systems of pure metaphysics elevate principles beyond all facts, take what is abstract for what is simple, and what is thus simple for what is primitive, in deriving the real from the possible, we will not leave the domain of the facts of human nature in order to find the principles of its

---

[22] *Quo magis vergit inquisitio ad naturas simplices, eo magis omnia erunt sita in plano et perspicuo,* Bacon, *Nov. org.* [F. Bacon, *Novum organum scientiarum* (Lugduni Batavorum: Wijngaerde, 1645); *The New Organon*, ed. L. Jardine and M. Silverthorne (Cambridge: Cambridge University Press, 2000), book II, chap. I, aphorism 8, p. 108: 'The more the inquiry moves towards simple natures, the more all things will be in a plain, transparent light.'].

State of the question *as considered in various systems of speculative philosophy*   63

constitution. If we do leave momentarily this inner field where reflection turns in on itself in order to know its own laws, where inner sense distinguishes its own facts, if we are obliged in the end to adopt an external point of view so as to trace from the outside the limits of the *self* and circumscribe its own domain, we will merely change the system of facts in coming into contact with the science of the phenomena of life and of physical sensibility. Based on two species of different observations, we will study the order of succession or coincidence and the parallelism of the two sorts of facts that are related to them, without ever wanting to assimilate or confuse them, and still less to penetrate into how phenomena corresponding to two very different senses can be linked, senses whose simultaneous products cannot be confused.[23]

Let us summarize briefly the means appropriate to the enquiry or to the determination of the primitive facts, and those also that we consider it necessary to employ in the resolution of the different parts of the problem posed.

Observing before *classifying*, studying each order of individual facts in its own respective source, each specific sensation in the sense that is proper to it, before generalizing or erecting as a principle any one of its abstract characteristics; attributing to each mode or intellectual product, each state or act of the feeling and thinking subject, to the faculty or to the proper sense that corresponds to it; applying the external senses and the imagination to things felt or represented, immediate apperception to the primitive forms of inner sense, and a concentrated reflection to the knowledge or to the determination of the proper acts of the will and intelligence, separated thus from the sensory results with which they are intimately combined in experience; circumscribing also the limits of each sense or faculty without any one domain impinging on another and in not confusing the limits assigned by our nature itself to each order of external or internal facts and to the two sorts of observations relating to them. Such is the method of which I should like to provide an example as well as the precept. It is by this method that we can learn if there really exists in us a fundamental state or act of

---

[23]   Those who materialize thought want to apply a sense of representation or intuition to the facts and to the ideas of inner sense or reflection; and *vice versa*, those who idealize external nature want to subject what belongs exclusively to representation to the inner senses of reflection. The philosophers who continuously work their meditative faculties seem to have only an inner view; it is thus in and by it that they perceive all phenomena. Those, on the contrary, who have exercised only the representative faculty can see only what is outside, and limit the sphere of realities to this. The former resemble a blind person denying that colours exist because touch cannot grasp them; the others are like men who, having always seen without ever having touched, would deny the reality of solid bodies in supposing that there exist only ever mobile coloured images that have no permanent foundation. These illusions derive from the fact that no one has yet adequately circumscribed the domains of each of our diverse faculties, and it is to this goal that the question posed leads us.

the thinking subject that bears the name *immediate apperception*, and come to know the characteristics differentiating such an act or mode from what bears the name *intuition*, in taking these terms according to the *analogy* of a language, itself grounded on the real analogy of the primitive facts of human nature that form the real and unique basis of the distinctions already established or to be established, and no longer according to the arbitrary divisions or categories of an artificial logic, which are as mobile and varied as the systematic and abstract views dependent on them. In this way, we will ascertain, in the primitive facts deduced from the analysis of the functions of the diverse senses, the real differences separating *intuition* from *sensation*, and the latter in turn from *feeling*.

After having traced thus, in reflective experience, the characteristics of *facts* that allow us to distinguish the primitive acts or states of mind constituting the three first parts of the question, it will not be difficult, perhaps, to respond to the fourth, in determining the relations that such primitive acts or states can have with notions or ideas, for the relations required have to depend on the very nature, or on the intrinsic character, of each of the acts or modes in question. The same relations, determined in the order of impressions or primitive facts of direct and simple perceptibility will therefore have to be the same in the system of notions and ideas, derivative products of the intelligence developed according to the progressive laws of its perfection.

To give an example here in anticipation of what will follow below, I will say that free effort, movement or the voluntary act (to which, I hold, internal immediate apperception is bound, and as applied to the first modifications of sensibility with which this conditional effort is intimately combined) will be the very same condition to which is bound, in the intellectual order, the same apperception but as applied to the notions or to the diverse ideas of the understanding. Here, spoken or written signs at the disposition of the will – without the intervention of which, perhaps, the intellectual idea would not even exist or, at least, would not come into the awareness of the thinking subject[24] – these voluntary signs, I say, take the place

---

[24] The response to this part of the problem, which concerns the relations of immediate apperception with notions and ideas, will give us cause to apply a fundamental principle, of which Condillac can be regarded as the author: that linguistic signs are required for the mind to be able, not just to order its ideas and *make use* of them, but also to conceive and apperceive them as *ideas*, and that is to say, to think, in the full sense of the word, and to employ freely the acts of attention, reflection and memory, etc.

Condillac's discovery – the depths of which he does not seem to have plumbed himself, since in his later work (the *Treatise of Sensations* and the one on *animals*, and his *Logic*, etc.) he misconceives its results and even the principle itself – seems to me to bear the imprint of genuine philosophical talent, which consists, as a German metaphysician has put it well, *not only in being able to repeat freely a series of acts, but above all in being able, within this free repetition, to gain an awareness of the power producing them*. (I add: and of the means that this power can employ in its free exercise.)

of the original movements, and finding themselves associated naturally to sensory impressions, bring them into the sphere of knowledge. It is thus that the fundamental act of *apperception*, or of the *will* on which it depends, remains always the same in all the orders of operations of sensory and intellectual ideas with the only change being the circumstances and the objects or terms of application of this primitive act.

Signs instituted voluntarily belong to these primary means; they alone can make the exercise of our faculties *available* to us. Condillac signals this principle; and thus he recognizes an *activity* outside of primitive, fundamental sensation. But why would any such signs, taken as a means of activity, not be employed in the first *ideas of sensation*? The analogy seems to entail the recognition of this original use of signs. But, further, what are the means, the instruments and the conditions of the availability attributed to signs, and through them, to ideas? How is it particular to the signs of oral language addressed to hearing, and is it not grounded equally on the exercise of all the senses? There are thus specific or individual differences between sensations; in what does this difference consist? Is it not that some are essentially passive, while activity belongs to the others? ... If Condillac had posed these questions and sought to answer them, we would have a quite different *Treatise of Sensations*.

Second Part

Of the Grounds of a Real Division of the Primitive Facts of Human Nature

First Section

Division of Affective Sensibility from Voluntary Mobility

The science of the faculties of the mind supposes, following Bacon,[1] two types of enquiries or primary considerations: the first relative to sensibility and to what simply affects the *mind*, the second relative to voluntary movement that the mind produces by its own activity.

Such is also the plan of the fundamental enquiries that I have proposed in this section in order to bring to light a distinction or division in the *primitive* facts, considered in the two really distinct systems of the sensibility and intellectual activity of *the human being*, and, consequently, to provide an answer to the following question: *is there an immediate apperception different from intuition, sensation and feeling, and in what do these differences consist, if they exist?*

---

[1] See the *Instauratio magna* and *Nov. org.* [F. Bacon, *Sommaire raisonné de l'Instauratio Magna, ou grande Rénovation*, in Destutt de Tracy, *Éléments d'idéologie*, t. III, pp. 563–88; Bacon, *Novum organum*].

Chapter I

Of Elementary Affection, and How its Characteristics and Signs can be Determined in the Mind and Physiology of Man

§1

Division of Affective Sensibility and Voluntary Motility

The elementary mode that I have designated under the heading of *simple affection* is located on the periphery, so to speak, of the twilight zone of the light of consciousness, and is not to be found, by itself, in the field of the general faculty of *apperception* that Locke took as the essential characteristic of all the modes or acts that can really be attributed to the thinking mind, as an individual subject of *inherence*.

It is not a question here of the impressions that, according to the author of the critical philosophy, clothe themselves, in internal sense, with the forms of space and time inherent to *pure sensibility*. On the contrary, what distinguishes the type of element that I want to speak of is precisely the complete absence of all the *forms* that can bring a sensory impression up to the level of an *idea of sensation* (in Locke's terms), that is, those forms under which the individual immediately apperceives his own existence in a time, and those which, representing to him external existences, transport his point of view into a space where the *self* does not exist...

Nor is it a question of a generative sensibility, such as Condillac conceives it, as if it were complete from the beginning, but rather of sensation as, precisely, incomplete and as it really is, according to the hypothesis that it is first of all without any personal form. This is affection as we conceive it, of which Condillac himself presents the example to us when he says that his statue is *odour, flavour, sound*, etc., and that identified with its modifications it wholly exists in them. Condillac, however, is not yet thereby thinking from the perspective of a simple living being: or, at least, his expression and his thought are not entirely in agreement. For what with one hand he takes away from his hypothetical phantom, he gives back to it with another, and, instead of putting himself in its place, or of lowering himself to it by the simple, immediate affection to which he reduces it, he tends rather to raise it to his own level, through consciousness and the individual feeling that he always tacitly grants to it, not ever really being able to conceive of the statue without the latter.

It is quite difficult to, as it were, denude ourselves and to ascribe to a being a nuance of life or sensibility, without ascribing to it also our *self*, without animating with our spirit the thing that we are thinking about, without conceiving it, according to an internal model, as a substantial or individual subject of inherence of modifications, however obscure or confused this conception may be.

Nevertheless, in spite of the difficulty that this sort of, as it were, *antireflective* abstraction presents to us, in which the *self*, the subject of perception, attempts to know what remains of this perception or complete sensation after having totally separated itself from it, and removed its constitutive forms,[2] we are no less justified in concluding from our own experience, our innermost experience, and from certain observations, which though constant are delicate and hardly accessible for the common man, that the phenomenal *self*, considered according to the internal, immediate apperception in which it consists, is not always associated in the same way to the diverse modifications of our sensibility, is not combined so narrowly with all of them, and does not always adhere to them, as it were, with the same degree of intimacy.

Now, in seeing that a composite varies in the more or less intense aggregation of its elements, we are led to conceive them in a state of total separation. Simply noting the differences in question, and, above all, enquiring into the causes or circumstances related to them, would therefore suffice to announce the possibility of a type of sensory or affective mode in which the self would find itself entirely excluded, which would consequently be simpler (under a *material* relation) than any of those that served as terms in the analysis of *sensation*.

But, before characterizing more precisely, and in its own signs, this type of mode, it is important to cast a glance on the efforts made by some philosophers to analyse this point and to draw it from the shadows in which it is enveloped.

---

[2] This difficulty stems from the fact that the material sense of immediate affection, like that of intuition, though distinct and separate from the inner sense or apperception, as much perhaps as touch is separated from sight, have constantly been exercised together, as far back as we can remember. Their products or modes can thus no longer be conceived in isolation from each other, just as it has become almost impossible to conceive forms without colour, etc.

§2

Diverse Signs Through Which We can Know a Purely Affective state

1. Immediate Affections Constitutive of Organic Temperament

We have already said it: man begins to feel before *apperceiving* and *knowing*.

This wholly sensitive existence, these penchants that are observable in the nascent individual, all these determinations that we vaguely relate to *instinct*, cannot be attributed to the source of all immediate *evidence*, to the inner feeling of what is in *us* and belongs to *us*. Consequently, these primary determinations, effectuated and conceived outside of the *will* and thought, cannot have received their imprint, nor be reproduced, under the intellectual form of memories or *reminiscence*.

This impotence of memory, which is attached in our experience even to the most lively sensations of internal or external sensibility, is one of the characteristic marks of any perfect, simple (*simplex in vitalitate*) affective mode, and of a sort of affective *matter* that is separate or separable from any personal form of *time* as well as *space*.

The whole of the determinations that we are right to understand under the heading of *instinct* are not limited to the first age of human life. The sphere in which this blind power continues to exert itself, far from being limited, can extend itself, in several respects, to that of our habits; but beyond that there is still a sphere of *activity* of a being that has now become double (*duplex in humanitate*).[3] It is not a single force, a single sensory power that can produce effects that are so often contrary and opposed. They are *two* which, without transforming themselves into each other, act together, each in its own domain, conspire, oppose each other, fight and triumph in turn. Who among us is not, at each moment, actor and witness of such internal scenes?

'There is not a single one of the parts of our body', as says Montaigne, he who is such an assiduous and judicious spectator of these scenes, 'that does not often exert itself against our *will*; they each have their *own passions*, which awaken them or put them to sleep without our concord'.[i]

---

[3] The sphere of instinct and that of habits seem wholly to *enclose* the animal. Only man is endowed with a power that tends necessarily to make him emerge from this circle, to the degree that it grows, so as to envelop all its acquired faculties. This power, which is the ground of all intellectual and moral perfectibility is but that of the will or of action, to which the apperception of free acts is immediately bound, whose power is located beyond the sphere of instinct as well as outside of the infringements and alterations of habit.

We can recognize the character of simple affections or the most immediate results of a sensitive property in the *partial* passions of which the author of the *Essays* speaks, in the brusque appetites of a particular organ, such as the *stomach*, the *sixth sense*, etc., whose influence, increasing sometimes by degrees, ends up by absorbing any feeling of the *self* and by guiding, unknowingly, all the movements or acts, that have thus become quasi-automatic. This is how can we recognize truly animal sensations.

From the more moderate support of the immediate impressions that are produced in the organs that affect each other by *consensus*, there arises the fundamental and absolute mode of a sensory existence, which can be said or conceived to be *simple* only following the *model* of a *resultant* of forces that are multiple and *variable* at each moment. This is not consciousness, for it does not *know*, does not illuminate itself; and, while it changes or dies incessantly, so as not to be reborn, there is something that *remains* and *knows* this.

The fugitive modes of such an existence, now happy, now baneful, succeed each other, push each other like mobile waves in the torrent of life. We thereby become, without any other cause than the simple affective dispositions to which any return is forbidden to us, alternatively sad or cheerful, agitated or calm, cold or ardent, timid or courageous, fearful or full of hope. Each age of life, each season of the year, sometimes each of the hours of the day[4] sees the contrast of these intimate modes of our sensory being. They fall under, for the observer grasping them, certain *sympathetic* signs; but, located by their very nature and intimacy outside of the field of perception, they escape the thinking *subject* by the very effort that it would make to grasp them. Thus the part of ourselves about which we are the most blind is the whole of these immediate affections that result from *temperament*, of which what we call *character* is always something like its *physiognomy*.[ii] This physiognomy has no mirror in which it could be reflected for its own eyes. . .

Such affective dispositions, associating their unnoticed products to the exercise of the senses and of thought, always impregnate things or the coloured images that seem to belong to them. This is a sort of organic refraction that makes nature manifest to us, now with a gay and graceful aspect, now covered with a funereal veil, which makes us discover in the same objects, now motives of hope

---

[4]   *Quod caeli mutatur in horis temperies, hominum simul quoque pectora mutant.* [M. G. Vida, *De Arte Poetica*, Romae, Vicentinum, 1527, book II, vv. 396–7: *Seu quod coeli mutatur in horas tempestas, hominumque simul quoque pectora mutant* ('Whether the sky shifts with the seasons, as the hearts of men change too')].

and love, now subjects of hate and fear. Thus is hidden, in the secret dispositions, the source of almost all the charm or the disgust attached to the diverse instants of our lives. We bear it in ourselves, this most real source of goods and evils, and we accuse fate or we erect alters to chance!... But regardless, indeed, of whether this unknown power be within or without us, is it not always the *fatum* that pursues us?... Let us dare to say it: it is not in the power of philosophy, of virtue itself, all powerful as it may be on the *actions* and the thoughts of the good man, to create any of these lovely affections that render so sweet the immediate feeling of existence, nor of changing these baneful dispositions that make it difficult and sometimes unbearable.[5] But does virtue itself not consist in this happy and ineffable feeling of existence, that is noticed and thus *redoubled* by reflection and the memory of all the great, generous and kindly actions whose inexhaustible source it is? Let us love and celebrate the good man, but let us also deplore the fate of the bad person, unhappy in the immediate impressions that he suffers, unhappy in apperception, unhappy in remembering and in foresight...![6]

Under the law of instinct, in the simple appetites, the penchants and primitive needs of the organism, the sensory being, *becoming* all of these affections or identified with them, immediately enjoys happiness or suffers the unhappiness of being. If a more developed intelligence observes these interior scenes, it is too often unable to distract them or change their course. This is not the proper field of the will and intelligence, which cannot go beyond certain limits that nature assigns to them.

2. Of the Signs of an Affective State During Sleep

In sleep or the complete inaction of the external senses, and even of the central organ of the imagination, there is often a surfeit of activity in the internal organs that allows the immediate impressions of which they are the seat to predominate,

---

[5]   If moral or physical medicine could manage to fix these happy impressions, or the organic state which corresponds to them, and to heal these baneful sensations which are a true sickness, those who possessed this precious art would be the greatest benefactors of the species, the veritable *dispensers of the sovereign good*, of wisdom and, I repeat, of virtue itself, if it is possible to call virtuous the one who is always good without effort, since he would always be calm and happy. It is this felt truth that J.-J. Rousseau drew from observing himself, and to which he often returns with such a great force of persuasion. It is also a truth of feeling for all men who, with the gift of an organization delicate enough to be always close to these immediate affections, have at the same time enough *force* to raise themselves above them. There is still for them, in this state, a certain consoling charm in *studying* them, in following their progress into even afflictions and sorrows, either in standing in relation to themselves as a sympathetic witness, or as envisaging in cold blood the internal enemy and in placing themselves by reflection out of the reach of its blows.

[6]   We will see, in what follows, how these simple affective dispositions can modify the exercise of the intellectual faculties and constitute the ground of all the mixed passions of the moral agent.

and that converts their *organic* impressions into veritable *animal sensations*. The animal, indeed, is thus determined to various co-ordinated acts or movements that are *necessarily proportionate* to the nature of the affections experienced and are, for the foreign observer, *signs* of the latter, while the *self* or the absent person completely ignores what the sensitive being alone does or experiences. Such a state doubtless hardly differs from *native simplicity*.

When the internal sense of the imagination, excited by the impressions that come to it during sleep, comes sympathetically into action, the images that it produces, following and merging into each other in a thousand strange ways, remain foreign to *thought*. The feeling of identical personality and, consequently, the *form of time, memory*, are not joined to these spontaneous and irregular productions of the brain, and the images, which we can call in this state of passivity *intuitions*, are, in this centre, like the immediate affections in the internal organs that correspond with it; these are *elements* of the same nature.

It is this absence of personal feeling, and also the momentary suspension of the particular conditions to which it is bound, which constitutes the veritable *sleep* of the *thinking* being; for there is complete sleep for the *sensory* being only in *absolute death*. The principle maintaining life and affectability in the organs is always awake (*active excubias agit*);[iii] it goes through, together or successively and in an order determined by nature or habit, all the parts of its *domain*, which awaken or fall asleep in turn. But the animal can be half-asleep while several organs are awake; the animal can also be awake while thought and the *self* are still asleep. It would not be impossible to observe these gradations, and, perhaps, in bringing them back to their organic causes, to explain some part of the quite surprising effects of *somnambulism*.

The phenomena of sleep studied in their successive linkages, the numbed state into which the various senses fall one after the other (from the moment when, the will ceasing to act, apperception and consciousness cease with it, to the point when all the external organs are completely asleep, and, in an inverse order, from the awakening in each particular sense to the point where the *self* becomes aware of itself in the plenitude of functions that are proper to it), the nature of the dreams that arise in a more or less profound sleep, the products of intelligence that sometimes break into the vague obscurity of the images and impress on them the character of an imperfect *reminiscence*,[7] joined to the observation of what

---

[7] We surprise ourselves sometimes when awake, in particular states that seem to us to relate confusedly to some anterior mode of our existence, though we cannot link them to it by an explicit act of reminiscence. These are perhaps old *dreams*, reproduced in the waking state following an organic state similar to that which determined them in the first place.

Of Elementary Affection, and How its Characteristics and Signs

happens analogously in diverse nervous, lethargic, cataleptic or ecstatic states, when their invasion is also gradual or successive – all this seems apt to reveal the simple character of these affections or images that Buffon calls *material*,[iv] and to make us aware of a *composite* in perception, that must admit an extra element.

3. Other Signs of a Purely Affective State in Cases of Mental Alienation

Whatever the cause may be that suspends the *perceptive* faculty in its conditions or its own motives, the impressions can be received, the animal can be affected and consequently move, but the *self* is not present, consciousness is *enveloped*, and for as long as such a state lasts, it is impossible to distinguish in it any of the characteristics that constitute for us the intelligent being endowed with apperception, will, thought.

The state of *idiotism*, for example, is one in which the *self* is asleep, while the impressionable or affectible organs are awake, and sometimes even adopt, by the concentration of their own life, a superior degree of energy.[8] The state of *dementedness* corresponds again to that in which the brain spontaneously produces images, which are sometimes linked but more often unrelated, while thought sleeps or comes to awareness briefly from time to time.

The *idiot* lives and feels; his life is composed of numerous impressions that he receives from inside and outside, and of movements that are *proportionate* to the nature of these impressions. He goes around, in a word, the whole of the circle of sensory existence; but beyond this circle, there is nothing. This degenerate being *becomes* all of his modifications more than he *perceives* them; there is no *time* for him; the *matter* of thought exists, but the *form* is lacking.

In the maniac with delirium, the principal instrument of intellectual operations is completely removed from the active and reflective force constituting the *person*. Images in him adopt by themselves the diverse characteristics of

---

[8] Barthez observes, and each of us can confirm this in himself, that a noise that suddenly awakens us strikes our ears with much more force than it has when we are awake, even in a very calm situation. 'The sounds that violently interrupt sleep', says this philosophical doctor, 'strike particularly the sense of hearing, because it is then more concentrated in its own organ, and more isolated from the other senses'. This example is apt for making us understand how there can be *affection* in a particular organ while its sympathetic communications with the brain are partially suspended. It also shows the difference in character between *animal* sensations, which occur by the play of *diffuse spirits* [*esprits diffus*] or by a *nervous* property, and perceptions that depend on the play of *celled spirits* [*esprits cellulés*] or particular modifications impressed on the organs by the will, as we will have occasion to show elsewhere. [J. Barthez, *Nouveaux éléments de la science de l'homme* (Paris: Martel aîné, 1778), chap. XI, section II, p. 237, note. Quotation slightly modified by Biran].

persistence, vivacity and depth that the immediate affections adopt in their particular seats by the sole effect of the organic dispositions. It is here that the effects of a sympathetic correspondence between the internal organs and the brain considered as the seat of passive imagination can be signalled – a correspondence so clearly demonstrated and so well described in its *signs* by great observers.

But will we go as far as to look for the signs and the proper characteristics of a division of intellectual phenomena in a state that excludes the primary and fundamental condition of intelligence itself: apperception, the *conscium* [consciousness] and *compos sui* [self-control]?[9] Can the exercise of the faculties of *attention, memory, comparison, meditation*, etc. be supposed in a being that presently is ignorant of itself, and which is deprived of the real power to *understand* ideas as well as to *will* its acts? It is certainly possible to transport to the state of complete mental alienation certain *faculties* that are defined and characterized (from *within* sensation) under the conventional headings of *attention, judgement*, etc., as Condillac has done with the hypothetical phantom that he takes for the term of his analyses. But are these the operations whose internal *model* we find in ourselves, whose singular ideas we obtain in reflecting on ourselves? Is it from this source that we can draw the knowledge of primitive facts?

In order to attempt to circumscribe the limits and the nature of the first *element* of sensation, I have selected examples in certain general states, where affectability, either alone or predominating, really *envelops* all the faculties belonging to thought, without allowing them to *reveal* themselves. It would have been easy to take these examples from the more particular modifications of the external senses, which prove that the impression can affect the animal without being perceived by the *self*. I could also cite cases where habit carried out by itself, as it were, the separation or the *analysis* of the two *elements* of the perceptual composite, in obscuring gradually the one to the point where it is completely effaced, while it conserves for the other an unalterable clarity. But I have presented these facts elsewhere[10] in sufficient detail; and they could find their place when we carry out a thorough analysis of the functions of each particular sense.

---

[9] See Pinel's *Medico-philosophical Treatise on Mental Alienation* [Ph. Pinel, *Traité médico-philosophique sur l'aliénation mentale ou la manie* (Paris: Richard, 1800), trans. D. D. Davis, *Treatise on Insanity* (Sheffield: Cadell and Davies, 1806)].

[10] See *Mémoire sur l'influence de l'habitude* [Maine de Biran, *Influence de l'habitude sur la faculté de penser* (Paris: Heinrichs, 1802), trans. M. Donaldson Boehm, *The Influence of Habit on the Faculty of Thinking* (Westport, Conn.: Greenwood Press, 1970)].

In order to discover the characteristics and the signs of an affective mode, a material element of complete perception that is foreign in its isolation to the individual person or *self*, we have had to draw from this primary source where physical sensibility, alone or just predominating, entirely excludes the will, in which all human power resides, all its thinking force. It would be easy for us to multiply the particular examples apt to illuminate the material character of these affections, which we were happy merely to signal in the most general states of the sensitive system. We could cite, for example, the particular modifications of the external senses, such as the sense of smell or taste, in which the predominant affective part can either absorb, in becoming enthused, the formal or apperceptive element, or leave it to itself as, so to speak, naked, in becoming gradually obscured by the frequent repetition or prolonged continuity of the same sensory impression or the same organic tone that is proportionate to it. The phenomena of habit – considered in each species of *sensations* in which one part fades away and the other, in contrast, becomes more intense or remains unalterable by repetition – would thereby teach us to distinguish the two elements of sensation and, by the two contrary influences that it exerts on both, would itself effect the separation of a multiple and variable matter, always subject to its deleterious action, from the apperceptive form – one, constant and invariable – that remains at a remove from its alterations.[11]

But these facts, which cannot find their place here, would not add much to the certainty of the results that can be deduced from everything we have said so far, and that we present briefly thus:

1. Affection can constitute, outside of the *self*, a mode of existence to which we can be reduced in certain states, and to which are probably reduced the multitude of living beings, distributed between the two ends of the scale separating the simple zoophyte from the feeling and thinking, mixed being.

2. Complete sensation, or the *perception* that serves as the object of philosophical analysis, is not a simple mode but already a composite of the first order, whose two elements, the one *material*, the other *formal*, do not rally to the same *principle*, are not in the same relation of dependence on the same cause, and perhaps do not even have the same, unique subject of inherence.

---

[11] See the dissertation already cited on the influence of habit, where this analysis is presented in great detail.

3. There can therefore be affection without perception or (in Locke's terms) *sensation* without an *idea of sensation*, or (in more recent terms) sensory matter without *form*, and this denies Kant's general claim about the forms inherent to *pure sensibility*, with which every material impression is clothed by necessity, without condition or exception.

4. Finally, the purely affective sensation that envelops the *self* or immediate apperception, as Condillac puts it, is not a real source of *ideas* located outside of the sphere of inner sense. It can arise before the latter in the order of time, without belonging to the sphere of its primitive facts. It is not an element generating science, though it precedes the latter in the absolute order of a passive and subordinate existence.

After having traced the contours of the shadow in order to know the point at which the light begins, we thus finally come to the question of what internal immediate apperception consists in. And since we have just seen that the act of the mind thus designated, if it really occurs and if it is not a vain abstraction of the mind, is not essentially united to all the passive modifications of sensibility, we have to ascertain whether, among all the modes of our felt existence, there would not be a special one serving as a ground for this original apperception, to which this title itself were applicable. . . This is what in the following chapter we are going to ask, with all the care and attention to detail that such a subject deserves, a subject that we consider as truly primary or fundamental in the science of principles. I have to say, indeed, and in order to justify in advance the details that will follow, that an attentive comparison of the diverse systems of metaphysics would prove to any impartial mind, I think, that the incertitude and the obscurities in which these systems, in both their form and their ground, are enveloped, as well as the oppositions, real or apparent, that exist between them, derive above all from the different way each expresses or conceives this primitive and radical fact of consciousness or the existence of the *self*. The latter is admitted by some under the hypothetical title of *substantial thought* and realized by objective hypothesis, outside of the senses and prior to their common exercise, where the phenomenal *self* does not exist and cannot yet exist, while it is confused and identified by the others with a *passive* impression of sensibility from which they suppose it to be indivisible. Another group of philosophers nominally distinguish it, but still admit it without *condition* and as a necessary primary fact, a truly primitive given, in the absolute order of nature as well as in the relative order of science. It is, in a word, almost always hypothesized where it is not, and misrecognized where it is, and exclusively ignored in its origin, its constitutive mode, its own character, and its internal or external signs of manifestation. . . And I said to myself that it was necessary either to illuminate and circumscribe this primitive fact of inner sense, better than anyone has done previously, or to renounce a *science of principles*. In addressing under this heading the question proposed, I am aware that I am not approaching it by its easiest and clearest side. But judges who have themselves plumbed these depths will appreciate my efforts, and their indulgence will recognize them, even should these efforts not meet with complete success.

Chapter II

On the Power of *Efforts* or *Will*: Origin, Grounds and Primitive Conditions of Immediate Apperception

§1

The diverse living combinations, subjected in their growth and progressive development to varieties of organic or animal affinities, belonging to an order doubtless higher than those presiding over composites of brute matter, are no less determined by their laws with a blind necessity. They follow to the same extent the circle that nature has traced for them, without the anomalies or continual excursions whose principle becomes manifest as one climbs towards the sphere of active intelligence, which impresses on itself its own direction and follows knowingly its own laws.

Uniting in himself, indeed, two sorts of faculties, and something like two sorts of lives, the human being also participates in two systems of laws: as an organized and simply sensory being, its absolute existence is composed of several internal or external functions, to which just as many species of immediate affections correspond, which constitute its instinct and determine its first automatic movements, in a way that is as certain and infallible as it is blind.

But in its quality as a moral and acting individual person, the human being is endowed, in addition, with a life of relation and consciousness. Not only does it live and feel, but it also has the apperception of its own existence, and the feeling or idea of its sensation. Not only does it maintain relations with everything surrounding it, it also apperceives these relations, distinguishes between them and things comparable to them. Moreover, it creates for itself new relations that extend and enlarge its existence, in the continual exercise of an activity, of a power of efforts, that subjects external nature to it, and, before that, the sensory instruments by means of which it perceives phenomena.

All the modes that this power produces or in which it co-operates have the character of internal reduplication that makes them belong to consciousness and determines its apperception. Everything that happens, on the contrary, in the sensory organs, outside of the proper and natural sphere of activity of the same power, remains at the obscure level of organic impression or animal affection, without being repeated as idea or perception in inner sense, without rising to the level of the *self*. This point of doctrine is fundamental, to my eyes, since it is on it that I base the whole theory of primitive facts as well as the reality of the distinctions enunciated by the terms of the problem posed, and, consequently, the way to arrive at the solution that they allow.

The fact of a human power of action and will is just as evident for him as is his own existence and his own inner sense well observed; neither of the facts can be distinguished from the other.

How, then, can the systematic spirit have been able to misapprehend or hide the real title of this power, in reducing all human faculties to sensation, and then subordinating the whole of sensation to the material or passive impressions of objects?

As if the individual, who feels and acts by means of diverse senses, found himself constituted in them by a relation of exclusive and necessary dependence on causes external to him! As if the will was not itself a cause and the first of all the causes or forces able to appear in inner sense! As if, finally, the subject that feels and acts could not be, and was not really, in certain cases, the real maker of his modifications!

If any perceptive or apperceptive faculty is identical in its origin with a primary will, as I hope to show, how have so many philosophers been able to agree on ordering, in two wholly separate classes or categories, the system of ideas that belongs to human understanding and that of acts that belongs to will? As if ideas came themselves, from *outside* or from *above*, ready made into the understanding! As if the operation or the whole of the operations that together form, recall and ceaselessly compose and recompose ideas was not, wholly or in part, a product of the activity essential to the human mind that already manifests itself in the exercise of its original perception!

Is it not the case that, of the known doctrines, perhaps none has descended deep enough into the natural and true origin of this perceptibility, into the fundamental fact of this immediate apperception whose existence is now being brought into question, to the first lineaments of the personal existence of the primitive *self*, identified perhaps with a primitive will?

Is it not the case that the real, individual idea attached to the term *willing, will* [*vouloir, volonté*] – the first, the most important and doubtless the most difficult idea to determine in the system of our reflective ideas – floats uncertainly among the metaphysicians, who employ it in different senses, senses always more or less distant from the one that would specify the true character of its primacy as a fact of consciousness or inner sense? To clarify these doubts, let us attempt to reveal the ground of the diverse meanings of the term *will* in the principles and language of a variety of philosophers. Moreover, among so many different meanings, let us determine or choose which can be true and fundamental.

1. Systems that Deny the Identity of the Motor and Thinking Principles

'Anaxagoras', says the historian of the systems of philosophy, 'is the first to have observed the identity of the motor and thinking principles in animate beings'.[12]

Of course, in order to make this *observation*, Anaxagoras needed to return only in the simplest way to the feeling of his own existence; and, in order to apprehend the evidence of the principle, it would have been enough for him to put to one side any systematic conception in order to listen to common sense alone.

The philosophical contemporaries or predecessors of the sage in question had doubtless already covered with a blanket of clouds this fact of feeling that is the identity of the motor and thinking principles, since this simple observation or testimony of the inner sense was able to appear as a discovery. And we should not be surprised by this if we consider that it is hardly due to the most renowned metaphysicians in the actual period of the progress of the sciences of the human mind that the evidence of the same principle, still just as undeniable as a *fact* of inner sense, has not been completely erased by the abstract or hypothetical theories that misapprehend or deny this testimony.

The opposing metaphysical dogmas concerning the essence of will, and the natural ties uniting its effective exercise as a *cause* to the felt acts or movements as effects, offer us the most instructive example illuminating the pitfalls, when reversing the order of the generation of human knowledge, in attempting to penetrate *ex abrupto* into the absolute essence of first causes, and to derive from

---

[12] See Degérando's *Comparative History of Systems of Philosophy* [J. M. de Gérando, *Histoire comparée des systèmes de philosophie, relativement aux principes des connaissances humaines* (Paris: Henrichs, 1804)].

them the laws of their possible action, by placing oneself beyond the frontier of primitive facts, far from the source of all real evidence.

1) Let us ask first of all the Cartesians what the will consists in, or what determines precisely an *act*, a *movement* that we call *voluntary*. The will, as these philosophers respond, can be only a *desire*, a *wish* (a simple inclination of the soul) for the act or movement to be carried out. But, as one proves *a priori* that the soul substance is simple or immaterial, and that its essence consists wholly in *thought* or *feeling*, it is consequently demonstrated that it cannot be applied to a composite, extended being such as the body, and that there is no real action or possible influence of the one on the other. The inner feeling that we have of the *efficacy* of a real force, now applied to moving the body, is therefore merely an illusion. The truth is that the supreme force, *God*, is the unique and really productive cause[13] of all movements, voluntary movements as well as physical or organic movements, in the machines that he has created. The soul can therefore only *desire* the movements of its body, in virtue of *an innate idea it has of its union with it*, and, on the occasion, the first mover intervenes, the act is carried out, and the soul or the *self*, which feels the movement consecutive to the desire, adopts the *necessary illusion* of a real influence of the one on the other.

Where, I ask, is the illusion here? Is it in the fact of inner sense? But if the illusion is there, where is the *truth*? What revelation could teach us that we are mistaken in affirming as *true* what we feel, namely that the *self* or the subject of thought is the identical subject of effort and the real, effective *cause* of the movement produced? But what foundation could add more confidence to this revelation (even if it were divine) than our own feeling? Is it not always to it that we have to return in order to discover the basis of all belief as well as the source of all truth? And by what right can a hypothesis claim to deny this internal testimony in arrogating to itself the title of truth against it? Physicists also advance hypotheses, but they are careful to compare them to the phenomena, to modify them until they conform to the phenomena, and to reject them when they oppose the phenomena... By what right do metaphysicians arrogate to themselves a different privilege? And why do they not engage with inner sense like physicists engage with nature?

2) In Leibniz's system, the soul is indeed endowed with *force* or, rather, is itself merely an active force, but its activity does not extend beyond its own domain,

---

[13]   If you admit, as in Leibniz's thinking, that all substance will be resolved into a force and is absolutely identical with it, you will see how Descartes' system leads straight to Spinozism.

On the Power of Efforts *or* Will 87

and consists only in *appetites, desires* or tendencies to a change of state. But since that applies to all the *composing* monads, that have also their own tendencies and movements co-ordinated or pre-established in a *harmonic* way with the desires or volitions of the *soul (central monad)*, it follows that all the movements of different types that are carried out in the body can be accompanied with volitions and *perceptions* that are more or less *obscure*, without any genuinely productive influence of the *unitary* force which attributes them to itself. This entails, for the idea of *will*, an indeterminacy that is identical to that which occurs in the *Cartesian* position.

3) It is true (as the partisans of *plastic forms* and the *vital principle* will say) that the thinking soul, being simple, cannot directly move the body. But in rejecting its *effective* force it is hardly necessary to have recourse to the action of God, nor to the spontaneous activity of monads. There are intermediate agents that, presiding over all the functions of life, over everything that happens in the body, effect in an immediate way the movements that are either *voluntary* or organic. The only difference between these two sorts of movements is that the soul *knows, desires,* commands those that we name *voluntary*, without being involved with the others, which are executed, however, under the same direct influence of *plastic* agents. . . I ask then how in the production of *effort* the master appropriates so perfectly the acts of its ministers or even identifies itself with them, while, beyond effortful movement, it is so completely separated from it. . .?

2. Systems that Attribute to the Principles of Thought the Movements of all the Organs without Distinction

We have just seen that the thinking or feeling subject neither effects nor wants, properly speaking, the movements that are executed in the organs, and that it simply *feels* them, or *desires* that they are carried out, as it could desire any other passive modification.

But now we have physiological metaphysicians who suppose, on the contrary, that only the soul, the identical principle of life and thought, is capable of communicating to the material and inert organs the vital activity that is impressed in the most obscure secretory function as well as in the most distinct voluntary locomotion. The soul has determined, they say, in its principle, the reciprocal play of the all the organic instruments by means of a feeling or an *anticipated*, inner knowledge. But habit weakens and ultimately destroys the feeling of the force that it continues to exert in the *perennial* acts of internal life. This opinion, fundamental in Stahl's doctrine, attacked by several philosophers, has been admitted or regarded as quite probable by others, who use it to explain the way in which they conceive a real *activity* in *passive* sensation (for consciousness) as well as in the will itself or the perception that it activates. Such is the opinion of, among others, Bonnet.[14] This seems to be also Condillac's view when he tells us that 'the principle of thought and voluntary movement is nothing other than a determination of the same principle that makes the organized body vegetate or live', and when he writes elsewhere that 'the role of the soul is only really in *sensation*; it is sensation that transforms itself, in vivifying itself, for example, to become *attention* in excluding all the others'.

It is doubtless the same when instinctive or automatic movements are transformed into *voluntary* movements. In all cases, it is the corporeal organs that tend and direct themselves after or with a sensation, but without the influence of any motive force, which does not exist as distinct from sensation.[15]

But how is it that a feeling of activity, of effort, always and only persists in the movements said to be for that reason voluntary, or that it can come back to life in them despite habit? If all the movements are or have been equally voluntary in their common principle, what is the origin and the sufficient *reason* of a distinction consecrated by language and so strongly supported by common sense? Whence do we draw the idea of *action*, of freedom, as opposed to that of *passion*, of *necessity*?[16]

---

[14] See his *Analytical Essay on the Faculties of the Soul* and his *Psychology* [Ch. Bonnet, *Essai analytique sur les facultés de l'âme* (Copenhagen: C. et A. Philibert, 1760); *Essai de psychologie, ou Considérations sur les opérations de l'âme, sur l'habitude et sur l'éducation* (London, 1755)].

[15] On all these details, see Condillac's doctrine, his *Logic* and his *Treatise on Animals* [1755], where he says at the end: 'Why, indeed, would one admit a motive force of which we have no idea?' [E. B. de Condillac, *Traité des animaux*, in *Oeuvres philosophiques de Condillac*, ed. G. Le Roy, *Corpus général des philosophes français* (Paris: PUF, 1947–1951), t. I, part II, cap. X. p. 378a]. If one understands by 'idea' an image, then no, it is perhaps not possible to have an image of such a force. But, as for the reality of that which we exert in effort, which is not to be found in passive sensation for that reason, I appeal to inner sense in order to know if such an idea exists or is merely a chimera.

[16] *Dum anima* liberum *motum producit voluntarium v.g. tunc* reflexione *facta actum suum potest deprehendere, sed dum necessarium motum peragitur consequenter ad certum corporis statum, tunc illum* (nec se ipsam) *agnoscere nequit.* ['When the soul produces a free and voluntary movement, for example, then it is able to discern its action as a reflected deed, but when an involuntary motion is provoked as a consequence of a certain state of the body, then it is unable to perceive that, nor recognise itself', J. A. Butini, *Dissertatio hydraulico-medica de sanguinis circulatione* (Montpellier: Martel, 1746), art. VII, n. 117, p. 29]. I found this remarkable passage in a thesis from the Montpellier school defended in 1747. One could search for the organic conditions of this distinction or explain it in some manner, but to deny its ground and reality seems impossible to me.

3. System that Re-establishes the Identity of the Thinking and Motor Principle

From the heart of the obscurity of these metaphysical hypotheses, opposed to each other and to common sense, I see some light emerge. I can hear a voice that confirms, reassures and accords with internal testimony. 'The only character', says Locke, 'in which we can recognize the modes or really attributive acts of a thinking subject is *consciousness* or *apperception*'.[v] Here I am wholly freed from uncertainty and the continual ambiguity that is born from a common sign given to two different subjects of attribution: the *soul* that is *me* and the *soul* that is *not me*. If therefore I remain invincibly ignorant of the absolute force that produces the movements of which I have no consciousness, although I give it a name (x) such as that of soul, *enormôn, impetum faciens*,[vi] etc., I know very positively, in contrast, that concerning the act that I feel or apperceive as producing it myself, it is indeed *I* [*moi*] who produce it,[17] and not another being.

'The will', says the same sage, 'is nothing other than a power or faculty of *moving*; it is an essentially active force. Vainly has it been confused with the *diverse affections*, and above all with *desire*; and it is this mistake that *causes the errors into which one has fallen on this question*. Do we not feel, indeed, that we can carry out *voluntarily* or freely an act, in *desiring* something opposing it? The will is related only to my own actions; *it ends there, without going any further*; and volition is this particular determination by which the soul makes an effort to produce, suspend or stop a movement that it knows to be in its own power.'[18] This is, indeed, I think, the true sense that reflection attaches to the simple idea of will.

---

[17] This is why we say, as de Tracy has remarked very well: it depends on *me* or on my will. But given that we do not say in the same way: it depends on *me* and on my *passions*, or on my *needs*, on my *desire*, etc., it follows that, in ordinary language, each of us understands by will this *sui juris* power with which he identifies himself, and separating it from everything that is *passion*. Condillac also recognizes this explicitly when he says, at the end of his *Treatise on Animals*: 'I want [*je veux*] does not mean only that a thing is agreeable to me; it means rather that it is the object of my choice; but, one chooses only among the *things of which one disposes*' [E. B. de Condillac, *Traité des animaux*, Part II, chap. X, p. 378b]. But what are the things of which we dispose? Are they the affections of unease, worry, etc. included nevertheless under the general heading of will? Can we dispose of anything other than movements or acts that are named *voluntary* only because of this availability? Why, then, equivocate endlessly about the word *will*? And why is it sometimes an *individual* faculty of movements and available acts, sometimes a *general* capacity to experience or to feel affections? The motive for this transformation is evident. In order to make a complete system of our faculties emerge from a single principle, it was necessary to reject or transform the reflective idea of will and of the power of action.

[18] Locke, *Essay on Human Understanding*, II, 21. [This is a paraphrase of Locke, *An Essay Concerning Human Understanding*, II, chap. XXI, §§ 28 and 30: 'We must remember, *Volition* or *Willing* is an act of the Mind directing its thought to the production of any Action, and thereby exerting its power to produce it. To avoid multiplying of words, I would crave leave here, under the word *Action*, to comprehend the forbearance too of any Action proposed [...]. This Caution of being careful not to

The metaphysicians had wholly denatured this idea. They denied the reality of a fact of consciousness in order to conserve the value of a hypothetical principle established *a priori*; and having thus lost any *criterion* of evidence they wandered blindly in the shadows. Locke came along to reinvigorate the natural principle of which Anaxagoras had had to remind the metaphysicians of his time... The thinking subject, the one who attributes to itself certain movements of the body, is also their productive cause. And it is this *conscious* force that is the will. No systematic point of view can prevail here over the fact of inner sense. Locke establishes it because he feels it, and does not explain it because he considers that useless or even impossible.

This same spirit of reserve seems also to have directed another philosopher, who, after having elaborated these issues, after having perfectly recognized and characterized the essential activity of *willing* as a fact of feeling, believes it necessary to limit to this bare fact all the subsequent researches on the nature and the means of action of this internal force.

'The word will is ambiguous;[19] often it is taken as the last judgment of the understanding, which is entirely *passive*; but we take it as the exercise of the self-moving principle that is entirely *active*. We have to put to one side here everything to do with *passion*; volition cannot be enveloped in any passive succession; it is, on the contrary, something that breaks the chains of the latter, *quod fati foedera rumpat* [which shatters the laws of fate]...[vii]

It is not mere *consciousness* of what happens. It is not an approbation of the understanding, or a desire or a preferential thought, or the pleasure taken in an event. All these things derive from antecedent things and contain nothing *active*. We can apperceive the effect of a foreign action, approve it, desire it, take pleasure from it, without any genuine action being inherent to it...

---

be misled by Expressions, that do not enough keep up the difference between the *Will*, and several acts of the mind that are quite distinct from it, I think the more necessary: Because I find the Will often confounded with several of the Affections, especially *Desire*; and one put for the other, and that by Men, who would not willingly be thought not to have had very distinct notions of things, and not to have writ very clearly about them. This, I imagine, has been no small occasion of obscurity and mistake in this matter; and therefore is, as much as may be, to be avoided. For he, that shall turn his thoughts inwards upon what passes in his mind, when he *wills*, shall see that the *will* or power of *Volition* is conversant about nothing, but our own Actions; terminates there; and reaches no further; and that *Volition* is nothing, but that particular determination of the mind, whereby, barely by a thought, the mind endeavours to give rise, continuation, or stop, to any Action, which it takes to be in its power. This well considered plainly shews, that the *Will* is perfectly distinguished from *Desire*; which in the very same Action may have a quite contrary tendency from that which our *Wills* sets us upon'].

[19]   See the essay by Merian on *Action, Power and Freedom* [J.-B. Mérian, 'Seconde dissertation ontologique sur l'action, la puissance et la liberté', in *Histoire de l'Académie Royale des Sciences et Belles-Lettres* (année 1750) (Berlin, 1752), pp. 496–7].

The sources from which our will springs and which lead to effort along the path that nature has traced, these sources, I say, and this path are mysteries on which the greatest philosophers have until now done no more than stutter.[viii]

Thick clouds will doubtless always cover the nature of the productive forces of objective phenomena, and, in analysing them as so many *volitions*, we would not come to know their essence or means of action any better. But for us it is a question only of knowing whether it is possible to develop the analysis of *will*, considered in the fact of the feeling of existence itself, in leading analysis to the point where Locke left it and then beyond that point to a place which philosophers with all his perspicuity have not thought that it could or should be led. In entering more profoundly into this subject, I will first offer some essential remarks on Locke's perspective and on the spirit of his method.

If the reflective idea of will seems to be quite well determined, when it is circumscribed in the feeling of the executive power of *movements* or *free acts in which it terminates without going further...*[ix] can we not still ask for a more deliberate analysis of the characteristics and conditions of these acts? If the will is limited to their exercise, where does this exercise itself end? It is always accompanied by a particular and individual feeling; but what distinguishes this feeling from any other sensitive or perceptive mode? From what circumstances does this feeling of individual power emerge as immediate apperception in all its clarity? In what circumstances does it become obscure and disappear for inner sense?... On what conditions do these differences depend? And are there not essential ones to be noted in the senses that obey more particularly the will, and in the play of the material instruments that work together in its execution?

Moreover, if by the ontological hypothesis the will as a motive force is *innate* to the substantial soul,[20] it cannot be said that the internal feeling of these free acts, or the immediate apperception of itself as producing them, are also *innate*, unless, that is, this feeling of freedom or this individual apperception is admitted into the first determinations of *instinct*, in the movements of the foetus and of the newborn, and, generally, in the movements executed with all the blindness of the mechanical habits of somnambulism, etc. This is, to be sure, a quite hypothetical assertion that, rather than finding its foundation in the facts of inner sense, is contrary to them.

---

[20] Following Leibniz, force does not differ from substance itself; we have to say therefore that the soul is innate to itself as a motive force.

But if, as we have tried to show with several examples, there is a whole system of impressions and movements in the living and feeling being before they arise in the *self* as *apperception, will* and *action*, and if, on the other hand, *consciousness* or immediate apperception characterizes all the modes or acts attributable to the soul as the subject of thought and the power of movement, it follows that the soul does not always act even when bodily movements are executed, and even when they are realized in organs that seem the most naturally subject to its motive force. These movements, which are voluntary or recognized as such by inner sense at present are therefore not innate or constituted as free from the beginning, and there must be a particular point in existence where this inner sense begins, along with the will, apperception and primitive egoity.

But what is this particular point? Or, if it is not given to human intelligence to clearly ascertain it, what are the possible limits in which it should be enclosed, from the completely blind determinations of instinct to the movements not yet *willed* but immediately *felt* as a result in a *sensory organic contraction*,[21] and from these movements thus felt to those that, accompanied by an individual feeling of force or personal causality, begin to be illuminated, in their determination as much as in their result, by the primitive light of consciousness?

This is what Locke does not tell us. For him, the only difference separating a *voluntary* movement from another that is not voluntary is that the soul produced the one freely, by virtue of its *innate* power, while it is foreign to the execution of the other. But how can we prove that it is the *soul* that acts in a *voluntary* movement? It is by the consciousness or the feeling of free effort that accompanies the act. And what explains to us why this consciousness, inherent to the execution of such movements, is excluded from the others? It is because in the first case the soul acts, whereas in the other case it does not. Thereby the action that has to be directly attributed to the *soul* is proved by the fact of consciousness, and this latter fact is explained in turn only by the action attributed to the *soul*. This is, I think, a circle from which it is impossible to escape, and the reason for that is simple.

The principle or point of departure of any science, if it is not a primary and positive fact, can be only an abstract *hypothesis* or a conventional principle.

---

[21] Bichat, in his *Treatise on Life and Death* distinguishes thus the simply felt organic contraction from the one that is produced by the will and perceived also as voluntary [X. Bichat, *Recherches physiologiques sur la vie et la mort*, Paris: Brosson, Gabon et Cie, 1799, trans. *Physiological Researches on Life and Death*, ed. F. Gold (London: Longman, 1815), part I, chap. VII, § 5, pp. 92–5].

In the latter case, all the deductions of which the same science is composed have only a *conditional* value, relative to the principle, and are hypothetical just as it is. Thus, if the law of logical identity is well observed, we must be brought back to the point where we started. The circle closes in on itself, and this is all that we can ask for.

But if the principle is a *fact*, then the whole of the facts of the same type, which constitute the *real* science in question, can find an explanation only in going back to the first fact that is homogeneous with them, without there being any need for further researches.

Now, let us pose the following alternative, applicable to the case in question: either the notion attached to the word *soul* carried with it something more than that of the real or phenomenal *self*, or it is restricted to the idea of the *self* in the primitive fact of consciousness.

In the first case, everything deduced from the abstract or ontological notion of *soul*, beyond the fact of consciousness, can be established only as *conditional truth*, relative to the principle. In this case, would not saying that the only characteristic of the operations that can be attributed to the soul is *apperception* or *consciousness* be to limit arbitrarily the value of a cause presented to us from another perspective as general and absolute? Indeed, if the soul pre-existed the *self*, why would its action not also have pre-existed? It is here no longer a matter of a question or factual principle; everything depends on the hypothesis.

In the second case, in which the word *soul* would carry at bottom no other idea than that of the *one* phenomenal subject of action, the principle enunciated comes back to this: the only operations that can be attributed to the *self* are those that it really attributes to itself as such in its own consciousness. This is the fact explained by itself; this is *absolute identity*.[22]

We have to stop there, unless we change our system of ideas or attempt to tie the order of internal facts to another order of facts, one provided by a different observation. It would thereby be possible to have more than logical *identities*, and to find a few signs or symbols capable of representing and limiting, from an

---

[22] The German philosophers have also been led back to this point by another route, as the judicious historian of systems shows us. The great circle of logical identities that they have circumnavigated with an often surprising mental force has ended up only with results like the following: the *I* is *I*, *it poses itself* (a = a), etc. The mathematicians are also led, sometimes, to purely *identical equations* of this form, but they know, by the insignificance of the result, that they have to abandon an insoluble problem, or change the method for resolving it, in taking the question in another sense. Why do the metaphysicians attach more reality and importance to their logical identities? Or why do they not draw from them the same conclusion as the mathematicians from their identical equations?

94   *Of Immediate Apperception*

objective point of view, the same ideas whose origin remains profoundly and necessarily veiled from a subjective point of view.

§2

On the Natural System Capable of Determining the Characteristics of Primitive Will as well as the Ground of Personality and Immediate Apperception

If there existed a means or a *natural sign* capable of establishing the still indeterminate idea of a truly primitive power or force of will and action (considered by certain philosophers belonging to a celebrated School as the very basis of personal individuality or of the primitive self).[23] I think that this would amount to covering it with a thicker veil rather than to discovering its ground in the very essence of a virtual force, abstracted from any actual product, from any experiential mode or fact, from any original modification in its exercise, from any organic term of *deployment*.

This natural *sign* of the *primitive will* can no more be discovered in generalizing from an abstract term or from the formation of a category employed by the metaphysicians who arbitrarily place under the same sign *will* all the *passions* or the blindest, impulsive causes of movements, even those removed from the empire and the apperception of the *soul*. Nor can the sign of the internal

---

[23] It is interesting to see how the philosophers of the French school and those of the German school, so opposed in their approaches and in the foundations of their doctrines, crashed, so to speak, against the same rock, in attempting to tie the unique and ineffable feeling of the *self* to a fundamental mode of human existence. 'The *self*, as two rightly famous philosophers say in unison, 'resides exclusively in the will; *the consciousness of the felt self, recognized as distinct from other existences, is acquired only by willed effort*' [See P.J.G. Cabanis, *Rapports du physique et du moral de l'homme*, Mémoire X, Section, II, § X, and A.-L.-C. Destutt de Tracy, *Éléments d'idéologie*, Part I, chap. XIII]. 'The first act that poses a *self* and that constitutes science', says one of them, 'is *voluntary*; no other basis can be sought for it than the will enclosed in itself' [Fichte, quoted by J.-M. de Gérando, *Histoire comparée des systèmes de philosophie*, t. II, pp. 299–300]. 'The action by which the self reflects and knows itself', says another [*Schelling*], can be explained only by the *determination* that it gives to itself, and this determination is a primitive act; it is *will*. Thus, the *self gains consciousness of its action only in the will, and the exercise of the will is the first condition of consciousness of onself*' [F. Schelling, quoted by J.-M. de Gérando, *Histoire comparée des systèmes de philosophie*, t. II, pp. 303–4]. 'Individuality', as a philosopher [Bouterwek] who advances onto our terrain says in a much more precise way, 'is nothing other than the principle of a living force, but which can be known only by the effect of a resistance. Effort and activity can be known or reflected by the separation of the subject that makes an effort from the objects that resist it.' [F. Bouterwek, quoted by J.-M. de Gérando, *Histoire comparée des systèmes de philosophie*, t. II, p. 320]. This is what is for us all practical reality, the origin of all our knowledge of ourselves and of things. All that remains for me to say is only the development of, in particular, the latter two perspectives.

manifestation of a conscious, free being be found in the acts that it determines, regardless of whether it is posited as an element of a class of affections, such as desire, or extended to a whole order of composite and mixed modes, in which it is so difficult to assign the exact proportion of *action* and *passion*. Among all the diverse modes of our existence, there is one that is quite particular and individual, capable of being alternatively felt or perceived in its objective result, as well as of being produced and apperceived in its subjective principle.

I mean to speak of the mode that accompanies the exercise of motility or, more generally, of muscular contractibility, which can appear to consciousness, following certain organic or *hyperorganic* conditions that it will be necessary to account for, either simple, direct and passive, like a received impression, or active and *redoubled*, as effort produced and apperceived at the same time in the free determination that effectuates it, as well as in the muscular sensation that is its result.

Now, if the light of consciousness is born, above all, and perhaps solely, from a contrast beyond which all uniform and continuous perception becomes gradually obscure and ends up by being eclipsed entirely, where could we find a sign able to bring out the original character of the active and efficacious will, if it is not in this simultaneous contrast, so rapidly successive, of the characteristics of passion and action with which the same specific mode is clothed, in remaining either at the level of passive impression like sensation, or in rising to the heights of consciousness, like action and effort?

Where elsewhere could we find, I say, the real origin of a power of effort, if it is not in the primitive mode in which or by which it was able to pass from the *virtual* to the *actual* [*effectif*], and which bears its essential characteristic of activity in such a way as to manifest itself either immediately to inner sense, or even indirectly to a sort of external observation?

Physiological observation teaches us, indeed, to distinguish with sufficient precision the organs whose movements are or become voluntary, in being contracted with effort that is felt, from those whose contractions are always effected without effort, and also without apperception or the individual feeling of power. An even more in-depth study of the particular organs serving the functions of motility and sensibility has taught us to recognize and explain, by more or less probable hypotheses, what happens in the different circumstances of *voluntary* or *involuntary* movements, and to recognize the different instruments put into play, those from which the action departs, those that transmit it and receive it. If, therefore, physiology could determine, through experiments or appropriate observations, the organic condition corresponding to the effort or the willed movement, and distinguish it precisely from the sensory effect of organic contraction occurring without *effort* or *will*, would it not have found the symbolic sign able to clarify the origin of this primitive fact, grasped externally to inner sense so as to be more exactly re-established in the true primacy that it must have in that source?

Having arrived at this point where two different sciences, which consider the same living, sensory and motor being from two different and separate perspectives, come together, limit each other, and nearly merge into each other, I think it is permitted to borrow a few facts from one and transport them into the other. I will therefore try to form a chain, so to speak, as woven from two species of elements, or from facts drawn from two different domains, in order to discover, if possible, the true symbol of primitive effort, and to go back thus to the source of *apperception* and egoity itself.

Beginning with the fact of inner sense, and summarizing here the preceding, I consider first of all that the movement or the effect of the contraction that I produce or feel always the power of producing, in the different parts of my body subject to the direct influence that I call my will, is the result of the same effort, which is always available for as long as the state of wakefulness or the individual feeling of my existence remains.

Since all the other modifications that come together in the unique feeling of existence succeed each other and vary in a thousand ways without ever being reborn absolutely identical, while the fundamental mode of effort remains veritably identical or varies only by the degrees of the energy of the will, I find, in the constant identity and the unity of this mode, the real characteristics of the phenomenal *self*, and I identify them completely with each other in the primitive fact of my existence as immediately apperceived.

I consider, in second place, that the same circumstances or conditions that clarify or develop the feeling of effort, or that constitute voluntary movement, felt or apperceived, develop or clarify for that reason the phenomenon of consciousness or of the individual *self*; and, *vice versa*, that in all passion where free effort is obscured and disappears, the *self* remains really enveloped in its obscure affections and seems, to *itself*, as if it did not exist... I therefore have reason to deduce that if it were wholly governed by the passions that envelop egoity, the latter could never have commenced, which signals to me the necessity of searching for the origin of knowledge and the truly primitive fact of inner sense outside of the circle of affections or blind determinations of instinct, which, far from being its source, positively exclude this fact.

But it is supposed that physiological experiments, for as much as they can imitate and reproduce the acts of living nature,[24] assure us that the brain (or, more precisely, the central point where the nerves, instruments of sensibility and motility, terminate) works in its own way, from the first stirrings of life, to execute various instinctive movements, in all the cases where organic contractions, capable or not of being sensed, are effected in the muscles without the express action or participation of the will. Now, these contractions, even when they can be sensed, are accompanied by no effort of consciousness, from which I conclude that the very particular case in which the movement, having become voluntary, begins to be apperceived has to be attributed to the action properly so called of an individual force or cause other than the sort of vital energy or blind force that the physiologists are in the habit of drawing back to the cerebral centre, and from which all the determinations of perceptibility and voluntary motility seem to depart.[25]

This *hyperorganic* as well as *hypersensible* force, present to me in the inner and radical feeling that accompanies its exercise in the actual effort that *I* create and in the phenomenal movement bound to it, cannot be *imagined* or *localized* in any part of my material organization without denaturing the very idea of it.

It is no more capable of being present to me *a priori* under some ontological or noumenal concept, a concept that has its basis or its primitive archetype in the truly primary fact of inner sense in real existence.

It is therefore from here, in this origin of all *practical* and not absolute reality, that I take the idea of force or of will, of the *self*, which is something more than a *virtuality*, a *form* or *category*.

---

[24] See, on this subject, the series of quite curious experiments recorded in the work of Bichat already cited.

[25] Despite the efforts of the physiologists to reduce to material images everything truly hyperorganic in the sort of phenomena which concern them, they are forced to go back to the hypothesis or to the explicative conception of a quite incomprehensible force or cause that produces the movement or the animal contraction, which they do not distinguish from effort or from voluntary movement. (See, again, Bichat's work, where the sort of contraction operated by the will is expressly designated by the name of 'animal contraction'.) The physiologist differs here from the metaphysician only in so far as the latter conceives the motive force in a substance (or even, as a substance) separated from its term of application, namely: in the *noumenal soul*, while the latter considers living force, which it attributes to the organization itself as a property inseparable from it, just like the veritable attributes or objective properties (extension, solidity, etc.) through which we represent to ourselves the complex idea of a body. This last illusion belongs to the forms of language, as we have remarked already, rather than to the ground itself of thought, where two sorts of ideas will always remain distinct no matter what we do, of which one is purely reflective and the other representative by its nature: the idea of force or a productive cause of the phenomenal movement and that of a quality inherent to the objects of our intuition.

The problem being thus circumscribed and removed, as much as possible, from the imaginary quantities or roots that complicated it and made it unsolvable, it remains for us now only to add, to the physiological findings concerning the phenomena of voluntary movement and the play of the organic instruments that have a role in its execution, the necessary condition that they lack in order to express, even symbolically, the original fact of consciousness, identical with the first willing or the first effort.

§3

Hypothesis on the Origin of Personality and Internal Immediate Apperception

1. For as long as the brain or the organic centre (to which the physiologists attach immediately the motive impulsion) reacts on the impressions that provoke it and that come from the organs of interior life with which it is in a sympathetic relation, the instinctive movements produced by this reaction, remaining consequently unperceived by the individual person, which is not yet present, cannot in any sense be held to be voluntary.

    For real knowledge, it is of little importance whether it is a *vegetative, sensitive* or *thinking soul,* a *vital principle,* or an *organic centre* that determines these blind movements! In any of these cases, it is merely a matter of a hypothesis, of a sign without an idea. It would perhaps be better to say, with Locke, that the *soul* does not yet act, since there is no will that is exercised, in concluding that there is a total absence of will from the absence of consciousness and apperception. One could also say that not only is this apperception not present in the organic movements, but also that the conditions for such a possible apperceptibility are not even present. In this way, we should note in passing, we could destroy an objection behind which the disciples of Stahl as well as Descartes can still hide.

2. At the point where the absolute and exclusive empire of instinct terminates, the affections weaken and the muscular resistance increases. The centre of motility begins spontaneous action by the vital energy developed in proportion to resistance, or even by a series of determinations that it might have contracted and the relations established between it and the mobile organs. And from this, muscular contractions result that are then felt or simply perceived. But up to that point, there is no willed effort, no genuine action.

3. Simple muscular sensation, becoming clearer to the degree that it is disengaged from the affective impressions that envelop it, is also distinctly transmitted to the common centre. The hyperorganic force, the *soul* – that it is necessary to admit here under the heading of *noumenal* or as an explicative, absolute, necessary cause, in considering it objectively in relation to the organic centre, as the physiologist considers this centre in relation to the motor nerves that it holds under its dependence – this soul, I say, notified and as if awakened[26] by this first sensation, can consequently retain from it a sort of reproductive *determination*, comparable to the imperfect reminiscence that is still attached to the vague images of a dream, immediately after waking.

4. In virtue of the determination thus conceived, the soul will be able to repeat by itself and *begin the* right contractive *action* to bring about the muscular sensation. It *will begin* it, I say, in virtue of a principle of spontaneity (I do not quite say of *freedom*[27]) essential to it, and in the absence of a sensory cause of the excitation, whether external or internal, that could determine the organic and blind reaction of a centre of instinctive motility.

It is here, and in the case alone, that we can recognize the essential condition of a complete and genuine *action*. It is in this case alone that there will be an effort of the soul (therefore *self*), immediately apperceived in its interior principle, at the same time as it is perceived or perceivable, in a *mediate* way, in the result or the objective term of this very effort. From this departs the first ray of the light of consciousness that clarifies the *self* arriving in the interior phenomenal world.

I said that the present hypothesis includes the intelligible conditions of a truly *complete* action. We should observe, indeed, all the *symbolic* circumstances of which this action is composed.

---

[26] Occasionally we are drawn suddenly from the state of sleep and dreaming by a brusque movement or by strong aspirations of articulated speech in dreaming. These movements, determined perhaps by a force different to that whose exercise constitutes the phenomenal *self* in the stake of wakefulness, belonging to the *self* as habitual acts free of the will, cannot, consequently, remain absolutely foreign to it in its results, even when it was not their determining principle or their efficient cause. Would one not say that the soul receives here passively the impression that awakens it in providing its ordinary impulsion to act? And does this not offer an image of what could have happened in the first sensations of movements that preceded and brought about the first willed effort and, with it, the real birth of the person?

[27] Freedom presupposes the possibility of *choosing* between two opposing options (here, between action and non-action), consequently, already clarified intelligence, experience, etc.

The soul begins the movement in acting spontaneously on the organic centre to which it is united or that serves it as immediate term of application.[28] This communicates the action to the motor nerves, which immediately transmit to the muscles the contractile influence.

This series of actions, and primarily its first impulsion, finds no similar example in any sensory impression whatever, whose cause or primary occasion is always placed outside of the soul and its own centre of action, as are quite generally all our sensations, either affective or representative. Accompanied muscular sensation, in all movement that is felt or apperceived as voluntary, is the only sensation that can and must be considered as having its primary cause or its truly initial principle in the unitary and individual hyperorganic force that attributes that sensation to itself in its quality as *cause* in the primitive fact of consciousness, which is identical to that of its existence itself.

Let us trace the circumstances of the complete action to which we attach the originary internal apperception.

The contraction operates in the muscle under the immediate influence of the motor nerves and under the mediate influence of the soul, and the muscular organ reacts in contracting. The product of this reaction is transmitted to the soul following an inverse progress to that of the initial action, namely from the contracted muscle to the nerves, from the nerves to the organic centre, and from the latter to the soul that perceives or feels the contraction and the movement as a result of the preceding action, or as an *effect* of which it is the *cause*. Such is, in its source, the essential and truly primitive relation of *causality*, which does not differ thus, in its primacy, from the immediate feeling of existence itself. . .

We should stop here: we have spent enough time and taken too many detours to arrive at a point that has escaped until now the metaphysicians, by its smallness, which makes it invisible, as much as by its obscurity and the shadows that seem to cover it. If we have not been able to illuminate these obscurities and penetrate all the way into the real origin of the phenomenal *self*, or establish the true beginning and the means of exercise of internal *sense*, in which and by which this *self* exists as *subject* or *object*, indivisible from the fundamental act that we call *immediate internal apperception*, we will have shown at least that there is an act of this type, a particular internal sense to which it is tied, finally a

---

[28] It is impossible to conceive an acting force without such a term of application or deployment.

beginning or a *principle* in the exercise of this sense, and necessary means or conditions that correspond to the origin of personality in time. We will have sharply distinguished the fundamental active mode of personal existence from all the other accidental modes or passive states of the soul, under whatever general or individual title we can name them. After having proved thus that there is an immediate apperception of *self* and having examined in what it consists, we find ourselves now able to recognize the differences that separate it from *intuition*, as well as to bring out the real characteristics distinguishing the latter from *sensation* and *feeling*, and this in always following the analogy *of language*, and the order of filiation as well as the consequences of the facts presented in these two chapters.

But, before that, and without departing from the perspective that we have adopted, we should examine a few questions that follow from the last one, and which also divide metaphysicians. In attempting to solve them by the means that we have just employed, we will put to the test the certitude and the practical utility of the results that we have established, and we will thus complete what there remains to say on the fundamental subject that it is our goal to clarify.

§4

Responses to a Few Questions Subordinate to the Preceding One on the Origin of Immediate Apperception and the Principle of Causality, etc.

1. In considering the existence of the *self* as *absolute*, the metaphysicians could only transport into an abstract order of the possible the real conditions of individuality itself. Hence the purely logical distinctions of the categories *unity, identity, causality*, ... vain and multiple simulacra of a single real archetype, different expressions of one and the same *fact* that is denatured and lost in the whole of the abstract forces from which it is impossible to rediscover the primordial archetype.

   Everything depends, indeed, as some philosophers have observed more recently, on recognizing the original value of the principle of causality. But one had not yet observed how such a principle is united and confused, in its source, with the very feeling of personal individuality, from which it is inseparable.

   Beginning with the abstract idea or from the sign of 'cause' so as to erect it *ex abrupto* as a *category*, taken for a *form* internal to our understanding, is to put a logical principle in place of a fact. It is to exit the circle of all practical reality; it is to cut the knot of the question concerning the order of the generation of our knowledge, or rather to invert this order... From another perspective, being concerned only with the simple passive succession of phenomena, and limiting all our ideas of causality to it, is to denature the real value that this principle always conserves, despite ourselves, in our mind. It is to want to reduce the whole intellectual system to images, and to destroy the principal tie that unites all its parts.

But in this latter case, as it is very easy to demonstrate that the relation of *causality* is quite different to that of *succession*, the uselessness of the attempts that one might make to assimilate these two fundamental relations, or to disguise the real value of the former, could always lead us to think that it involves some impenetrable mystery and to accredit, in some way, the opinion of the metaphysicians that establish it *a priori* as a form innate to our mind and independent of all experience. That alone would suffice, I think, to justify our procedure and to give some weight to the apparently minute considerations that we have gone into here.

We can suppose in fact that the feeling or the idea of a cause is currently part of all the modes that we can *feel, perceive* or *apperceive*, in relating them to our organs as affections or already composed *sensations*, or to the outside as images, or to ourselves as immediate producers of our activity. If this is not the case or if this liaison does not exist, personal individuality does not exist either and the impressions are thus simple and purely affective. Consequently, there is no place to distinguish this feeling of *causality*, in the primitive exercise of effort and of the *will*, from that of egoity itself.

Would it therefore still be a question of knowing if, independently of effort or of some exercise of a *muscular* sense, it would be possible for there to be the production of some idea of exterior force or primary application of the *principle of causality*? In other words, if the passive impressions of sensibility can, by themselves and abstracting from any other circumstance, be first perceived as *effects* of some foreign cause or force, already known by anticipation?[29] Or if the *strangeness* of these impressions is recognized by contrast with the activity belonging to other modes, where the *self* is found and feels itself as a cause? In the end, if this individual *self* can know its existence as a simple *power of feeling* before apperceiving itself as an

---

[29] This is the view that seems to be generally followed, in their famous School, by Thomas Reid and Smith, etc.

individual motive force? If it is personally constituted in the simple feeling of its passivity, or in the reflective feeling of its activity?

The solution to the problem of the generation of knowledge seems to me to depend on the choice of one or the other of these options.

Suppose that all sensation is completely passive, deny all power of effort or action, and admit a *self*, a pre-existing soul, capable of apperceiving modifications of this type; from where could the idea come to it of a cause or force capable of acting on its organization? In this hypothesis, it must be the case either that the idea of cause is *innate*, or that its value is reduced to a simple succession of modes or images, abstracting from any active, effective linkage or production. I cannot see any middle ground. Re-establish, on the contrary, the fact of existence such as it is manifest to our inner sense, and you will find in the *unitary* and permanent *effort* on which it is grounded the primitive archetype of any idea of cause and foreign power, the archetype that is clear in its source, but which is obscured and can be denatured in being combined with *images*, and being objectified entirely along with them.

A famous sceptic, whose works have very often furnished opportunities for meditation to philosophers who have introduced diverse doctrines, will furnish me here with the particular occasion to apply the preceding principle and to justify the path that led me to it.

2. *Hume*, looking for what the notion of *power*, of *causality* or of *force* outside of ourselves could be grounded upon, wonders if this notion might not have for its basis the *internal feeling* of a characteristic force or of an empire over the organs of the body, as well as over the operations of the mind, which we attribute to our *will*. But this philosopher, as subtle as he is profound, preferring to gather clouds rather to dissipate them, seeks to attenuate the force of the principle, and seems even to fear finding in it a far too easy way of escaping the labyrinth of sceptical doubts in which he moves with such satisfaction.

The influence of acts of will on the bodily organs, he says, *is only a fact of experience like the operations of nature.*

That this is a *fact* is sufficient for us: but is it a fact of experience of the same order as the other operations of an external nature? I deny the equivalence. It is precisely this that seems to me to be the source of all the illusions that provide such opportunities to the sceptics: 'in either rising up into the skies or descending into the abysses, I only ever contemplate myself or my thought'. This is true, if the internal feeling of the *effectiveness* of acts of will in effort or the movement produced is a *fact* of the same order as the operations of an exterior nature; and *vice versa*, if the latter is not true, the former is not either. Condillac and Hume share here the same point of view.

Our sceptic continues: *We would never have been able to predict the effect in the energy of its cause*. This requires explanation. The internal energy of the cause in question here is quite directly *felt* in the effect or the movement produced. This is precisely what distinguishes, in our inner sense, voluntary movement and that which is not voluntary. One can also say that from the first willed effort, the movement is as if *predicted in the energy of its particular cause*: energy that consists in the feeling of a *power to act*, to create at each moment the same effort. This is the sole effect able to be *predicted* in this way, and we search in vain for analogies in the *facts of external nature* or in the general notions that we can constitute from foreign causes.

'We are condemned eternally to be ignorant of the means of the production of voluntary movements, so far are we from having an immediate feeling of them.'

This argument is quite apt to make us feel the necessity of a distinction unknown in the exclusive systems that want either to *objectify* all laws and faculties of the thinking being, or to *idealize* the whole of external nature. The knowledge acquired by the representation of things or of images outside of us is not at all the same as that which is bound to the facts of inner sense or to the purely reflective acts of intelligence. What relation is there, for example, between the images that the anatomist or the philosopher construct of the position of the different organs, or of their interplay in a phenomenon such as that of muscular contraction, and the feeling that the individual has of the contractions produced, or of the power that effectuates them in a freely determined relation? Are there even any relations between the secondary, *objective* knowledge that the individual acquires successively from the external parts of his body in traversing them by touch and sight, and the *internal* and necessary awareness of the parts obeying the same will acquired in the first deployments of *effort*, an awareness without which the *self* does not begin to exist for itself? We have already seen, and we will see still better, how great thinkers have either confused these two types of knowledge, or attributed all reality exclusively to the second. But in limiting ourselves to Hume's particular assertion, we will say that when it makes the reality of the effectiveness of the will depend on the possible perception of the means or instruments put into play so as to effectuate it, this is as if he made the reality of perceptions of colour outside of ourselves depend on the immediate vision of the luminous fluid or of the cause that makes us see.

On the Power of Efforts *or* Will
105

And here again, the case is more unfavourable, for we have a quite positive, thoroughly internal, it is true, awareness of the cause which moves the organs, since this *cause is me*; while in reality, we never know the cause that makes us see; and just as in order to have at one and the same time the immediate direct perception and that of the luminous fluid in itself it would be necessary to have two eyes that could see at once inside and outside of ourselves, so too in order to know the efficacious means of the will on the muscles at the same time as we feel this effectiveness, it would be necessary, at one and the same time, to be *ourselves* and other than *ourselves*.

But here is the strongest, and, so to speak, the key point by which the sceptic ends his arguments: *the idea of force and of power does not derive from any internal awareness, since we do not really feel any power in producing movements in our body, and in applying our members to their diverse functions.*[xi]

What! When I exercise a general or partial voluntary locomotion, I do not have the awareness of an action other than the passive mode attached to the beating of the heart, of the arteries or to whatever automatic movement of a machine; I do not feel more effort or power when I act on a body in pushing it, as opposed to being pushed by it, etc. Where does the distinction come from, then, between an actual *voluntary* movement and one which is not, either by nature or because it has ceased to be so? Previously, one had not gone so far as to deny the fact; the Cartesians themselves in avowing all its reality in *feeling*, only denied it in its absolute foundation by rejecting as illusory the testimony of inner sense.[30] Hume here goes beyond all the limits of scepticism. To decide to deny the evident fact on which a principle is based is to recognize tacitly all its force; it is to honour it.

No other philosopher has shown more strongly that we must renounce the idea of finding outside of ourselves a real foundation for the idea of *cause* or power and of necessary connexion. Consequently, we have to conclude that it remains for us to look for it in ourselves and in this very

---

[30] 'It is true', says Descartes in one of his letters, 'that we are not conscious of the manner in which our mind sends the animal spirits into particular nerves; because that depends not only on the mind alone but on the mind's union with the body. We are, however, conscious of every action by which the mind moves the nerves in so far as such action is in the mind, where it is simply the inclination of the will towards a particular movement. The inflow of the spirits into the nerves, and everything else necessary for the motion, follows upon this inclination of the will. This happens because of the way the body is constructed, of which the mind may not be aware, and because of the union of the mind with the body, of which it is certainly conscious. Otherwise, it would not incline its will to move the limbs. That the mind, which is incorporeal, can set the body in motion – this is something which is shown to us not by any *reasoning* or comparison with other matters, but by the surest and plainest everyday experience. It is one of those self-evident things which we only make obscure

106 *Of Immediate Apperception*

same inner sense of an acting force that scepticism seeks in vain to envelop in obscurity.

The sole necessary connexion is that which originally takes place between a living force and a resistance or a vanquished inertia. This liaison is beyond the habits of the imagination. It is not founded on it and cannot find in it a sufficient reason that would explain it.[31]

§5

On Immediate Apperception in the Relation to the Feeling of the Co-existence of One's Own Body and to the Circumscription or Distinction of its Different Parts

The sense of effort, which we can call also the sense of immediate apperception, and to the particular exercise of which we attach the feeling of causality and of permanent individuality, *resides* in all the parts of the motor system that, directly influenced by the will, circumscribe the proper domain where this power is exercised. Everything that is effected within its limits is immediately apperceived as an act or result of an act *willed* by the identical *self*; everything outside of it, no longer depending on the same power, is no longer appropriated by the same mode of apperception.

To general locomotion, or to the simultaneous contraction of all the mobile parts that obey the same will, there corresponds first of all the fundamental feeling of an *organic resistance*. Now, could not the feeling of uniform and *continuous* resistance, inseparable from the common effort deployed on an inert

---

when we try to explain them in terms of others...' [R. Descartes, *Letter to Arnauld*, 29 July 1648, in *Philosophical Letters*, trans. A. Kenny (Oxford: Clarendon Press, 1970), p. 235]. This is the first fact of the physical influence of this will that is the *self* expressly recognized. How, then, was Malebranche able to attempt to destroy it by *reasoning*, as he did in his system of occasional causes? We *feel* that the soul or the *self moves the body*; this is what Descartes recognizes. The soul or the *self* does not and cannot really move the body; this is what Descartes seeks to establish ontologically. What should we believe and what should we trust: the proofs of feeling or the those of reasoning, grounded *a priori* on the nature of substances?

[31] I have the advantage here of being able to cite the authority of a philosopher on whose ideas one might think I have modelled my own, if it were not demonstrated that we could not agree, even though we met each other in the deduction of the principle and the choice of the example employed to confirm it. (See an essay of M. Engel on the idea of force, inserted in the collection of Berlin, 1801.) [J. J. Engel, 'Sur l'origine et l'idée de la force', in *Mémoires de l'Académie Royale des Sciences et des Belles-Lettres depuis l'avènement de Frédéric Guillaume III au trône*, 1801 (Berlin: Decker, 1804), pp. 160–1].

mass that is harmoniously mobile in its diverse points, be considered as the primitive interior mode that already corresponds to a *space* or to a sort of vague and indeterminate *extension*, belonging to one's own body? And is it not here that we have to assign the origin of the complete apperception that will subsequently represent the same body in a form of determinate objective extension, where the contiguous sensory parts will be found limited each in relation to the other, as their ensemble or their own body is limited in a space in relation to the foreign body?

Now, if extension is only the continuity of *resistance* foreign to a willed effort,[32] could we not also consider the perception originating the type of interior extension constituting one's own body as enclosed in the fundamental and continuous feeling of resistance or of inertia that the organs offer to the same individual force that tends to move them?

This *interior space* of one's own body, from which the phenomenal *self* is distinguished in its immediate apperception, without being able to separate itself from it by external intuition, will be the place of simply affective modifications. These cannot be felt or perceived in another *form* or without the individual relating them outside of itself to some part of its organization, since exterior space is the *place of objects*, or of the non-affective modes, like *colours, figures*, etc., which can be perceived only at a distance, completely outside of the *self*. We have to go back, I think, to the fundamental distinction of the two primitive forces of *sensation* and *perception* in order to find the possible origin of *knowledge*, and embrace in all its extension the problem of existence.

If the human body were composed only of a single mass, capable only of receiving impressions and being moved consequently by a general will, in admitting even that the *unitary* subject of effort can be distinguished from the composite that thus resists as a whole, it would have no means of perceiving, in this internal continuity of resistance, parts juxtaposed each outside of the other, and, consequently, of relating sensory impressions to them.

But to the division of the muscular system into separate organs, or to that of the nervous branches that effect its partial contractions, there can correspond so many homogeneous muscular sensations. . ., as distinct between themselves as are the successive acts of the motive force that gives birth to them. Each individual

---

[32] Leibniz defined extension as a continuity of resistance (*resistentis continuatio*). I do not think that any better definition has been furnished since.

effort, or each particular act of the same will, *will localize* in this way one of the immediate terms of its application, and mark a point of division in the resistant *continuity*. As the same fundamental mode is reproduced under these forms, varied in their very uniformity, personal existence is affirmed and developed, and the motor subject is individualized more completely, in the apperception of the relation of its *unity* to the *plurality* of the *mobile* terms. In putting itself outside of each of them, it can learn to put each outside of the other, to distinguish their common limits, and to relate to them the passive impressions of sensibility (these, diffused by themselves in the living combination, and absolute or general in their affective character, would become particular and relative only in being associated with the successive modes of the same effort that appropriate them for the person and constitute them, indeed, in relation to it).

Although this last assertion is a direct consequence of the preceding hypothesis concerning the origin of personality and immediate apperception, I think, nevertheless, that it could be justified in some way, as a *fact*, by examples of certain extraordinary cases, related by observers on the body and mind of man who have attached themselves above all to grasping sensory nature in its anomalies and absences, which are often more instructive than its ordinary functioning. They cite, for example, certain quite remarkable cases of partial paralysis where, with external sensibility no longer existing, the faculty of moving or acting remained in its entirety.

In other contrary cases, where sensibility remains and motility is diminished, it was thought, since the soul loses knowledge and the memory of its motive force or of the availability of its effort relative to the paralysed parts, that the impressions made expressly on these parts did not produce more than general affections, which are not localized in any determinate seat.[33]

---

[33] The necessity of a motive influence, or of a present effort exerted on the sensory parts so that the impressions made on these parts can be directly related to them seems to me to be confirmed by a curious fact, related in a little-known work (*Histoire naturelle et raisonnée de l'âme* by Rey Régis, doctor at the Montpellier Faculty of Medicine): 'Having seen', says this doctor, 'a patient who seemed paralysed in half of his body, after a recent attack of apoplexy, I was curious to know if he had any remaining feeling and any movement in the parts affected. For that, I put my hand under the cover of the bed and pressed one of his fingers hard, which made him give out a cry. In doing the same to each finger, he felt each time a very sharp pain, but without relating it anywhere. I therefore put my hand in his and told him to grasp it; he couldn't do it. This man needed several days of practice in order to learn once again to use his hands, to move his fingers one after the other; and, consequently, he knew perfectly how to relate the pain to the fingers squeezed.' The author concludes that 'in paralysis of this type, the soul loses knowledge or memory of its motive force, of the proportion of its effort to the movement required, etc.' [See J.-J. Rey Régis (Cazillac), *Histoire naturelle et raisonnée de l'âme* (London, 1789), t. I, p. 27], which amounts to saying that the subject of this effort, the *self*, loses the idea or the immediate feeling of the particular terms of its application, which are

We could deduce from such experiments that a child born in this way, paralysed in all his members for movement though not for feeling would have a purely affective existence if he could live in this state. None of his impressions could be localized; he could be said to feel them, without perceiving them. In the end, since the relation of his force to resistance would have no foundation, personality would not have one either, and would remain *enveloped* in sensation, without being able to be developed or to be born.

Such is the man who sleeps, with all the impressions received in this state of complete passivity. Such are we, though awake, in all the internal impressions that, having their seat in organs that are wholly foreign to effort, are nor circumscribed in any particular seat and remain thus always vague, general and unapperceived.

We can conclude from this that all affection related to a part or to a place of the organic body must be considered already as a composite of the first order, and, then only, as a complete sensation or *idea* of sensation; and that these first composites admit a common element, or, if you will, the same *form* that is united with some variable matter in each type of sensation. Finally, we can conclude that this form is not inherent, as is said, to passive sensibility, but that it is referred to the special or individual sense of effort, and has the same extension, the same limits, the same original conditions as its exercise.

This leads us to examine briefly two famous doctrines. One viewed as innate knowledge the primary circumscription that occurs in the parts of one's own body, and, consequently, the local relation of the impressions that affect the soul, while the other, wanting to explain this relation or this original knowledge, considers it as the exclusive result of the exercise of a particular *external* sense, that of the touching of solid surfaces.

1. 'This confused reasoning or this *natural judgement*', says Malebranche,[34] 'that applies to the body what the soul feels is only a *sensation that can be described as composed*'. Here, we find the outline and the beginning of a true analysis, which needed to be further developed. For it is here a case of

---

organically affected. And if all the partial terms, or the body as a whole, were in the same state, would not any apperception find itself suspended, as in sleep, although passive affectability could remain? The direct relation of the impressions to a seat would be a product of the same conditions as voluntary motility. Now, if this separation is recognized in perhaps the first of all judgements, it will have to be admitted in all the others. Besides, are we not, as to the impressions of the internal organs, in the case of Régis' paralytic?

[34] *Search for the Truth*, I, i. [N. de Malebranche, *De la recherche de la vérité. Livre 1-3*, in *Œuvres*, t. I (Paris: Vrin, 1972); *The Search after Truth*, ed. T. M. Lennon and P. J. Olscamp (Columbus: Ohio State University Press, 1980), book I, chap. X, § 5, note].

employing Leibniz's argument: wherever there are composite beings or modes, there are simple modes. If the sensation related to a corporeal seat is really a composite, we have to distinguish two elements in it: pure affection that, by itself, does not relate itself to anything else, and judgement or the simple act, unitary and truly elementary, in virtue of which the simple impression is localized.

But Malebranche begins to establish *a priori*, with the other Cartesians, that the soul has an innate idea of its union with the body. Consequently, sensation is born composed and does not become composed. There is therefore no origin to be found for this judgement or confused reasoning that composes sensation.

But if this judgement is innate, must it not also be necessary and general or common to all sensory impressions, internal or external? Why therefore are there, in actual fact, so many cases of exceptions and distinctions in this primitive relation? Why are these wholly passive interior impressions not related to anything else although they affect general sensibility? On the other hand, if this way of seeing or perceiving is unique and absolute or necessary, how can we know that it is an illusion, and what is the supposed reality here?

Without going further concerning this system, we should recall on this occasion what we have observed many times before, namely that the supposition of something *innate* is always something like the final desperate act of an analysis, and that in beginning thus with certain *a priori* principles, it is necessary either to abandon such real effects without explanation or to disfigure them and confuse them so that they can be forcibly fitted, without consultation, into an established hypothesis.

2. In his work on the human understanding, Locke, adopting a method of experimental analysis, thinks it necessary to begin this side of the more distant limits that had offered themselves to the Cartesian perspective. For him, the idea of sensation is a simple element, not only when the affective impression is related to the organ that receives it, but also when the representative mode is related to an external cause, like the image to its object. It is in this way that Locke *presupposes* the first naturally formed knowledge, and does not explain it.

But when Condillac had the idea of going back to the origin of all ideas to anatomize, so to speak, the different species of sensations in order to recognize the part that each contributes to human intelligence, he was led by an ingenious hypothesis to step back to the point that can really open the circle of knowledge. He had to recognize first of all that, since the direct impressions of a passive external sense, such as that of smell, for example, do not have in themselves or in their simply affective characteristics anything that carries in itself, so to speak, the stamp of the object that occasions them or of the organic place that they occupy, this knowledge of the object or of the seat, which enters now into all our diverse sensations in composing them as relative sensory ideas, had to have its origin in some primitive mode, thus perceived or naturally felt in a necessary relation. He also had to recognize that such a mode, being associated next with the other purely sensory impressions, had to communicate to them its characteristic or its own relative form, and *compose* them, in Malebranche's sense, or raise them to the rank of ideas, in Locke's sense. In this way, the Cartesian point of view was brought back for the first time within the limits of experience, and the principles of the English philosopher were able to receive their necessary complement.[35]

I cannot stop here to follow in detail all the steps that the statue makes to get out of itself in transporting wholly interior modifications, either to parts of its own body, or to the foreign bodies that it clothes with these same sensory impressions. It is *identified* with each in turn, moment by moment, in the exercise of olfaction, of taste, of hearing and sight. It is now, as is known, by the primitive exercise of a passively *sensory* organ on the outside rather than voluntarily mobile on the inside, that the external world of phenomena is born and will develop, a world that will be, however, only an objective composite of the same sensations.[36]

It is the *tactility* of the hand that, alone, circumscribes in one's own body each of the parts where it finds the *reply* to feeling, and separates them thus from the portions of dead matter whose *bare* solidity gives no reply to the feeling of the hand that delimits them, and figures them out by its successive application.

If Condillac had gone back to the truly primitive and fundamental sense of knowledge, the fundamental sense of the *internal apperceptive idea* as

---

[35] See, in the *Reasoned Excerpt of Treatise of Sensations* [E. B. de Condillac, *Extrait raisonné du 'Traité des Sensations'*, in *Oeuvres philosophiques de Condillac*, t. I, pp. 333b–334a], the definition that Condillac gives of the word *idea* in remarking that a judgement always enters into those that seems to be the most simple. This is what Locke only very vaguely noticed and only in the particular case of the association of ideas of tangible forms with visual images.

[36] For it is well known that, 'in either rising up into the skies or descending into the abysses, I only ever contemplate myself or my thought', which is nothing other than my *sensation*'. [E. B. de Condillac, *Essai sur l'origine des connaissances humainest*, Part I, Section I, chapter I, §1, in *Oeuvres philosophiques de Condillac*, t. I, p. 6a, trans. *Essay on the Origin of Human Knowledge*, ed. H. Aarsleff (Cambridge: Cambridge University Press, 2001), p. 11].

much as of the perceptive or *intuitive* external idea, he would have seen perhaps that this transport of our modifications to an organic seat and thus to an external *spatial* place must find its principle in the necessary reply of a willed effort to an opposed resistance,[37] much rather, perhaps, than in a feeling which, as passive, cannot be redoubled or *reply* to itself.

But the author of the *Treatise of Sensations*, occupying himself instead with the means of objective knowledge, had no regard for the immediate products of the action of an internal force, impalpable as much as it is invisible, which not only applies itself to extended surfaces in order to delimit them, but which also penetrates into the inside of the masses and even to the elements of resistant matter, as if to be complicated or combined with the force opposed to its elements.

Given that the wholly internal sense of effort, such as we have considered it in its determination or original form as well as in its immediate results, has to associate itself in a more or less intimate manner (as we will see in a moment) with the diverse external senses of which it plays a more or less notable part, and that external touch itself, at which Condillac stopped, is only its primary appendix, it is clear how much its omission in the origin of knowledge must have left incomplete, vague and uncertain elements in the analyses that failed to grasp it.

Just as the omission on the part of the old chemists, in taking no account of the influence of the air or of a part of the air on the phenomena of combustion and the acidification of bodies, meant that all the analyses had to be remade or checked by our modern *pneumatists*, who discovered in the analysed air the true principle of these phenomena, so too the distinction of a new sense that can be united with all the others without being confused with any one of them, having been absolutely neglected or misrecognized by the author of the *Treatise of Sensations*, would impose today the task of recommencing all the analyses, or of producing a new verification for them. This is the work that we would have in view if time permitted, and whose sketch we are going to trace for the sake of completing the solution of our problem.

---

[37] Supposing that two hands were paralysed for feeling, it would be enough for them to be able to be moved the one against the other and to resist each other for this reply of effort or resistance to determine them as distinct each from the other and belonging to the same *self*. If only one of these hands could not feel, the one that conserved sensibility could feel the other hand as foreign in this way; but if the two efforts encountered each other once again, the *strangeness* would disappear and this case would return into the preceding one. One sees clearly here the clear division in the two functions.

Let us now conclude, from everything that has been the object of this long chapter, and from the last section in particular:

1. That beyond the *perception* or the primary knowledge of the limited and figured form of the parts of one's own body or of a foreign body, to which the external touch that Condillac speaks of is applied, there is an immediate *apperception* of the co-existence of this body, which is grounded on a general and continuous resistance (*continuatio resistentis* [*organici*] Leibniz), relative to the same individual effort.

   That this sort of corporeal *extension*, initially unlimited, cannot be figured by any external sense and cannot be the immediate object of any *intuition*, but that it has its own *muscular* sense, which acts and knows itself only on the inside; that it is to this special source that has to be related the primitive *form* of *space*, which, in its very *purity*, cannot be generalized and attributed thus to any passive exercise of a sensibility in which it would be supposed to be naturally inherent.[38]

2. That, outside of the initial exercise of the sense of effort, all the impressions of sensibility, including those of touch itself, are passive, *materially simple and absolute*, or without relation to any personal or foreign existence; while with this sense alone, distinct and separate even from all the others, the individual subject of effort (*self*) is constituted in the fundamental and necessary relation to the resistant organic term. Consequently, the immediate internal apperception of this *self*, which is associated more or less intimately with all the accidental modes (mixed results of passive impressions that have come from the outside and of movements produced by a will in the organs appropriated by the two sensory and motor functions) is always distinct from the varied elementary products with which it is associated, and which alone motivates the distinction, established in the very ground of the inner sense, between the *subject* and the *object* of an *intuition* or complete *representation*.

3. Finally, that since the feeling of the power of effort enters, as an essential part, into the modes of the external senses that are each subordinate to it, the mere absence of this feeling, in such passive modifications where *will* and *desire* are in opposition, would suffice to reveal, by the contrast itself, to the motor and sensory being, the reality of some foreign existence or cause, which would have as much power to modify it as it has itself to impress

---

[38] Critique of Kant.

movement on its body, as the sensiferous impulsion on certain organs. The double problem of *personal* and *foreign* existence would thus have one and the same solution, deduced from a single, truly primitive fact, from a unique and fundamental condition.

It is, above all, this unique solution to two problems that are too often separated that we had in view in going back to the source of immediate *apperception*. It remains for us now only to bring out the unity of these characteristics, in distinguishing it from everything that is not it in the composites of experience.

We are thus led to seek, in the secondary facts of our sensory and intellectual nature, the differences separating *apperception* from *intuition*, as well as those separating both from *sensation* and *feeling*.

Second Section

Chapter III

Application of the Preceding to an *Analysis* or Division of the External *Senses*

How it is possible to deduce from this the real distinction between the faculties or states of the soul whose differences are to be accounted for? Division of the three systems: *sensory*, *perceptive* or *intuitive*, and *apperceptive*.

The sense of effort, whose exercise constitutes the life of *relation* and *consciousness*, once active, continues to exert itself in a uniform and invariable manner in all the parts of its own domain. Although absolute and sensory life, carried forward in the perpetual flux of the impressions that compose it, remains uninterrupted and never returns to itself as it was, the fundamental mode of individual personality, periodically suspended in the sleep of the *self* and of thought, is always reborn the same: it is always the same relation of force to resistance, the same immediate apperception, the same self.[1]

---

[1] If it is true that all the diverse modifications of the being that feels or apperceives correspond to particular and present circumstances in the play of the organs, according to some relation of conditionality (even a *pre-established harmony*), we will discover, in the instruments serving to effectuate or to reproduce continuously these two sorts of elements (the sensory affections, on the one hand, and the modes of *effort*, on the other), a few obvious signs of the diversity and change, or of the uniformity and constancy, which characterize respectively these modes inside ourselves. Now, physiology teaches us, from one perspective, that the organs affected by external and internal impressions from a variety of causes differ markedly from each other in the physical properties of consistency, size and subtlety, of the envelopment or exposure of the nervous fibres that work together to form these organs, while the cerebral nerves serving in particular the functions of voluntary motility in different senses, offer everywhere the same aspect and apparently homogeneous properties. From another perspective, we discover through reflection that the modes of this effort, which persists or is reproduced in the same way, differ only in its degree of intensity, while all the sensory affections, singularly varied in their own specific characteristics, are in a perpetual flux and never return absolutely the same. It is manifest, therefore, that there is a quite striking parallelism between the instruments and the functions, on the one hand, and the products of consciousness, on the other. Is not the difference of the latter in some way confirmed by the diversity of the former? We should observe again that the more the external senses are subordinate to voluntary action and appropriated by effort, the more they also conserve fixity in the impressions and constancy in their sensory dispositions. They are not, like the internal organs, susceptible to these great anomalies or perturbations of sensibility that offer no hold for judgement, no constant form. Besides, as a natural relation binds these senses to certain physical forces, they have to be governed by a power maintaining them and making them proportionate to the tone of the external agents. Otherwise, the latter remaining the same, each organic variation, each unevenness of sensibility, would have destroyed the relation, and judgement could never have been born.

In order to conceive this phenomenal *self* in the unique and individual sense of its immediate apperception, separate from everything that it is not, let us suppose all the voluntary muscles contracted in the immobility of the body, eyes open in the shadows, hearing tensed (*acuta*) in the silence of nature, the ambient air at rest and the external temperature in balance with that of the surface of the body, all the internal impressions reduced to the natural tone of organic life, unable to be sensed in their continuous uniformity... Effort alone remains, and with it, the pure phenomenal *self*, reduced to its immediate internal apperception. For as long as this invariable mode persists, for as long as the wakefulness of the *self* endures, sensory and accidental impressions coinciding with it can participate according to diverse laws or conditions in its reproductive activity and in the light of consciousness that springs from this source.

But among these diverse modes of our successive existence in time, there are some that coincide with *immanent* effort, and participate only accidentally in the apperception that belongs to it.

There are others that, without arising from the same source of apperception or consciousness, come to combine with it, so to speak, or to adapt themselves to it in *results*, while they remain foreign to it in principle.

There is, finally, a third species of sensory mode that, as if projected from the very source of effort, participates fully in all its characteristics and is inseparable from the person as the internal object of complete, unitary apperception, in which this person finds himself constituted as an individual.

Hence, there are three classes of fundamentally and essentially different modifications, and three corresponding systems to which we can relate all the individual or specific modes of the feeling and thinking being:

1. *Sensitive system* (passive) that includes all the internal or external affections of sensibility, without the support of the will or the active participation of the *self*.

2. *Perceptive* or *intuitive system* (mixed), that includes all the modifications relative, on the one hand, to the initial action of some cause, external or internal, foreign to the will, and, on the other hand, to a consecutive reaction determined by the will itself.

3. *Apperceptive system* (active), by which I understand all the modes or *acts* properly so called that are immediate and exclusive (or even only mediate and partial) products of the same living force that creates effort, in taking and in conserving, in this case, the initiative of an action that no longer accepts the law of external objects.

Application of the Preceding to an Analysis *or Division of External* Senses   119

In analysing separately these three systems in order to apprehend the different types of sensations that are included in them respectively, we will have to reveal the real characteristics to which are attached the principal distinctions that we are seeking to establish, as mixed up with several other, incidental characteristics that we are not.

§1

Sensory or Passive System

The faculty or rather general receptive capacity of all immediate impressions made on the nervous extremities by some cause (x), external or internal, includes all the facts of living and simply sensory nature that can be observed, either from a physiological point of view and wholly outside of the *self*, or from the perspective of immediate tactility [*tact*] whose relations we have already studied, and which, though related to consciousness, do not enter into the domain of the latter since they remain on the limits that separate our two natures.

If analysing completely this system of impressions, or recomposing it anew from its primitive elements, was our express intention, we would go back down perhaps to the living points, organized monads that are affected or intensified reciprocally in their reunion or co-ordination in a system, and that, continually reproducing these variable affections, these *material sensations* (Buffon) or *obscure perceptions* (Leibniz), never rise to the height of the idea of consciousness, because they are wholly beyond the sphere of activity that constitutes the latter.

The immediate passive impressions at issue here have their own seat in the nervous extremities of the internal organs. It is to them that is attached the play of *elective affinities* on which depend the secretory functions, the primary instinct of nutrition and conservation, and, finally, all the determinations of the organism and all the blind appetites manifest in the newborn animal.

Outside, we find again those impressions that spread themselves across the whole surface of the body, where they constitute general *passive* tactility, which, modified in a particular way in each separate external organ, becomes the immediate seat of the affective part constitutive of all our external sensations: the *matter* that is transformed not into ideas or original knowledge, but into all the variable degrees of force or weakness by which the human being or the spontaneity of the organism can conduct them.

Corresponding to this passive tactility, the primary sensory functions of smell, of taste and hearing, and sight also, in so far as they are considered in their immediate dependence on the action or impact of odorous, sapid, sonic and luminous fluids, that come to find, as if by a sort of attraction or elective affinity, the respective organs that are appropriate to them, and, tend to combine themselves with the latter, according to hyperchemical laws.

In this way, in the local impressions of the sonorous or luminous fluids in particular, it cannot be doubted that there enters, beyond the *perceptive* part that is represented to the soul, a truly immediate affection that remains confused in the total fact of objective representation and cannot be distinguished by the *self* since it does not rise up to the level of the latter, but which nevertheless can emerge in certain cases where experience and observation find it isolated.

Such are those cases, for example, where the material, and so to speak, inanimate part of the sound impacts sensibility internally, without there being anything distinctly perceived by the sense of hearing. It is in this way that completely deaf individuals have been observed to experience particular affections in different regions of the body, when sounds were made by a nearby instrument. It is also clear that certain sounds, certain tones of voice, certain accents, are naturally apt to excite diverse passions in the animals hearing them, and even to heal them or give rise to certain nervous diseases, etc....

The direct impressions of the luminous fluid on the retina seem to be, by themselves, the most devoid of the characteristics of immediate affection, beyond cases where the rays act *en masse* on the external organ, and it is clear that in that case there is no vision or intuition of any sort. Nevertheless, what makes a certain colour simple, or a certain combination of colours more agreeable than others doubtless depends on a specific affectability, even though it is subordinate in the sense of intuition.

We should clarify straight away that these *feelings* of pleasures or pains, of attraction or repugnance, which often accompany the complete exercise of visual or auditive perceptibility, should be distinguished from direct or immediate affections of which we have just spoken. These feelings – whose characteristics we will have to re-examine in the full development of our faculties and in the superior source that gives birth to them – of joy, admiration, love, for example, that *beauty* or the *good* (even when sensory) inspire, can arise only following the perceptive action or judgement of the soul, from which the immediate impressions of physical sensibility are always independent; and it is on this essential ground (which we indicate here only provisionally) that we will establish the truly distinctive characteristic separating *sensation* and *feeling*.

Coming back to the class of purely passive impressions at issue in this essay, I think that one could reduce the phenomena of *external intuition* to a sort

Application of the Preceding to an Analysis *or Division of External* Senses   121

of vibratory property, quite particular to the immediate sense of sight. Independently of the laws of knowledge, to which it is prior, and foreign, in the spontaneity of its exercise, to apperception and to the fact of consciousness, this subsists by itself, like all instinctive determinations, in virtue of organic laws and of the type of cerebral affectability that reproduces it. Such are the phenomena, indicative of a passive and spontaneous faculty of representation, of which the instinct of many animals at birth provides so many remarkable examples, when before any experience, they grasp the visible object that is naturally appropriate to their nutritional needs and thus to the conservation of the species. Such is also the spontaneous appearance of phantoms, forewarnings of a troubled sleep, that succeed each other in our vision in the obscurity of the night, phantoms that pursue us, envelop us in myriad forms, without the will being able to distract from them the intuitive sense that they occupy or that produces them. Such are, finally, the images, now changing, now persistent, which, in delirium and mania, by their vivacity and truth, overcome all the impressions of real objects, the images corresponding to the diverse vaporous states and that are proportionate, in their periodical apparition, to certain needs or organic appetites, coming back to life in intervals by nature or habit. In all these cases, the organ of imagination, according to the law of internal impressions, seems to be completely removed from the empire of the hyperorganic force from which apperception is inseparable. In limiting intuition to the spontaneous exercise of the material sense of *images*, we see clearly enough that it differs from apperception by all the distance that separates a complete *passion*, dependent on the organism, from a free *action*, illuminated by intelligence. But it is not here that we have to delimit an internal faculty of intuition that, in its very spontaneity, can fall under other laws and adopt a more intellectual form.

We should observe now, since the impressions or the images that constitute the matter of this type of simple intuition are able not to be affective, that this faculty ought to be distinguished from *sensation*, whose basis is constituted by its affective character.

§2

Perceptive or Intuitive (mixed) System

We have seen, since the sense of effort is fully exercised in all the parts of the body to which the influence of the will extends, that any one of these parts can be immediately *localized* as a distinct term resisting a determinate effort, and even before any foreign impression comes from the outside to excite its specific sensibility. Hence when such an impression arises, the immediate affection, if it is not strong enough to absorb all other feeling, can be associated with the mode of resistance of the organ that is its seat, and be localized in it and with it. From this derive the primary composed sensations and the primitive simple judgement, regarded as natural or innate by profound philosophers who have returned to it. It is not surprising that analysis should have found here limits that are difficult to overcome, since the obstacles are born from our most intimate and oldest habits.

It is sensation thus composed that, forming the first idea of *sensation* and bringing necessarily with it the *participation* of an individual, unitary sensing subject, could be very well designated by the term, which is indeed individual, 'sentiment'[2] if this term were not employed to designate an in some way more intellectual sort of affection, one more foreign to the material organs, closer to the soul, than the sort in question here.

I will continue therefore to call *sensation* every mode composed of an immediate, variable affection together with the unitary, identical feeling of personality, in so far as the impression is related to an organic seat that is therefore in some way separate from personality, just as the latter is separate from the body or the organ to which the impression belongs. It is not in this way

---

[2]   The term *sensation* is ambiguous, and, deriving from the Latin *sensus*, can serve to indicate only the function of *sense*, identified by physiologists with that of the organ, whereas the term *sentiment*, deriving from the [French] term *sentir*, carries with it the idea of the necessary participation of an individual and conscious subject. Also, the physiologist who, adopting a language established before him but looking to render it more precise, had distinguished an *animal sensation* and a different *organic sensation*, would not have distinguished, I think, an *organic sentiment*, nor even an *animal sentiment*. The esteemed author of the *Elements of Ideology*, Destutt de Tracy, to whom science owes a great deal and whom I will never cease to honour even when I adopt an opinion contrary to his, employed for the first time this formula: *to feel sentiments* [*sentir des sentiments*]. I doubt he would have dared to say also: *to feel sensations* [*sentir des sensations*] [A.-L.-C. Destutt de Tracy, *Éléments d'idéologie*, part I, chap. I, p. 35]. The pleonasm would thus be real, since, given that the object of the verb is contained in the verb itself, it would present only an absolutely identical idea, repeated twice in different forms. It is as if we said: *suffer suffering, to be pained by a pain* [*souffrir une souffrance*], or *speak a speech* [*parler une parole*], etc., whereas in taking *sensation* as the immediate result of the function of an organ, and designating by the verb 'to sense' [*sentir*] the express participation of the subject in the sensory organic impression that it receives, there is no longer a pleonasm. And the formula 'to sense a sensation' [*sentir une sensation*] expresses even quite energetically this fact of consciousness in which the *self* is unified to its modification, from a certain perspective, while it separates itself from it, from a different perspective, in order to perceive it, to *judge* it, in relating it to an organ or a term outside itself. There is at the heart of the expression 'to sense a memory' [*sentir un souvenir*], a *relation*, a kind of operation of mind that, indicating more particularly the consciousness of the *self* in certain acts or products, can be referred to this higher feeling that Locke calls *reflection*. But one had to distinguish perhaps the different uses of the term 'to sense', and to find their grounds and conditions in the very characteristics of the felt modes...

that it distinguishes itself from the acts or the modes that belong to it as constitutive of its own phenomenal existence.

All the complete sensations of odour, flavour, colour, sound, touch, considered as affections, are fitted to particular organs that enter more or less directly into the general sense of effort and are localized as terms of the action of a motive will.

But there is here an essential distinction to observe between these external senses. Some are constituted in a relation of dependence on the occasioning causes of immediate affectability that always predominate in them over voluntary motility, while in others (this affectability being quite subordinate and almost nothing) the *perceptive* part – that I name thus as entering more directly under the influence of the will and, consequently, into the horizon of consciousness – predominates in the total sensation and, isolating itself from all affective composites, can alone constitute this complete, mixed mode that I call *perception*.

The first senses of which I have just spoken belong above all and originally to a life that can be called *animal*; such are the senses of smell and taste, which even in the full development of our active faculties are always related to the nutritive instinct and to its laws. Such is also the universal sense of living and animate nature: the passive sensibility of the whole body.

The second belong to life that is almost wholly intellectual; they are the senses of knowledge, the instruments or means of all physical and moral communication, to which the progressive development of our highest faculties is bound. At issue here are the senses of sight, of hearing and of touch, all three considered in relation to fully active functions, from which they gain the *perceptive* character that is common to their products. In this, indeed, they are not limited to the immediate impressions or to the passive modes of representation or spontaneous intuition with which we began a moment ago. They do not always wait for objects to seek them out and apply themselves to them. They have their own force that makes them fly above those objects, master or modify their impressions, give to them the form that makes them fitting for intelligence as available materials for its later elaborations.

I will go into some detail here on each of these three instruments that belong to perceptive activity.

1. Visual Perception

And, first of all, as for sight, there is nothing more clearly recorded or easy to recognize than the difference in characteristics and in their respective products of a wholly passive vision, that simply reflects the images outside of it like the polished surface of a mirror, and the *looking* that is activated by will, which penetrates, so to speak, the interior of objects and draws from them the elements of a real intuitive knowledge. When vision is, indeed, activated by an express will (*vivida intentione actuantur* – one of Stahl's organic expressions[i]), its organ adopts a particular expression, for it is as if the life and penetrating fire of intelligence (*ignis intelligens*) shines within it; but the expression that thus animates looking does not come from the organ itself. It is an irradiation of the force of the soul, of which the eye becomes in turn the *mirror*. It is this force that directs the visual point, fixes it on the different parts of the object one by one, that agitates and turns the organ in all directions, electrifies it by rubbing or communication, thus giving to it all the essential conditions of distinct *perceptibility*.

If the sense of sight did not fall under that of effort – if, in other words, the eye was immobile like the organ of smell or even that of hearing – there would be no voluntary guidance, no active and intentional looking, no visual *perceptibility*. The luminous impression would be limited to the immediate affection, as when the rays act together overwhelmingly on the organ when we pass from darkness into daylight or open our eyes for the first time. Even when habit weakens the force of the affective impression and the rays make the fibres of the retina vibrate only slightly, to the degree required for distinct vision, complete perception has still not taken place. The matter is there, but not the personal form, and passive intuition, as foreign to effort, would also be foreign to a *self* that alone can be said to perceive the impression or the object, whatever it may be, from which the I distinguishes itself by placing it outside of its own self.

Thus, just as immediate affection, which is associated collaterally to effort, and, for that reason, to the feeling of the *self*, constitutes sensation properly so called, so too intuition, combining itself in a much more intimate[3] manner with the personal mode, constitutes an equally complete perception, in its immediately higher order.

Among the diverse characteristics that perception thus considered can adopt, with regard to the initiative or to the predominance possessed by either of the two elements of which it is composed, we will discuss the following:

---

[3]   In the immediate intuition of the images related to the passive sense of sight (the impression of the highly subtle luminous fluid seeming to be propagated by itself and almost without intermediary to the central point of the brain, hypothetically considered as the organ of the soul) we could suppose, from an objective perspective, that in this instantaneous transmission there is something more than material contact, that there is an intimate combination and something akin to a penetration of the elements or *monads*, reduced to their state of greatest simplicity, which on the one hand compose the organic centre of intuition and, on the other, the luminous fluid that actualizes its force of spontaneous representation, by virtue of truly harmonic relations and without the support of mental activity.

Application of the Preceding to an Analysis *or Division of External* Senses 125

1. Simple intuition, which can constitute all by itself the wholly *passive* mode of vision, being stripped of affective character, or having it only in the lowest degree, is not subject to the sort of sensory exacerbations that obscure and even completely eclipse consciousness in *sensation*. This is a quite distinctive characteristic that separates intuition from *affection*, and, consequently, sensation from perception.

2. Attention, which is a more deliberate and more *intentional* exercise of the sense of effort, can always, in the looking that is *activated* by the will, lift simple intuition up to the rank of complete perception, which does not happen in the same way in sensation, where the affective element, taking on by itself or through spontaneous sensibility an excess of *tone*, can, on the contrary, absorb effort, active attention and the *self* as a whole.

3. But when the external sense of intuition takes the initiative over and above the internal motive force, effort, though activated by a more express intention, is not *apperceived* in itself in its own determination, nor in its most immediate result. It can be apperceived only in its *mediate* result, in the image or intuitive mode on which attention or the force of the soul focuses and is concentrated. This is a quite notable difference that separates, in the perception that we are considering here, the faculty that will be called perceptive *attention* and what, in internal apperception, is called *reflection*, the latter wholly attached to the internal acts of the will and the self, the former following the path leading it outside, and which is particularly attached to the modal results of these acts, or to the sensory effects that they can produce outside of the *self*... This observation is quite general and applies to the exercise of all our most diverse faculties, to all the states of the soul where action and passion are combined, succeed or replace each other in turn. This is what blinds in such a particular way the mind of man about the nature and the characteristics of his most intimate active faculties. This is what makes *philosophical* talent so rare, in so far as it consists, not in repeating *a series of operations freely*, but in being able, even in the course of this free repetition, to *gain awareness of the power that executes them*.

   The sense of perception, and that of intuition in particular, predominate in the human organization, and even in its intellectual nature. The more we find facility and pleasure in representing or imagining what is outside, the less are we disposed to *apperceive* or to reflect on what is in us or what is *us*... It is thus in images and heterogeneous impressions that one attempts to analyse thought and grasp the secret of its operations. It is when carried on the wings of the imagination, which take us up into the skies or take us down into the abysses (Condillac's expression), that we think we contemplate and grasp it... Should we be surprised that the facts of inner sense escaped an organ that takes us so far from them, so far from ourselves? Should we be surprised that in taking this predominant external *sense* as the model or primordial type of knowledge as such, and in immediately generalizing the results of its representative function, we have been led, either to a sort of materialism that established feeling and thought in a necessary and absolute dependence on *objects*, or to an idealism that annihilates these objects in replacing them with images, mere phantoms, spontaneous creations of our intuition, which have no need of an external support in order to subsist, to *be* in their quality as ideas.[4]

We have just traced the principal characteristics of the perceptive faculty, in taking as a model the sense of sight in particular, of that of intuition, associated to effort and activity by the will.

The truly distinctive characteristic consists in the fact that will, effort or the activity of the soul that lifts simple intuition to the rank of the idea, is itself not noticed in its own determination, or remains confused with the modal result to which it gives, however, the perceptive form by which intuition, otherwise material and passive, is fitted to the consciousness of the individual subject, and thus becomes the object or final term of diverse intellectual operations like *attention, memory* or *reminiscence*,[5] comparison or judgement, etc. All of these lie outside of reflection, which in them finds itself removed from its basis, for it cannot be applied to an object heterogeneous to its own nature.

---

[4]   *Dialogues of Hylas and Philonous* show how he grounds the best part of his reasoning against the existence of bodies on examples drawn from the sense of sight [G. Berkeley, *Dialogues entre Hylas et Philonous*, trans. J.-P. de Gua de Malves (Amsterdam, 1744, reprint 1750)]. After that, we can see in the *Treatise of Human Nature* how the sceptic Hume, pushing these considerations to their conclusion, used the same weapons in order to destroy all substantial reality, including that of the *individual* thinking subject. This philosophy has reasoned quite thoroughly, like an intelligent being possessing only the sense of sight, if such a being could reason at all. The *real* or permanent substantial unity is obscured indeed, and seems to be entirely effaced, in the sense of intuition or in the mobile and composite images that it presents. The constant relation to the fundamental *unity*, without which there is no intellectual *plurality*, seems no longer to have any basis in existence... Everything is a *mode* or accident; nothing is *substance*... There can be a ground of the *tableau* that remains for some time and to which the transitory colours are attached; but this ground itself passes in turn, dragging everything with it in a perpetual flux. The sceptic triumphs here indeed. We will not attack him on this terrain that he has chosen as the most favourable for him; we will only attract him into another field of experience where his machete, a *harmful* instrument of universal ruin, can find nothing to cut.

[5]   It is necessary to remark, as an essential fact that seems to have escaped those who have confused wholly sensory imagination with intellectual memory, that there is no, properly speaking, *reminiscence of images* or simple *intuitions*, but only of complete perceptions in which an act of consciousness or an express will, an effort, is there at the beginning. It is this conscious part that,

2. Perceptibility of hearing and touch

Wherever the same conditions of perception are produced, namely 1) the *initiative* taken by a foreign force, or by some cause of an impression applied from the outside to a sense, prior to that of the force of the will, whose action is thus only consecutive to the external impression; and, consequently, 2) the absence of immediate apperception (this apperception can take place only when the soul initiates movement or when effort is truly initial) of an effort, perceived thus simply in the mode that is its partial result – we can recognize the characteristics of perception, such as they have just been exposed in the sense of sight in particular.

Thus, the conformation of hearing, considered only in its external organ and independently of its correspondence with the vocal organ, is such that the action of the sonic rays, like that of the luminous rays, comes always to impress and thus to provoke the sensibility of the organ, initially with the support of the active force of the soul, which, able to lend itself to perception and complete it by a truly active *auscultation*, has no direct means of preventing mere passive *audition*.

Although the sense of effort extends to external hearing, as is shown by the muscular apparatus involved in its organization, and above all, by the act of will that distinguishes *auscultation* from passive audition in the way that *looking* is distinct from mere *vision*, it seems that within it effort plays only a secondary role subordinate to the external impression. The will, far from taking the initiative, might never enact, on the material or the purely affective part of the sounds that strike the external ear, the type of secondary influence that it exercises on other sensory impressions, such as those of taste and smell, if nature itself had not associated hearing to another organ, seizing on these passive impressions, redoubling and repeating them, impressing on them its characteristic activity, as we are going to see.

The same would apply to the sense of touch, were it considered as passive or as receiving from the outside the diverse impressions fitted for its mode of

---

alone, comes back to life by itself in genuine *memory*, or in the feeling of the same, identical and continuous personality. And how could the *self* recognize or rediscover a sign of its reminiscence or of its personal identity in the purely sensory or intuitive modes, where it has not been, which it has not supported, neither as an agent nor as a witness? All the distinctions that could be deduced from our principles, applied to a complete theory of the intellectual faculties, cannot be noted in this essay, which already goes beyond the ordinary limits, and it suffices here, particularly given that it concerns such clear-sighted judges, to indicate the principal points of division for all the others to become apparent.

sensibility, that bring to it ready-made, tangible images of extended shapes, with the truly tactile sensations of heat, cold, smooth, rough, etc. But it would be a grave mistake to limit the functions of touch in this way. It would be to fail to grasp touch's own, original characteristics, and to apprehend only the one that is impressed on it by the most inveterate of habits, in the state where the immediate apperception of effort that initially determines these functions disappears beneath the results of the act, where the consequent of the primitive relation of *existence* and causality takes the place of the antecedent, where the *object represented* appears before the *subject* of *representation* and seems independent of it.

We can recognize here the characteristics of intuition that we have deduced from the simple images of the sense of sight, which are rightfully described as *intuitive*; indeed, the term *intuition* can, in being generalized according to real analogies, express very well all that the soul sees or perceives *spontaneously*, in itself or beyond itself, without any *effort* on its part or without any apprehended activity (either because effort is not exercised, or because it is confused with the composite result of the sensory mode and effort). Here, it is clear that the faculty of intuition – grasped from a general point of view and considered in the complete development of all its faculties, whose proper domain it becomes so difficult to assign – would hardly be distinguished from *perception*, in its outer limits, and above all in the high degree of facility and rapidity, and, for that reason, obscurity to which habit ceaselessly leads originally necessary acts and movements, so as to give to the impressions, passive in the organs, the form raising them to the rank of complete perceptions.

It follows that in considering our faculties in their habitual state of exercise, we could understand under the heading of intuition all the modes of *colours, forms* and *sounds* that objects themselves seem to bear, in the first apprehension that we have of them with each external sense. Complete perception would thus require an express, intended act of *attention* that, in focusing on the object of representation as the natural term to which this faculty tends, is not yet apperceived in itself, but only perceived in its result. It is here in the new deployment of *perceptive* activity, that we can discover the particular characteristic that we wanted to specify in this article.

Let us come now to consider, in the full and active exercise of the sense whose functions have not yet been analysed as they should be, the new characteristics of apperception, composed by experience with other sensory products to which it communicates its characteristic activity, and let us complete our study of the primitive facts of all the differences highlighted.

Application of the Preceding to an Analysis *or Division of External* Senses   129

§3

Active Apperceptive System

1. External apperceptions, functions of active touch

We related internal immediate apperception to the individual feeling of a hyperorganic force, applied to a living, organic resistance. Let us now substitute for this living resistance a dead, foreign resistance... The fundamental mode of effort will not be altered in the principle of its *determination*; the antecedent of the primitive relation to which the fact of consciousness or personal existence is bound will always be the same *self*. But the consequent of this relation will be complicated by a new element that, being the source and the basis of all our *objective* knowledge, demands to be delimited in its nature, its limits and the veritable order of its primacy, with more exactitude and depth than perhaps it has yet had.

We should separate from the *active* sense of touch, first of all, everything that does not depend on the voluntary motive function that constitutes it as such. We should also put to one side everything relating to the sensibility of passive tactility in order to find, in their purity and prior to any admixture, the two elements related in it: the unity of resistance as essentially *relative* to the unity of *effort*.

In this object, we could suppose that the tactile organ, instead of being shaped like the human hand, was reduced to a sort of extremely sharp nail, deprived of external sensibility but moveable at will, under the exclusive direction of a hyperorganic force capable of determining its acts and of perceiving its results.

Ending in a *point*, this mobile finger, moved successively or continuously over some portion of this matter that we would realize outside of ourselves, in the phenomenon of an extended, *shaped solid* (such as it is reproduced in the normal interaction of our senses and under a flexible hand, itself with an extended surface), would find nothing more than mathematical *points* whose *continuous resistance* would offer it the *phenomenon* of the mathematical *line*, where the intelligent and motive subject could not prevent itself from apperceiving these resistant unities, *discrete* or *continuous*, as being *outside of it*, since they limit or stop, in the direction from which it encounters them, the freedom of the same movements in any other direction, and since what can stop or limit effort or the *will* in this way is *opposed* to this *will*, is not it, is not the *self*.

The intelligent being, reduced to a sense such as the one we have just *supposed*, would have its own geometry. The mathematical object, unity, the point, the line without material extension, which are for us only intellectual abstractions, would appear, as phenomenal objects, within the horizon of its immediate apperception, and would be for it genuine, real existences. It would find itself naturally much closer than we are, in the most advanced intellectual progress, to what perhaps constitutes the absolute reality of things, or to the perspective, eminently abstract to our eyes, from which a superior intelligence could contemplate them. For it, at least, the primitive fact of consciousness would find itself reduced to its *most simple expression*, and the two elementary terms of the fundamental relation constituting it, cleared of the heterogeneous mixture that adulterates it in our experience, would emerge in all the purity and simplicity of the original fact where the *self* is established as *subject* in relation to a resistant term.

The *metaphysical* subject and the *mathematical object* being thus bound to each other, within a single, simple relation, with the first as the unitary, unique *antecedent*, and the second as the equally unitary and simple *consequent*, the two terms could in some way replace each other or be represented each by the other. The object could be conceived from the perspective of the subject, just as the subject could be represented under the attribute of the object. . .

Such is the intellectual *symbol* (grasped in the most concentrated reflection, and also, in part, by the most extensive imagination) that a genius of the first order conceived and dared to employ. It is here that Leibniz attached the first ring of the great chain of synthetic relations of which he composed the system of beings, the longest and densest chain that it was possible for the human mind to grasp and follow to the end. . .

From a hypothesis (which neither time nor the nature of the subject allows me to elaborate) established in order to arrive at the simple and primitive fact of external existence, identified in the same source with the fact of consciousness, I think that one can deduce the following consequences, applicable to the reality and to the original constitution of our cognitive being:

1. That the essential attribute or the very essence of what we call *matter* or *foreign body* consists, really and intrinsically, only in a force of resistance opposed to effort, which can be known or conceived fundamentally only in or by this freely determined effort. This entails that this free determination, in a movement that the will or the force of the *soul initiates*, is the true principle of knowledge, of the *subject* as of the *object* included in the same apperception.

2. That this apperception, considered in the exercise of the genuinely *active* sense of touch, presents the condition and the real characteristic to which we have attached the actuality or the fundamental state of the soul, expressed by the word *apperception*, since, in the primitive fact of foreign existence as we have

Application of the Preceding to an Analysis *or Division of External* Senses   131

just conceived it, the effort of the soul is truly initial, and is neither preceded nor determined by any other foreign action, as we have seen in the preceding cases where we established the characteristics of perception and sensation.

Consequently, this effort is not only immediately apperceived in its free determination, but also *mediately* in the dead resistance that, offering a support or a natural term to the living force of the will, realizes it or effectuates it in giving it the character of internal intensification that constitutes consciousness and complete apperception.

3. Given that this same apperception indivisibly comprises, in one and the same primitive fact and in the essential form of a *simple, fundamental* relation, the *self* and the phenomenal object, it follows necessarily that we are as *certain* (neither more, neither less so) of the existence of our *self*, the subject of effort, as we are of the *body* or of the term, either organic or foreign, resisting that very effort and included in its apperception. Now, since this *belief*, itself a primitive fact of the inner sense, is based on the bare feeling of effort or resistance as its proper and natural ground (and not on the superficial and mobile forms, or on the group of variable qualities and modifications, that are associated with each other and with this primitive *ground of being*, in the simultaneous exercise of all the senses[6]), it also follows that all the doubts promoted by a sceptical idealism attached solely to these mobile forms cannot unsettle in any way the true ground of *real* existence, as *objective* as it is *subjective*.

---

[6] The real existence of bodies is not an idea either of sensation, such that it would be a modification of sensory being, or of reflection, entirely concentrated in the feeling of our free acts, or in the consciousness of what is us or belongs to us. To what origin, then, can we draw back the knowledge of bodies, and this intimate certainty that we have of their real existence? A famous metaphysician, who attempted to reduce the whole of philosophy to what he calls *common sense*, that it would perhaps have been better to call *inner sense*, established that by virtue of a primitive principle, one inherent to our nature, all our sensations, whatever they may be – odours, tastes, sounds, colours, tactile impressions – are nothing other than *natural signs* by which we immediately pass from the sensory modification to the knowledge of the *object* or of the thing signified, that we do not feel, properly speaking, by any sense, and that we do not reflect on either, nor conclude from any reasoning, since the idea that the object or the thing exists is immediate, primitive, and the very basis of all our deductions from experience. The author of the philosophy of common sense here cuts the knot of the difficulty. It remains to determine whether he has gone back to the true *primitive fact* that serves as a ground for this belief, and if he has not followed habit rather than nature, in attributing to all sensations, even considered as wholly affective, the immediate property or function of serving as a sign for real existence. This may well be the case in the present phenomena of our sensibility, almost identical with our judgement, at the right time! But is there not, originally, and even presently, a mode or act on which is genuinely grounded the belief in a permanent reality, whether objective or subjective, that subsists absolutely and beyond its present modifications? Is it not in effort and the resistance opposed to it that we find the primitive sign of the two substances or *noumena* that *we believe*, without perceiving or feeling them, without having, properly speaking, an idea of them? Examining whether this is the case is worth the trouble, but we cannot know of it by generalizing according to the habits of the senses and the imagination.

Immediate internal apperception, which includes the feeling of the co-existence of our body and the still immediate external apperception, which makes us believe in rather than feel an existence foreign to us, therefore come together and coincide (according to the order of time) with the primordial exercise of the same living force. Is this exercise free and immediately apperceptible in organic resistance? This is the self and its body, object of *immediate internal apperception*.

Is it constrained by a fixed obstacle? It is still *me* and the foreign body, object of mediate external apperception, in which the absolute resistance of matter obscures, in consciousness, the proper, *relative* resistance of the organs obeying the same will.

This entails that if there were no invincible resistance facing us, or if the terms foreign to the application of effort opposed to it merely the degree of inertia necessary to effectuate its complete deployment and to make it apperceptible, then the two limits separating immediate internal apperception of what belongs to us or is in us from the external apperception of everything else would tend to come together and to merge into each other. Our will would seem to be the *soul* of external nature, as it truly is of the portion of matter that is submitted to it.

It is perhaps such a supposition that, at the inception of philosophy as identical with a sort of poetry, bound so many *souls* or individual principles of movements and will to these luminous bodies that move above our heads... The same hypothesis, realized outside of the inner sense where it finds its source, is related to the more philosophical idea of a *soul of the world* that all the parts of this great *whole* called the universe would obey, just as our body obeys the will that is a kind of parcel and emanation of the supreme active force.

And for whom would it be more fitting to conceive in all of nature an *intelligent* motive power than the stoics who, after having annihilated everything that is *passion* in the human being, granted the most unlimited empire to the exercise of the will, appending to it all the idea of morality and virtue, of greatness and force!...

If, as our ideologists quite generally have believed since Condillac, the sense of touch is the only one that, by virtue of its specific sensibility more than its individual motility, could make the passage from our internal sensations or modifications to the objects that occasion them or are represented by them in experience, then this sense would also be the only one able to provide a permanent basis to mobile images or intuitions, which could only succeed and replace each other in the organ or the internal sense belonging to that organ. Touch would only, so to speak, activate and complete a type of specular *reflection*,

Application of the Preceding to an Analysis *or Division of External* Senses   133

in which the *self*, the subject of the representation, brought into relief outside of itself, as if looking in a single mirror, attempts to see itself, to feel itself where it is not, and becomes more distant from the concentrated reflection that, alone, can make known its own *forms*.

However, if it is true that the mixed sense of touch, constituting an *object* that is stable in thought, carries the latter with it into the world of foreign existences, then it is also no less true that, as a special sense of effort, the type of support that it gives to the *will* and to thought can promote the reaction that the subject enacts on itself in learning to know itself and to limit itself.

We find, indeed, in the characteristics of the impressions or active modes that are related to this sense a sort of equilibrium between the two elements of apperception, an equilibrium that we have not yet seen exist in the perceptive order, where the object took the initiative over the subject of effort, where matter could dominate the form.

When a wholly passive intuition does not envelop the feeling of the *self* and when the apprehension is activated by the express attention or effort of the soul, this attention, escaping itself in the very act of its determination, remains concentrated in the modal result, which can persist without it and despite it, solely by the energy of its external *cause* or by a vibratility proper to the very organ of intuition.

But, in active touch, nothing can be perceived on the outside if the will does not begin and continue the movement. Any external impression stops when this will ceases to act or to deploy itself by its own sense. Besides, the tangible object, the resistance to which touch is applied is truly *dead*; it does not emerge by itself at the forefront of its sense, but waits passively for the will's action, and presses on it only in so far as the will acts on the object.

Sight (which, under the guidance of touch, and in so far as it is subordinate to the same *active* force,[7] takes such a precocious part in the delimitation of forms or figures, and replaces so promptly the wholly geometrical sense whose object it composes and often denatures) remains foreign to the fundamental mode of resistance and cannot reach its heart, since it stops at colouring the surfaces, etc., and drawing the *plan* of external forms. And, consequently, in abstracting from what in a group of tactile qualities constitutes their true linkage and external support, namely the permanent and *singular resistance* which is manifest solely to the sense of touch, and in reducing, finally, all that constitutes body to this

---

[7]   'Necesse est consimili causa tactum visumque moveri' (Lucretius). [Lucretius, *De rerum natura*, trans. A. Stallings, *The Nature of Things* (London: Penguin, 2007), book IV, vv. 232–233: 'sight and touch have to be trigged by similar causes'].

grouping of qualities or modalities that the sensory contact of the hand discovers in it, when it traverses or touches the surfaces, we would find only the simple characteristics of perception or of *intuition*, such as they are apprehended by the sense of sight, in which the separation in question is effected...

But when it is deployed by its own sense, the living force of effort also directly meets dead resistance and is thus *complicated*, so to speak, with it, when touch, instead of sliding over the surfaces, tends to penetrate bodies and to make them move, and in this way immediate apperception, internal and external at the same time, wins out and predominates over simple perception, the reflection concentrated in the very act taking over from the *attention* that follows outside the result of this act.

In the double function composing the special exercise of the sense that we have just examined, there are therefore two primitive relations that, governed by our habits, tend without fail to merge into each other, but which a reflective analysis must recognize as distinct. In one of these relations, which is truly primitive and synthetic, the *unitary* subject of effort is to be found in relation to the resistant term, which is also unitary and permanent. This is immediate apperception, which can be described as internal from a certain perspective, and as external from another. The second relation, genuinely analytic, and doubtless also primitive in the order of its nature, has as its antecedent the unitary resistance that is the genuine substance[8] of the body, and, as its composite consequent, the

---

[8]   I fear here that I will be accused of wanting to resuscitate vague ideas and denominations that our philosophers carefully exclude and which they claim to be able to do without. But I observe that the notion of substance, which, despite ourselves, enters into all the forms of our judgements, and which is correlative to the notion of *mode*, seems vague and obscure only in so far as one attempts to bring it, like all the others, into a representation or to penetrate the *absolute* nature of the thing designated by the term. Now, first, it is essential to all reflected ideas not to be able to be represented or conceived in images, and it is the forgetting of this principle that has produced so many errors and misunderstandings among the metaphysicians, who have tried even to represent the *soul* or *thinking self*, for example, with the image of a *subtle fire*, of small ethereal bodies, etc. Second, we are constituted in such a way that we can never *feel* or *perceive* or *imagine* the true agents of our sensations. Thus, it is not the luminous fluid that we see, but the bodies or objects that its rays reflect or decompose. We do not touch resistance, but the sensory and composite forms. Motive force is not apperceived either in itself, but in its application to the resistant organ or the term moved. The forces that act on us and against which our own force exerts itself are therefore conceived only in their necessary relation to certain produced effects. We cannot exit this circle of relations, nor isolate their terms in order to penetrate their individual nature. ['The ocean has its depths that can put the sound to the test, just as the sources of rivers that fertilize vast plains hide in hollows of overhanging rocks; so too, the principles of action that produce, animate, and change the universe and ourselves present only certain of their aspects to us, eternally hide from us their depths and their mode of operation'] [approximate quotation from: J.-B. Mérian, 'Dissertation ontologique sur l'action, la puissance et la liberté', in *Histoire de l'Académie Royale des Sciences et Belles-Lettres* (1750), p. 478]. But, although our thought is attached above all and even exclusively to effects or *consequents*, it is no less invincibly led to suppose and affirm the existence of *antecedents*, so much so that it is the latter alone, the forces or fixed permanent causes, and not the effects or the variable and transitory modes, that are said to *exist*; for to exist is to *act*, and only forces or substances act.

Application of the Preceding to an Analysis *or Division of External* Senses   135

sum of variable qualities or modalities reunited in this complete group where the senses and the imagination realize bodies and the entire phenomenal universe.

It is solely with regard to the first synthetic relation that it is possible to attribute to the special exercise of the active sense of touch (which is only the appendix of the more general sense of effort) the origin of simple ideas such as *external force, cause, unity*, substance, etc. Thus conceived in the fundamental relation of existence, these can be *objectified* in the external world from which the geometer and the cosmologist borrow the elements of their compositions. At the same time, they are *subjectified* or reflected in the genuine heart of the thinking subject..., the living model of the ideas wherefrom the metaphysician and the theologian gather the real elements of their systems, transform them subsequently by *abstraction* and, in misapprehending their origin, attempt to find them in a mysterious region of essences and even in the *divine understanding*.

2. How Internal, Mediate Apperception is Grounded on the Active Exercise of Hearing and the Voice in Particular

There are no known members of our species who, endowed with the faculty of hearing, do not also have the faculty of imitating the sounds that strike them and of reproducing some of them. However, it is known that a few individuals having lived to a certain age, who, deprived of all commerce with their peers and in complete isolation,[9] with their vocal organ in a kind of paralysis by lack of use, have lost for that reason not the faculty of hearing or of being struck by different noises that could affect the external sense of hearing, but the faculty of perceiving and distinguishing sounds that they are no longer able to imitate or reproduce.

A small number of observations of this type would already suffice to make us suspect that true auditory perceptibility is related at least as much to the eminently voluntary functions of the *repetitive* organ as it is to those of the passive sense that receives the sonic impression from the outside.

In touch, the two sensory and motor functions are reunited and even identified in the same sense. Here, they are separated in two different organs, but they do not correspond to each other any the less intimately, or co-operate any

---

[9]   Most notably, the wild boy of Aveyron, about whom we have precise observations written by the philosopher-doctor who is still concerned now with his education. [See P. J. Bonnaterre, *Notice historique sur le sauvage de l'Aveyron et sur quelques autres individus qu'on a trouvés dans les forêts à différentes époques* (Paris: Veuve Pancoucke, 1800).]

the less well, since the sensory organ brings the motor organ into operation, with the latter communicating to the former, in the repeated sound, the activity that was lacking in the direct impression.

At the very moment, indeed, that the sonic disturbance strikes external hearing, a determination of the same order is joined to the consecutive motor reaction that is necessary to complete the sensation, one that will put into play the corresponding touches of the vocal instrument. By virtue of this active determination, the sound directly repeated, imitated as if by an echo, is redoubled in the internal sense of hearing and the voice, and makes itself known, simultaneously or in an indivisible instant, by two equal but distinct impressions, the first felt or perceived as coming from the outside, the other apperceived or reflected as the immediate product of effort or of the activity of the soul that makes it.

Putting to one side any external cause of the auditory impression, the same activity can return to act on the vocal instrument, which is wholly subject to it, whence derive new, purely apperceptive products, whose characteristics and conditions deserve a separate class in the analysis of the senses and of the classification of the phenomena relating to it.

The vocal sound, freely determined in effort, or as effort itself whose organ is its end, will also have to be apperceived in both its free determination and its modal result. But this result, quite different from the sensation that follows or accompanies the muscular contraction determined by the will, will also have a truly sensory character, appropriated, like the movement itself, by the activity of the soul, which cannot determine the movement without effectuating the sensation.

In this quite remarkable mode of the exercise of two corresponding senses, the soul has thus the power to modify the sensibility of the sense that is not directly at its disposition, in putting into play the motility of the other that is at its disposition, and this, by one and the same will, which is as infallible in its mediate result as in its direct or immediate product, without, what is more, the support of any external cause. For in the complete apperception of the internal vocal sound, the will, which can provide only the *form* of the sensation (the matter coming to it from the outside) provides here all the matter together with the form itself.

There is here a quite particular circumstance that ought not to have escaped the attention of the anatomists of sensation. Indeed, in the most active looking, the eye does not illuminate itself internally. In touch, if the resistance is apperceived only in effort, it is no less true, whatever the idealists may say, that

Application of the Preceding to an Analysis *or Division of External* Senses   137

the matter of apperception does not derive from the same source as the form, and that the subject, which apperceives itself this side of the object, draws the latter neither from *nothing* nor from itself.

But, in the simultaneous exercise of hearing and the voice, the vocal act and sonorous mode begin from the same subject, which reflects and discovers itself in the one as the modifying force or cause, and in the other as the modified product.

From this double relation, we can deduce two types of apperceptions, proper to the sense of hearing united to the voice, namely: one that is relative to vocal effort, considered in its free determination and which is distinguished under the already recognized heading of internal immediate apperception; and one that corresponds to the result of this effort or to the sound produced, which could be called an internal mediate apperception. These denominations, used to distinguish truly distinct facts in their own condition and character, are not hypothetical or conventional. Inner sense, consulted well, in abstraction from our habits, would doubtless find enough to justify them.

The sense of hearing, activated by the truly intellectual exercise of speech or the articulated voice, is indeed *doubly* apperceptive or reflective. It is this sense that listens to everything, restates everything, even the most intimate modes to which it provides signs allowing for their distinction and recollection. The sense of memory borrows its own, truly available materials from this source, namely the *articulations* addressed to internal hearing, that come from the voice and are repeated in it voluntarily, and not simply the audible sounds that come from the outside and stop at the external sense whose sensibility they immediately excite.

It is also the sense proper to the understanding, of this superior faculty that includes all the others and through which the thinking and motor subject *understands* [*entend*] (in the full, proper sense of the word) all the ideas that he conceives, all the acts that he determines.[10] Other perceptive senses can replace hearing and even do better than it in relation to everything that is represented or imagined on the outside; but none can replace it when it is a matter of reflecting

---

[10]   Also, in the sense in which we take the term *apperception* and with regard to the character of the primitive fact of inner sense that the term represents, it would perhaps be better to replace the phrase 'immediate internal apperception' with 'immediate internal understanding'. The sense of the word *understanding* would be, in this case, individual and singular, instead of being general and common, as it is in its ordinary metaphysical interpretation. Besides, the signs *perceive* and *apperceive* are taken figuratively from the sense of sight, which, dominant as it is in human organization, represents in such an illusory way the primitive facts of inner sense that it always denatures when supposedly representing them.

or understanding what happen inside ourselves. Thus the fact is that the privation of this sense leads almost to that of all intelligence; without it, the individual, deprived of the primary means of social communication, languishes in a state close to imbecility. When due to an education led by the genius of a benevolent philosopher, he finds himself initiated into all the means of communication that his state can bear; when, in possession of a complete system of signs borrowed from sight, he thinks by means of these images, conceives and expresses everything by sensory figures, either directly or metaphorically, it is still permitted to doubt that this being has risen to the full dignity of the thinking being, to the high functions of intelligence that consist above all in *understanding* or in apperceiving the intellectual acts that the mind executes, and to reflect on itself, to think on itself in this free execution.

Let us draw this from the preceding (perhaps apparently too minute) details, whose useful application will soon become clear: the voice joined to hearing provides to the individual the sole means of modifying himself sensibly by the successive acts of his will without any external cause. In the exercise of this double sense, the sensory and motor subject is concentrated in its redoubled modifications on the inside, and does not have to follow the torrent of objects that drag him outside. With the other senses, the effort beginning from the soul, which grants the form of consciousness to impressions, merges into the intuitive result, and it is for this reason that reflection can abstract from it only with difficulty. Here, the very act producing the apperceived form in inner sense as a motor determination, returns into the same source and is again reflected there as a sensory modification identified with the will itself.[11]

---

[11] For the deaf and dumb who have learned to articulate or pronounce series of words, by the first method promoted by the famous abbot of Epée (see his *Instruction of Deaf-Mutes*, etc.) [Ch.-M. de L'Épée, *Institutions des sourds et muets par la voie des signes méthodiques* (Paris: Nyon l'aîné, 1776)], the vocal movement would be the exclusive term of the will. There would be no associated and resulting modification that could, in whatever way, lead away from or rather push away the goal (for the will always bears on the final result, above all when this result is a sensory mode, and all the acts or intermediate means are more or less unapperceived, although they were originally genuine *volitions*). If such *talking deaf* people came to recover the sense of hearing, they would feel in principle, much more than we can now, the real distinction that exists between the *vocal* or *oral* movement and the *sound* that is its product. It would be the first that they continue to will, and the second would surprise them perhaps, first of all as an unexpected modification produced in them spontaneously, until the repetition of the same act, constantly followed by the same result, would have appropriated this for the will. Note that the vocal or oral movements in the speaking deaf person can be reflected only simply, like any other isolated product of the motive function. They do not have, as they do in ourselves, this characteristic of *redoubled reflection*. This is why they do not support better, and in fact only less well than gestures, the development of the faculties. It seems to me that we have to distinguish a purely *vocal* from a purely *oral* function, which work together in the exercise of articulated speech, but which nevertheless have quite distinct characteristics,

Application of the Preceding to an Analysis *or Division of External* Senses   139

In comparing the active functions of the three senses that we have analysed, we could say that the vocal movements are, to the direct and simple impressions of hearing, what the proper acts of the sense of effort, in the sense of touch, are to the simple tactile sensations; or, again, what the final acts granting a solid basis to colours are to the simple immediate intuitions of the sense of sight.

In the phenomenon of complete perception, such as it is realized with the mutual support of all of our active and passive senses, what depends on an initial effort of the soul or the acts that it immediately produces by the two motive forces belonging to it, touch and the voice, is redoubled in consciousness and, in adopting a genuinely apperceptive character, extends and communicates this character to all the modifications or ideas intrinsically capable of entering into the same sphere of activity. The heterogeneous passive impressions remain confused in the sense as immediate affections, following the spontaneous movement of intuition that the force of the soul does not direct.

It is thus in the field of its apperceptions, and not outside of it, that intellectual memory or voluntary recollection finds the sole grounds for its exercise. The distinct memory of forms or figures leaves to one side all the passive impressions of sensbility and sight, like heat, cold, the smooth, the rough, and the affective part of colours, which are not reproduced in memory, or, if so, only confusedly. Thus also the memory of articulated sounds does not stretch to the physical aspect or material timbre of these sounds, or to the purely audible and affective part of external hearing.

particularly in relation to the more or less active role that the will has in them. The production of what we call *vowels* or *voice* belongs solely to a certain mode of emission of air from the lungs; it is a manner of breathing or more deliberate aspiration than is ordinary in sighs, cries, yawns and laughter, etc., in the interjections that strong passions produce. These are voices or sounds that are rightfully described as *inarticulate*, which are formed without the participation of the will, and often even against its express action. This power influences more directly the tightening or dilation of the glottis, which modifies the air in exiting the lungs and thus determines the *tone* or the different degrees, from the grave to the acute, of vocal sounds. As for the timbre of these sounds, it belongs to the organic dispositions over which the will has no power, and for this reason a man can never entirely disguise the character of his voice, even if he voluntarily raises it or lowers it. But genuine articulation entirely depends on the *oral* function, and, in this part of the phenomenon of speech, all the mobile parts of the mouth, the tongue, the teeth, the lips, play an eminently active role. The will had to apply itself originally, and by an express determination, to move in detail each of these parts, in such a way as to form a particular articulated sound. Thus, these sounds, though having become profoundly habitual, always conserve this principal and original character. While sounds passively emitted will excite the sensibility of hearing, or put sympathetically into play other organs in the one that hears them, the articulations have to be *listened to* voluntarily in order to be imitated in the same way, and it is only by virtue of this imitation that they are distinctly perceived. We should note also that, in the regular action of thought, which is grounded on a sort of discourse that we address quietly to ourselves, the vocal function is unemployed, but the *oral touches* are struck and put into play. It is by this means that the intellectual organ is electrified, that attention is focused, and that thought finds, so to speak, a support in order to react on itself.

In a word, there is veritable memory and, before that, immediate apperception only of acts subject to the will, and, consequently, of the modes or impressions that can be *repeated* or imitated by the exercise of the same power. No affection, no product of any force foreign to the will, can be genuinely imitated. The hand and the voice joined to hearing are the only imitative senses. They alone communicate the form of apperception and reminiscence to all the sensations or intuitions to which they can be associated. It is therefore here and in these primitive facts, presented as a true analysis of our internal and external senses, that is to be found the origin of the pure forms of space and time within the sensory order, and of unity, of identity, of causality, etc., within the intellectual order, a formal origin that is no more to be found in artificial categories than in the abstract categories of transformed sensation.

Chapter IV

Of the Relations of Apperception, Intuition and Feeling with Notions and Ideas

The analysis of the functions of the senses, taking the latter term in its full extension, ought not to be (as several philosophers have thought) simply a necessary *introduction* to the history of the formation of ideas, and above all, to research on the origin and the generation of human faculties. Considered in the depth, in the number and variety of details, and above all in the true order of the facts to which it has to extend, this analysis should include the complete elements of the general history of the formation of ideas, and particularly everything that is fundamental, truly originary, in the generation as well as in the order of development of all faculties.

Indeed, our most simple ideas, as well as the most elaborate, those closest to the primitive source as well as those furthest from it, if they are complete ideas or perceptions, must always admit one of the personal or intellectual forms by which the feeling and thinking subject participates and co-operates in them, in joining the products of its activity to the type of passive matter furnished by the immediate organs of sensation or external intuition. This is the case in all the orders of ideas just as in all the modes of application or exercise of the same productive living force, which always remains identical to itself, from the origin of the *self* that is constituted in it and by it all the way to the complete development of intelligence, however one wants to distinguish these modes of the exercise of the same active force, in giving to each, in the language of reflection, the proper and individual name of a *faculty* of the understanding.

The result of this, and of the preceding analyses of the functions of our external and internal senses, active and passive at the same time, if I am not gravely mistaken, is that the complete separation of two orders or systems of ideas, the one *superior and pure*, the other *inferior and empirical* (such as it is defended by diverse metaphysicians that make of it the basis of their doctrine) is subversive of a *science of principles*, and must be absolutely rejected as contrary and opposed to the primitive facts, which are wholly unrecognized and confused by those who have established them *a priori*, or according to far too incomplete and superficial observations on the formation of the first sensory ideas and the primordial conditions of the exercise or development of these supposedly inferior faculties.

If the primitive facts had been truly recognized and distinguished at their source, one would have seen, perhaps, a whole intellectual system spread out progressively from the origin, accommodating itself to a primary ground that is common and invariable. Just as crystals grow, in developing into their complete form, when the secondary molecules come to adapt themselves to a primary core formed from truly integrated and primitive molecules, so too, in the system of the understanding, it would be necessary to distinguish first only the secondary forms (faculties or ideas) that are modelled, so to speak, on the truly primitive forms, so much so that it would always be possible to rediscover or recognize them in one another by ascending from the simple to the composite, as well as in descending from the composite to the simple, in the way that the ingenious *Crystallographer* proceeds.

The intellectual germ can indeed include, in its first sensory lineaments, the same formal elements that it offers subsequently in its whole development, but the microscope of inner sense is necessary to reveal everything that is hidden in this germ, which escapes vision because of its minuteness. It is doubtless more convenient to suppose that what cannot be seen is not really there, but comes to be added to it later, as if by a *transcreation* from a *superior* order of elements or forms, rather than to follow the continuous or successive progression from the same initially *inferior* order.

I have said that the complete analysis of the senses must include all the elements of the *formation of ideas* and of the *generation of faculties*. I now add that it includes both, in an indivisible way, and from one and the same point of view.

Those who admit a general and common derivation from passive sensation that would transform itself doubtless cannot recognize a *science* of faculties, distinct from that of ideas or primitive sensations. Everything for them can be reduced to a sort of logical analysis or to a method of classification of these diverse sensations or ideas, as is expressed by the technical term *ideology*, adopted most recently. But if they identify or confuse in this way the origin of ideas with the generation of faculties, it is because they abstract completely from the latter, or because they fail to apprehend their nature and real characteristics.

As for the metaphysical systems that admit intellectual operations as distinct from their materials or results, or faculties distinct from the actual, positive ideas that are its products, just as they suppose that the primary ideas of sensations are completely passive, and that any system of the understanding is consequently equally passive, it must be the case that these systems consider the faculties or powers purely *in abstracto* or in the abstract order of possibles, rather than in the effective or real determinations that form the experience of inner sense. It is also clear that they do not have to occupy themselves with the origin or the generation of the faculties, considered as a permanent attribute of the very substance of the soul, innate in it or with it.

Between these two opposed points of view, there is a new one to grasp, and I have sought to place myself there in elucidating, from the analysis of sensation or complete perception, the common principle of the originary formation of ideas and of the generation of faculties, the latter taken concretely or in reality, in the truly primitive acts that co-operate in sensation in adding to it an intellectual form or consciousness, and this without being confused with the materials to which it applies itself.

Now, it will be generally agreed, I think, that the fundamental operations or acts of the will and thought have to remain identical in themselves, whatever the objects or terms of their application might be. It follows, which we needed to prove above all, that the acts, modes or primitive states of sensory and thinking being, already recognized and distinguished in the formation of our first ideas, or the most direct results of the exercise of the senses, under the headings of *immediate apperception*, of *perception* or *intuition*, of *feeling* and *sensation*, should be identical in the progression of the intellectual system, in the formation of this order of ideas called *superior* or *pure*, and ought to enter into it in the same way, according to the same laws, conditions or relations, observed and determined in advance in the *primitive* or *inferior* order. From this, it also follows that we can, without fear of illusion or error, transport to the intellectual system the elements borrowed from the sensory system, and, far from separating the superior from the inferior, bring them together or unite them in a common perspective, by establishing between them a harmonic correspondence that will facilitate and shorten what remains for us to say to complete the solution of the problem posed.

I think I am able, first of all, to establish the correspondence in question by recognizing, in the intellectual order of notions and ideas, three systems parallel to those already distinguished, under the same headings as in the order of sensations and perceptions, namely: an intellectual *apperceptive* system, an intellectual *intuitive* system, and a *sensory* as well as intellectual system. We will examine successively the relations of these three systems with the ideas or notions of the understanding, as we did with the first ideas of the senses.

§1

Intellectual Apperceptive System

1. Relation of Apperception to the Notions and Ideas Associated to Signs and, first of all, to the Institution of these Signs Themselves

The relations that bind immediate internal apperception to ideas or notions, themselves considered as intellectual acts or as resulting from intellectual acts, are the same as those already observed in the primitive facts that indivisibly unite this mode or fundamental state of mind to the movements or simple acts accompanied by *effort*, and, consequently, to the perceptions or sensory ideas that result, as a whole or in part, from the same movements.

Thus, considered in the intellectual order, apperception should be grounded on certain characteristics, proper to the elements of this order, or added and associated to them in such a way as to be able to enter into the sphere of the will, to become completely available, or repeat themselves freely, with the *consciousness of the power itself that determines these free repetitions*, since this is what characterizes *immediate apperception*.

This characteristic of availability and, for that reason, of apperception is essentially grounded on the primary institution of linguistic signs, and particularly on oral language, on the truly intellectual employment of its signs, or on their constant association with our ideas of any order.

The institution or this secondary, artificial association of signs with ideas corresponds in a quite particular way to the primitive association established by nature, in the direction of direct perception, between the movements subject to the will and the sensory impressions that rise by means of this intermediary to the height of the idea.

These two effects of signs, each taken in its system, follow a constant parallelism within them and are perhaps closer to one another than might be thought by those who admit the absolute independence or complete separation of the two sensory and intellectual orders, as well as of the intellectual and the voluntary.

We can recall here what we have already observed in the sensory order about the characteristic of apperception and reflection, which can be inherent to the immediate production of the articulated sounds available to the will, though these sounds of the voice, considered in themselves or in the simple act of their emission, seem now to play only an accessory or subordinate role in the actual

Of the Relations of Apperception, Intuition and Feeling with Notions and Ideas 145

progress of developed intelligence. It is no less true, on the one hand, that this progress is grounded on the necessary employment of a few instituted signs that can establish between people, as well as between the mind and its present idea, the external and internal communications without which intelligence would not be possible... But, on the other hand, it cannot be doubted either that these signs of intellectual communication, in the human voice in particular, have on all those who can address themselves to different senses a type of reflective pre-eminence, as the first means for the activity of thought, the source of all intellectual progress in the individual as in the species.

In associating itself with our modifications and our ideas of any order, articulated speech impresses on them the eminent characteristic of availability and apperception only in so far as it carries the characteristic within itself, in the, so to speak, naked mode of its formation or exercise. It grants the will power over the diverse ideas lent to it by the signs of distinction or of recall, only because it is, by itself, the first motor of memory, and because its successive products in time are as distinct between themselves as are the very instants of the time that they measure. In the end, it communicates to the most intellectual ideas, in activating them, the characteristic that makes them sensory only because it is itself an intellectual *act*, a *willing made sensory*.

Metaphysicians exclusively attached to a superior or pure system of ideas, with its head in the clouds and no roots anywhere, who will doubtless scorn these minute (but not *pure*) details concerning the exercise of an inferior sense, cannot recognize the proper characteristics of the oral sign. It is not to this that they will reattach immediate apperception, considered in its relations with intellectual ideas and notions. But, when primitive facts are required, I am quite convinced that, without presupposing any *theory* or *pre-established system*, these facts cannot be drawn from a more real source.

No system of signs or instituted language creates for man new faculties. Its institution, or the very possibility of the primitive intentional employment of signs, much rather presupposes the pre-existence of an activity superior to sensation, by which the thinking being is placed outside of the circle of impressions and images in order to signify or note them.[12]

---

[12] Several philosophers agree that the principle cause of the difference between human beings and animals is that the latter have no instituted signs like we do; but why do they not have our signs, or why do they not institute any as we do?... One of our most distinguished analysts (Destutt de Tracy in his *Grammar*) attributes this essential lack to the fact that animals do not have, as the human being has, the faculty of noticing or distinguishing particular sensations that are contained in others that are more complex... [A-L.-C. Destutt de Tracy, *Éléments d'idéologie*, part II (*Grammaire*)]. This explanation seems to me to offer a vicious circle, for it is probable that the faculty of

But the usual employment of a regular system of instituted signs reacts powerfully on its cause or on the instituting faculty itself, and develops, extends, perfects and complicates in a remarkable manner the play of all the operations of the understanding. In this period of progress, the spirit of man is already so distant from the primitive source, though he is capable of returning to himself and of interrogating the principle of his operations, and now finds only the products of *art*, confused with those of a simple nature whose traces it can no longer discover. The mind of man attaches all of his intellectual existence, all his material progress, all his works, all his memories to this ensemble of artificial signs, the secret of the institution of which escapes him, and whose influence habit almost entirely hides from him.

Hence the difficulties and the slowness of a discovery, begun by Hobbes and Locke, but completed only by Condillac.[13] Hence also the limitations in Condillac's inventions, when, after having recognized all that the institution or use of conventional signs adds in availability and activity to the first operations of the understanding, he remained this side of the limits of the primitive fact of the institution of language, of which he observed only the secondary or subordinate effects.

In returning to the primitive fact that makes such institution possible, we will find that the immediate functions of two eminently active senses, such as touch and hearing joined to the voice, already compose, indeed, under the influence of the same motor will and prior to any human conventions, a system of natural and real signs that expresses, in the case of touch, the true ground of external nature, and, in the case of the voice, all the sentiments or the most intimate modes of the soul, which gain with it their most fitting expression, as well as their most direct and most assured means of internal or external manifestation. . . It is now only a question of gathering nature from the facts, and of continuing the plan traced out by it.

---

distinguishing or abstracting in this way the *content* from the *container*, as well as of subsequently joining it to the latter by a synthetic judgement, already presupposes the habitual use of some instituted signs. I think, for my part, that the primary cause of the lack of signs derives from the more essential lack or absence of *thought*; animals do not speak because they do not think, and they do not think because (or rather *in so far* as) they do not have the faculty of forming a simple and truly primitive or fundamental judgement of the intelligence, and that is to say of apperceiving from within the relation of personal *causality* in a willed movement, apperceived in its free determination at the same time as perceived or felt in its modal result – which could itself derive from the way that their movements are executed by sympathetic reaction from the cerebral centre, according to the law of instinctual affections or appetites, as well as to the law of blind habit.

[13] *Essay on the Origin of Human Knowledge* [E. B. de Condillac, *Essai sur l'origine des connaissances humaines*, trans. *Essay on the Origin of Human Knowledge*, ed. H. Aarsleff (Cambridge: Cambridge University Press, 2001).]

Of the Relations of Apperception, Intuition and Feeling with Notions and Ideas 147

But under the law of instinct and that of habits (which overlap without intermediary in beings stripped of freedom and thus without the apperception of movements that are determined by a blind principle), the plan of nature in question cannot be followed, since it cannot be apperceived or known. It is therefore only outside of these laws of the organism, and under the primary influence of a power of effort and will that these same movements or acts, already instituted as *signs* by nature itself,[14] apperceived in their free determination, will be able to be instituted secondarily as arbitrary or conventional signs, and thus acquire the broad and varied capacity for representation that has no limits beyond those assigned by the will that leaves its imprint on them, or by the intelligence which attaches its products to them, in order to come back to visit them and to enjoy once again their results.

Such is therefore the progress that the *institution* of intellectual signs can bring in the natural exercise of the senses activated by the will.

The individual already understands, and translates to himself, so to speak, two sorts of *mother* tongues that nature has taught him. He grasps these and apperceives their naked signs with the *power* of *repeating* them; he repeats them, and applies them with an express *intention* that comes from him, that is in him. Here, the first intellectual sign is understood, language is *instituted*, and, with it, an invariable and fixed basis grounding immediate apperception, the latter taken in the whole extension of the relations that it can have with the formation of all kinds of ideas, which recalls their comparison, their deduction – in all the intellectual acts applied to these ideas, which are transformed into purely reflective ideas with the help of the same signs that express and apply them... Let us examine here, with a few examples, these new relations of apperception with the intellectual notions that linguistic signs create for it and submit to it.

2. Relation of Apperception to the Sign of Recall or Memory

Memory properly so called, or considered as one of the principal active faculties of intelligence, is not, as an ancient philosopher said very profoundly, a simple

---

[14] The child cries first by instinct, and I do not believe that one should say that, from birth, it apperceives and wills the vocal movements that form its wails. But, sometime afterwards, we can recognize that he transforms these instinctive cries into voluntary signs, which he already uses to gain attention. At that point, he has made an important step, but how could he do this if the affections of instinct had always, as in the beginning, predominated and forced the vocal movement, and if there were not, in the course of the rapid progress of life, a few particular conditions or circumstances of the very production of the movements, to which belong the first feeling of power and, consequently, the first feeling of effort or primitive will?

depositary for images, but instead the very power that draws, from past operations, materials apt for new intellectual monuments: *memoria non est imaginum custos, sed facultas quae ex rebus mente conceptis propositum denuo promere potest* (Porphyry).[ii]

This capacity that the human being has to repeat freely acts already executed, for a present purpose that the understanding conceives and the will determines (and, what is more, to obtain in this free repetition, the feeling of the power that, having once produced them, sets itself to reproduce them again) is memory, which, thus constituted as *intellectual*, can be grounded only on the prior relations of immediate apperception to the signs or movements associated with the ideas or notions drawn from this past that it brings back to life. But, without these signs added to the preconceived ideas, the acts that had a role in the original formation of the latter would remain caught up in the most sensory results, and would find themselves outside the domain of memory, wholly in that of intuition or spontaneous imagination.

The signs that are attached to the acts or formal elements of the ideas or notions of the understanding can attribute to them, as well as conserve for them afterwards, a distinct and separate existence, in tracing around these elements something akin to a line of circumvallation that prevents them from losing themselves again in the composites of experience and habit. They assure thereby for the will the means of conceiving and repeating again these *formal* acts or reflective elements of ideas, which the will has at its disposal only when they are signified or noted separately from a sensory, intuitive matter, which, by itself, escapes the power of recollection and is not subject to the power of signs.

These reflective signs, serving to abbreviate all the longest and the most complicated intellectual operations, in conserving their results, thereby assure them, in time, of an infallible recollection that allows them not to have to be repeated in detail. They thus multiply the forces of intelligence, in focusing and concentrating them as if into a point where reflection finds the complement of its power and most energetic activity.

From here, we see the tree of science, having emerged from the germ where we were attempting just now to grasp it, magnified suddenly, now hide its head in the skies and cover with its expanses an immense surface whose limits we can no longer embrace... And yet, all the parts of this majestic tree were all hidden in the primitive germ, where, in order to distinguish and recognize them, the patience and the *microscopic* eye of *Lyonnet* would be needed, as would be needed now, in order to depict them or grasp them as a whole, the genius and the palette of Buffon!

Intellectual memory has too often been confused with a simple faculty of representation or spontaneous intuition. Sometimes, indeed, these images, products of this intuition, have been considered as carrying in themselves the characteristic or the intellectual form of reminiscence with which our inner sense can cloth them. Sometimes, in abstracting from this truly intellectual form whose origin one would have sought in vain in sensory impressions, where it is indeed not to be found, the purely arbitrary title of memory has been conserved for images passively reproduced, without any recognized identity in the object or in the subject of this spontaneous representation.[15]

In the first case, there is no regard for the real characteristic and the essential condition that constitutes, in the ideas or images, reminiscence that is distinct and separate, in its state of *purity*, from any intuition or sensory impression.

In the second case, the purely nominal title of memory [*souvenir*] is established on an artificial and false basis, on a condition wholly external to the subject itself, who *remembers* only in so far as he recognizes some *identity*, and first of all, his own. A hypothesis is substituted for a fact, or one takes this fact into the outside, where it does not belong. In a word, the sign is conserved and the idea is denatured.

It is in this way that intellectual memory comes to be confused with passive imagination, just as apperception is confused with intuition. How to apprehend the real differences that separate the positive facts when one desires absolutely to have everything fall under a single category, doubtless with the aim of simplifying language rather than of extending and making more precise our knowledge?

Thereby, the *apperceptive* faculty of *recall* or free repetition of intellectual acts has been confined in the narrowest limits, a faculty that plays the most constant

---

[15] Destutt de Tracy, in his *Eléments d'idéologie*, sees in *memory* only the passive faculty of being affected once again by an impression or sensation that one has already had, without having the fact of *recognized identity* enter into his definition [A.-L.-C. Destutt de Tracy, *Éléments d'idéologie*, part I, chap. III]. This fact must form the basis of the idea attached to the term *memory* when the analogy of language is consulted and, above all, the analogy of facts. In his *Treatise on Sensations*, Condillac had also considered memory as consecutive to a material shock that is persistent or renews itself in the organism, in abstracting also from the fact of inner sense, on which the recollection or recognized identity is grounded [E. B. de Condillac, *Traité des sensations*, part I, chap. II, in *Oeuvres philosophiques de Condillac*, t. I, pp. 225b–226a]. Bonnet's *Analytical Essay* displays the great pains and the detours that he took in order to find in a certain play of the fibres of the brain a material sign in which this inner feeling or immediate judgement could be attached, by which the soul recognizes and assures itself that it has been modified *in the same way* ... [Ch. Bonnet, *Essai analytique sur les facultés de l'âme*], as if a fact of pure inner sense, a reflective idea of this sort, could be represented by some image, or be translated, so to speak, by *movements of fibres*. The same reproach can be made to Hartley, in his *Observations on Man, His Frame, His Duty, and His Expectations* [(London: S. Richardson, 1749), trans. J. Jurain, *Explications physique des sens, des idées, et des mouvements tant volontaire qu'involontaire* (Reims: Delaistre-Godet, 1755)].

role and occupies the most eminent place in the operations of the human understanding, since, without it, the understanding itself would not exist.

Indeed, active memory occupies with regard to reflection a comparable office to that of sight in relation to touch. We have already seen how, in retracing and in recognizing the identity of our acts or of their results, this faculty can stand in for the complete repetition of the same acts, just as sight represents, with an extreme promptness, the results of the slow and profound analyses of touch.

But memory can still furnish the means to begin the same detailed operations with more assurance and facility. In this latter case, it is linked by intimate relations to immediate apperception, and is nothing other than this apperception itself, considered in the free repetition of completely effectuated acts. In the other case, it is a simple reminiscence that, wholly attached to the simple results of previous operations, has only the characteristics formerly attributed to perceptive *attention*.

In the two orders of ideas or operations, we always find therefore a perfect correspondence.

Memory, always based on the same active motives, can be limited to *bare* voluntary signs and considered according to the simple relation of the order of their succession and the systematic arrangement of their material forms. It can, then, turn in the circle of the same mechanical procedures, which end up begin repeated in a spontaneous way with all the blindness, I would say all the automatism, of habits. Then, indeed, the memory of ideas and signs, having degenerated into a veritable mechanism, exists no longer and, having ceased to be related to internal *apperception*, has lost, for that very reason, all its intellectual characteristics.

It is a law of our active and thinking nature (subject to all the influence of habit, which, on the one hand, activates progress, while, on the other hand, blinds it concerning its own operations, because of this vey progress) that, in a more or less long series of acts associated to ideas or intellectual notions, and serving the acts or each other as signs, the one that is placed last in the order of the *series*, if above all it is known or foreseen in advance, seems to become the term or the exclusive goal of a unitary will. All the other intermediary acts or signs, that are as many echelons or essential means for arriving at the latter, are gradually obscured to the degree that they are repeated. All the terms of the will thus enter into each other; and the primary means at the disposal of the will seems to touch the purpose that the understanding conceived or foresaw in advance.

It is in this law of habit that we can find the explanation of the promptness and facility with which even the longest and most complicated reasoning is

Of the Relations of Apperception, Intuition and Feeling with Notions and Ideas 151

executed, in the constant and repeated employment of the same methodological procedures. This is what, above all in the highest degrees of intellectual perfections, extends so greatly the limits of the rapid and seemingly passive intuition, which in a single flight travels over the longest chain of results and seems no longer to need to *act* in order to *think*, to *look* in order to *see*. It is here that an immediate intuition seems to enclose and to *envelop* all human faculties: *memory, judgement, comparison* and even *reasoning*, despite the great complication of its terms and means...

In taking the faculty of *comparing*[16] or reasoning in its primary elements, it would be difficult to say, indeed, to what point, brought back to the source of all perceptibility, this operation is bound to it and begins to be exercised. It can scarcely be distinguished from the principle that served to form or compose our simplest ideas, those that seem now to be the most direct. In this period of both progress and blindness concerning our intellectual acts (in which the existence of things or modes that presently escape the senses is *concluded* and internally affirmed on the basis of a simple impression that is associated to it, and that by virtue of a more or less long chain of images or memories, traversed with all the rapidity of our most inveterate and intimate habits), it would be difficult to distinguish what is in our mind in the form of reasoned deductions from what is there as immediate intuitions or in the simple form of an image,[17] so much has habit, a function of nature itself, complicated the elements of these primary sensory ideas and strongly cemented the ties uniting them.

---

[16] Comparison is, as has been said before us, only *attention* itself, actually applied to two modes or results of volitions and actions. These results can be considered either as simultaneous or as rapidly successive in two almost indivisible instants. I observe here that *simultaneity* can be in the results of the acts of will, although there is really *succession* in these acts themselves. It is in this way, I think, that we can resolve a difficulty that still divides metaphysicians and which has arisen recently in a celebrated school (in the Edinburgh School, by Dugald Stewart). It is a question of knowing if the thinking subject can have several ideas present at once, or execute several operations in one and the same instant of duration. We will doubtless always lack the data necessary to resolve such a question, since we can have no *absolute* idea of simultaneity or succession, which are purely relative to our variable way of existing or feeling. Nevertheless, in the order of passive faculties, I do not believe that it is possible to bring into question the real simultaneity of several received and immediately felt impressions. The perceptive results of the movements or acts of our will can themselves co-operate severally together, and persist thus for some time, by a sort of vibrality proper to the separate organs that are its seat and to the common centre where they are reunited, which does not stop the acts themselves, considered in the determination of the soul that precedes and animates the sensory results, being really successive. In short, everything that is or can be in our internal apperception is successive; what is in simple perception or intuition can be simultaneous.

[17] In a treatise on the faculties of animals, Lachambre, doctor to Louis XIII, distinguished with much wisdom the type of reasoning that is executed, as if all by itself, by the imagination or by habit. In comparing these spontaneous procedures to those of reflection in genuine reasoning, he brings to our notice the governing parallelism between the two orders of ideas or the two systems of operations: the sensory and the intellectual [M. Cureau de La Chambre, *Traité de la connaissance des animaux* (Paris: chez Pierre Rocolet, 1648; reprint: Paris: Fayard, 1989)].

It is by such a chain of causes and effects that from the origin to the complete development of all our faculties, the series of volitions or intellectual acts necessary to operate the formation, reproduction and diverse deductions of all kinds of ideas become obscure in their source and barely cross one's mind. It ends up escaping immediate internal apperception entirely, which is dulled by the lightness of its own operation, by the promptness of *succession* and the facility of its products.

In responding to this part of a question that only *the most philosophical talent* has dictated and conceived, we have just discovered and indicated a quite fecund source from which others could draw and perhaps find a negative solution opposed to ours, by clearer, much simpler and expeditious arguments than those we have used, in view of elucidating the terms of the *question* and of finding a *positive* solution to the problem.

§2

Intellectual Intuitive System

When the individual is in possession of the instituted signs, and when all of the faculties developed by their use have acquired the extension and regularity of exercise that constitute what we call human *reason*, the particular organ of the imagination, having been worked in all kinds of ways, finds itself endowed with a prodigious quantity of materials. It combines them again, often without subjecting itself to any law; it creates models and is governed by none; but its spontaneous products, in being tied to voluntary signs, take on a more intellectual and persistent character and can lend themselves to the new productions of the active faculties.

Whatever the extension that this mixed faculty of production and combination of sensory images can acquire, however far it seems to us from its source, when it rises up and looks over the marvels of an ideal world, it always bears the imprint of its primary origin (this is the most sensory part of ourselves, the part constituting our character and passions, the one that often inspires and contributes to the spontaneous creation of the wonders of art); it bears this imprint in the works of genius, whatever its material signs may be (*colours, sounds* or *speech*); we *feel* it, we sympathize with it: it animates the witness of creation just as it did the creator. This ineffable form of *inspiration*, source of the most amazing *powers* of man, is not itself in his power. What is more, it ceases to exist and loses its ability to influence and move us, as soon as the will tends to give it laws, or aims to reproduce and to imitate its supreme charm.

One could say of this faculty of creating by representation that it is defined solely by its exercise; opposed to tranquil and cold reflection, never do the two co-exist together. The one who now obeys the inspiration of genius is subject to its charm; he cannot account exactly for what he does or experiences; he feels, sees directly and does not apperceive; and when he apperceives, he no longer feels or imagines. But if genius does not itself belong in secret to one's own power, who could attempt to discover it?

Genius in the arts is in some manner like despotism; it is endowed with an *executive force*; that suffices for it. Its *legislative* force is in the execution itself. It is a kind of exercise of the faculty of intuition that, always more or less independent in its excursions and witticisms, is closer to the field of reflection by the character of its products, by the species of signs that it attaches to them, by the very methods that it makes for itself and to which it can remain faithful even in its boldest flights of fancy. Genius in the sciences, among the masses that are like the elements of an ideal world for it, and bearing on a small number of very complex and very general signs that redouble its energy in *concentrating* it, grasps at once the laws and the general relations of these masses, at the same time as it penetrates into the inner constitution of each. It sees the *abstract* in the *concrete*, and the *concrete* in the *abstract*, always guided in its procedure, its flight, by certain analogies. Often, the first one apprehended is a secret inspiration that seems to fall from the skies and that the genius cannot account for. Sometimes, they are suggested to him by the relations of the signs themselves; it is here that his sagacity apprehends or divines them, and it is from here that he departs to find an analogy of nature, one of these great laws that govern the system of beings.

Kepler, meditating on certain properties of geometrical solids, came to see, by a sort of truly intuitive inspiration, that there must be a parallel between the periodic times of the planets and the distances to the centre of their revolutions. He follows this idea, gropes around, tries different relations of numbers and their powers, and then finds the true one that observation transforms into a law of nature.

Newton sees the fruit fall from the tree; his genius rises up by a sort of spontaneous intuition to the sphere of the moon, foresees the identity of the force that makes the apple fall and retains celestial bodies in their orbit. Immense calculations again prove this inspiration.

What apparent analogies could lead *Franklin* to suspect the identity of lightning and the electric spark? *Several*, as he tells us himself: the *light*, the *colour* of this *light*, its *zigzag direction*, the *rapidity* of the *movement*, the *ease with which it is conducted by metals*, etc.[iii] Perhaps all these means confirm the first intuition of genius; they fill in the interval separating the sparkling clouds, the majesty of storms, and a slender electrical apparatus. But it was necessary that the imagination first spanned this distance, and who directed it in this bold excursion?

This indefinable creative faculty has the function neither of, so to speak, unboxing ideas or terms *closed inside* each other, nor of regularly following the thread of a supposed logical identity that unites them.

The imagination alone, carried away on a happy flight, fixes two distant points, and measures them with its ray. Sometimes, it creates the intermediate means that cross the interval separating them; at other times, it indicates only the possibility of their conciliation, and abandons the means to our technical methods. Can one reduce these diverse cases to the exclusive influence of such methods? Will it be affirmed that invention, in the fine arts as in the sciences, is always equally the slave of forms of analysis?[18]

Corneille and *Newton* are two *inventive geniuses* of opposed species. They can be compared, perhaps, by the very principle of invention, by the spontaneous intuition of genius that divines and *feels*, as if by a primary instinct, the *beautiful* and the *true*, so identical in their source, that hurls itself with enthusiasm towards this image, and draws from the joy it anticipates the forces necessary to make it real. The sacred fire that inspired the sublime traits of the poet perhaps also burned in the mind of the geometer who saw, for the first time, the admirable chain of relations that bind the turning spheres to each other. *Kepler*, who was transported with joy after having discovered a law that he sought with so much ardour also experienced this enthusiasm, the source of all discovery, in all its force, as did before him *Pythagoras* and *Archimedes*, whose transports, in joy and the contemplation of eternal truth, history has depicted for us. The principle that invents is the same, perhaps, whatever the objects or the products of the creative activity may be. This indefinable principle resides in a certain warmth of the soul, perhaps in a free and easy correspondence between the organic centre where the feeling is lit, and the seat where intelligence shines and rules; but in the exercise of the diverse faculties, the two foyers do not act to the same extent, nor according to the same order of influence. For the poet, everything begins with the *heart*, and everything comes back to it. It is by its impulse that the mind is directed. For the philosopher, the feeling that precedes or that follows the first intuition or joyful experience of truth, enters into him only as an encouragement

---

[18] This is Condillac's paradox in *The Language of Calculations* [E. B. de Condillac, *La Langue des Calculs* (Paris: C. Houel, 1797)].

Of the Relations of Apperception, Intuition and Feeling with Notions and Ideas 155

or recompense. It can embellish the entrance or crown the end of a career in the middle of which the mind remains riven to its own efforts.

Nothing is less alike, moreover, than the means of execution and the procedure of inventive genius in the two cases: the philosopher and the poet both employ signs, formula, but the sensory image arrives prior to the form in which it clothes itself and that it impresses with its own stamp, while the intellectual concept is inseparable from its sign, and often exists only through it. The philosopher feels that all his force is in his method; he relies on it with confidence. The imagination of the poet submits regretfully to the forms of language, fights against them, sometimes tames them, and, even in ceding to them, demonstrates independence. In the end, the one *strips* its signs to simplify; the other composes them in order to stir emotions. For the one, signs are levers; for the others, they are a talisman.

If it is proved, as I think it is, that *mechanical methods* do not enter into our reasoning about *facts* as they do in our reasoning whose sole object is the comparison of our ideas or abstract terms, it is all the more the case that these methods have to be limited in their influence when it is a question of a faculty that is all pictures and sentiments, of a power of creation that, depending in its exercise on the support of a multitude of circumstances, of which sensory dispositions are among the first, resists the weight of methods and all artificial *means*!

Among the diverse characteristics of this multiform faculty that is named *imagination* or intuition, the most stable perspective from which we can grasp it is that of the constant correspondence that is established by it between our affective and intellectual faculties. It is, so to speak, in the point of contact of these two orders of faculties that the creative imagination is situated and executes all its compositions. It soon forms, with the materials borrowed from the understanding, these archetypal ideas that lead it by new procedures, reveal for it a vaster horizon. We can see its influence in the bold and rapid insights of genius, which spontaneously take flight towards an order of truths placed well beyond the limits of the century, lays the grounds of a new science, and prepares the future progress of the next generations.[19] Often, the imagination borrows from a nature that is sensed, but more perfect than that which strikes our eyes, the elements of

---

[19] When a discovery is ripe, so to speak, usually several people reach it, each from their side, by the force of analysis alone. Several different mathematicians found at the same time the laws of movement and of the impact of bodies. Newton and Leibniz invented, independently of each other, differential calculus; but, as the germ of this calculation was to be found hidden within methods already known, such as Barrow's method of tangents, and Cavalieri's method of indivisibles, etc., it is possible that, sooner or later, less gifted mathematicians would have made the same discovery. There was, in contrast, only one man like Kepler, whose *imagination* was the dominant faculty, to discover this great law that could produce in its consequences the keys to the system of the world.

these compositions, prototypes of *ideal-beauty* in all the genres. Its living works excite all of your sensibility; a particular charm, a profound sympathy are attached to it; and in the emotion that they provoke, in the way that one *feels* rather than *judges* them, the source from which they depart and the dominant faculty that inspires them can be recognized. In this fleeting sketch of the traits that characterize a sort of intuition or intellectual imagination, we can recognize a spontaneous faculty whose active exercise is all in its *result*, and not at all in a principle of apperception or consciousness. Such is the character of this faculty that is exercised, so to speak, beyond the thinking being. It is also under this external relation, or in judging it by its results, that it can be *active*, as it is often said to be. Is it not in the same way that we recognize an *activity* of the *passions*? In this sense, it is when a being is the most completely passive, for himself or in his own apperception, that he is the most active in the eyes of the spectator; and here the opposition in the terms reveals an opposition between the perspectives, of which one is founded on a wholly internal intuition, while the other is concentrated in the most inner reflection. This is the secret of all the divergences between the metaphysical systems, and the source of the apparent obscurities. If we had a language appropriate for reflection, perhaps there would be a type of metaphysical evidence, just as there exists mathematical evidence. Indeed, the two orders of conceptions are drawn without admixture from the very source of evidence, and are both grounded in one of the elements of the same primitive fact, that of *apperceived* existence; but all the primary habits of our sensibility, and, consequently, those of language conforming to them, bring us out of ourselves, and objectify first of all our modifications and our ideas in composing them. It is apparent why the culture of the science of ourselves or of our own faculties must always be rare, difficult, off-putting and subject to a thousand sources of illusions, even for those who are the most and the most sincerely disposed to cultivate it.

The spontaneous creative faculty that we have just spoken of is always represented in language under the banner of *vision* (*intueri*, to see). We talk of the *piercing eye of genius*, etc., and it is indeed in the infinitely prompt, easy and apparently spontaneous operations of this sense that the discoveries of genius find their most faithful representation. Perhaps this last observation helps to justify the procedure that we have followed in allying not all *the same nominal faculties to sensation in general*, but a particular order of faculties to the exercise of *each sense*.

One of the characteristics most apt to distinguish intuition from apperception is reminiscence, which enters exclusively into the reflective products of one, but is not involved in the spontaneous products of the other. That an idea, a relation,

Of the Relations of Apperception, Intuition and Feeling with Notions and Ideas 157

strikes us vividly like a ray of light, as often occurs in certain happy dispositions in which ideas comes to find us without us having to try (for example, when travelling, walking, etc.), whatever their vivacity and sharpness may be, if we do not immediately tie them to some available sign that sentiment gives us, if they are not subject to a sort of incubation of thoughts, they escape us entirely, and soon after we are surprised to have to look for them vainly. If they present themselves again, they seem to us to be completely new. And is this not the reason for which the person of genius is often incapable of tracing out his route and of giving the description or analysis of his procedures? And are we not all in the same situation, in relation to these intellectual operations that we exercise in a more limited sphere? Is it not for this reason that the *science of our faculties has so little advanced*, and that the problem on which I have *struggled* for so long will have only an imperfect solution?

§3

*Intellectual Sensory System. Relation of Feeling and the
Passions of the Moral Being with Ideas*

We have just seen how a spontaneous, creative faculty, lighting its torch on the fire of feeling, can come to place itself, so to speak, on the point of contact between two natures, sensory and intellectual, and borrow from the affections of the one everything great, sublime and original that it carries into the intuitions or conceptions of the other.

We should tarry awhile on these relations of sensibility to intelligence, considered in different orders of operations and of the ideas that they constitute.

The individual feelings proper to the soul – that the moral person attributes to itself, and with which the *self* really *identifies itself*, for as much as it separates itself from a wholly physical sensibility – are secondary results of the exercise of the activity of the soul, and as united to the direct perception that they follow or accompany, are associated in the same way, and perhaps even more intimately with the ideas of reflection, or to the elaborated products of the intelligence. In both cases, they are homogeneous elements, by their nature or by the superior source from which they emanate.

Thus, just as there is a feeling of the *beautiful* and the sensory *good* that, in the direct order of perception, is immediately attached to the symmetrical proportions of the forms or figures, to the harmony of the colours, above all to the harmony of sounds in their compositions and melodies, there is even a feeling of the *beautiful*, of the *sublime*, of the *true* and of the *good* in intellectual and moral ideas. There is a pure and celestial joy that, in being united with the results of the operations of the mind and of all the works of thought, becomes the sweetest and the most noble recompense.

In that instant, quicker than lightning, in which a truth laboriously sought after finally emerges from the clouds, and illuminates with its clarity the mind perceiving it without effort, intuition and feeling seem indeed to be identical and to merge together in the joyfulness of this truth... and in this case, perhaps, the metaphysical precision that could distinguish them again seems to have almost no ground in the facts of intellectual and sensory nature.

But, in looking more closely at the primitive facts of this mixed nature, considered more particularly under this latter relation, we can recognize points where sensibility allies itself and brings itself into contact with intelligence, without merging into it.

The direct perceptions of our senses, like the images of our intuition and the most elaborate ideas of our mind, as received, produced and contemplated in turn with different affective dispositions (for example: with an *immediate* feeling of energy or of radical *forces*, or of weakness and languor, of serenity and calm, or of unease and trouble), seem to be tainted, so to speak, by the colours of these diverse fundamental affections... This is the sort of *sensory refraction*[20] that gives, to the ideas that have a common basis in the mind of all, certain variable forms that they receive in passing as if through the organization and the temperament of each. This is why the same individual idea, in two human heads, cannot be repeated identically in all points, in the same head; and this is why, let us note in passing, *moral ideas*, which belong all the more to these affective dispositions, and take root to a large degree in them, are so mobile or difficult to stabilize, while mathematical ideas, being the most foreign to our sensory nature, are also the most fixed, the sharpest and the most uniformly determined in all minds.

The role of the immediate affective feeling in the formation or the reproduction of the different species of ideas has never been and perhaps never will be fixed with exactitude, for the reason that, since it does not reproduce itself in our apperception or memories, we are all the more completely blind about these modes of our sensory being.

---

[20] See Part II, Chapter 1.

Hence the philosophers who aimed to apply a sort of mental calculation to the diverse elements of our moral ideas have never taken these modes into account, have never analysed or remade them, as one makes and unmakes the ideas of numbers and of extension.[21]

The metaphysicians aiming to *intellectualize* all human passions in attributing to the soul an active influence on the simple and immediate modes of pleasure and pain, as well as on the feelings accompanying its own operations, have understood just as badly the primitive relations of sensibility with intelligence.[22]

It was perhaps necessary to distinguish a fundamental affective state, which gives, so to speak, the tone, direction and form to the ideas relating to it, rather than being the result of the latter, from another, higher state of sensibility, in which will and thought, taking indeed the initiative of acting on accidental feelings, can exalt them and even give rise to them.

One cannot be concerned with the relations that the feelings of the soul can have with the ideas or notions of the understanding without being tempted to penetrate further into the nature and characteristics of the mixed phenomena that are called, in general, *passions*, in which the intellectual, moral and physical or organic faculties of man work together in such a remarkable way, influence each other, and take it in turns to take the initiative and become predominant.

It is from such an alternating order of influences (of mutual, diverse actions and reactions) co-operating simultaneously in the mixed facts of our nature that it is possible to deduce all the essential distinctions apt for establishing the diverse classes or species of passions, to which so many species of *relations* between *feelings* and *ideas* would correspond.

1. There are passions that belong to the *physical*, emerge from it as from their source, come back to it as to their home: such are instincts, appetites, the penchants and determinations of the organism or animality, instincts that are expressed and manifested by striking signs, taken in the physical side of the human being, though there they are less fixed and less infallible, perhaps,

---

[21] Locke, *Essay on Human Understanding*; Condillac, *Essay on the Origin of Human Knowledge*, and *The Language of Calculations*.

[22] Descartes, *Letters to Elizabeth* '*tota autem nostra voluptas posita est in alicujus nostrae perfectionis conscientia*' ['all our contentment consists in our interior awareness of possessing some perfection', Descartes to Elisabeth, 1 September 1645, in *Philosophical Letters*, p. 168]. See also Leibniz, vols. I and II [G.W. Leibniz, *Principes de la nature et de la grâce*, in *Opera omnia*, Dutens (ed.), t. II, § 17, eng. *The Principles of Nature and Grace, Based on Reason*, in *Philosophical Papers*, p. 641].

than in the inferior beings that are *simple in vitality*, in which there is only a sensory and organic nature, alone and without a counter-weight.

All the images or ideas that are engendered by such a source, or relate to it and even depend on it, in a higher order of progress, can and must be characterized as *physical*. The dependence of the mind that feeds on phantoms, the mobility and spontaneity of images, the nullity of the will incapable of changing or distracting them, and even, in extreme cases, the nullity of consciousness itself, which, not flowing from this source, can be absolutely separated from it...; such are the characteristics of genuine, *bare* and complete *passion*. Whatever the spiritual automaton may produce as results, he is still a machine, and can recognize himself as such when he compares himself to himself in the passage from passion to action.

2. There are purely *intellectual* passions, genuine *feelings* that the will cannot directly create, imitate or reproduce, but which arise only following an act or operation of intelligence. We have already seen this in the feeling of sensory and intellectual *beauty*, of the *good* and of the *true* in the intuition of ideas, of the *surprise* or admiration that grips the soul in the presence of great works of art or nature, etc.

In this reciprocal exaltation of the faculties of the mind and heart, we can recognize all the predominance of the initiative that belongs to the former. The feelings emanating from this source are distinguished above all by the characteristics of persistence and depth that belong to them or that they acquire in reflection itself, and in the assiduous contemplation of the ideas to which they are bound. It is in this way that the all-powerful will has, in order to maintain them unchangeable, and even to produce them, a *mediate* influence, derived from the one that it exerts *immediately* on the production of its ideas themselves, as well as on the memory or the relation of their signs.

3. There are mixed passions or sentiments that belong equally to two orders of faculties and, so to speak, to two different lives, without us always being able to determine to which of the two the initiative or predominance belongs, since they work together towards a common product. Such is, for example, the mixed sentiment of *love*, in which the senses borrow from the imagination, and the imagination from the senses, love as the attraction, the invisible charm, covering the object loved, in which the physical and the moral, woven together in the same chain, are held together, touch each other at all points, and cannot be separated from each other.

It is always, thus, in the points of contact of the two sorts of life, and in their equal or common participation, that our sweetest, our most ineffable joys are to be found.[23] So many sympathetic affects that are immediate and inapperceived in themselves react powerfully on all the faculties of the mind! And how much these affections manage to exalt the latter in turn!...

In the class of mixed sentiments or passions, we have to place also all the passions that, born from a certain state of the progress and institutions of the society in which one lives, seem wholly artificial in their development and their complication, although they always have their principle and their more or less profound roots in our sensory nature: such are ambition, glory, love of conquest, the thirst for gold, or greed, etc. To say that these passions are purely artificial is to recognize their primary motives in the imagination and intelligence, directed in a way by education and the chance support of circumstances in society.

But it is no less certain that such a disposition of the organic temperament, and such a fundamental mode of the immediate affections that result from it, corresponds to an appropriate mixed passion or sentiment awaiting the occasion to develop, but which all the activity of thought, all the force of the imagination concentrated on its object, cannot elevate to the tone of a dominant passion, without this sensory predisposition that is its natural principle.

There is more: the artificial passions in question cannot rise to this persistent tone constituting them by any other cause than an analogous disposition of sensibility, accidental first of all, but that becomes fixed, permanent and transformed by habit into a sort of secondary or acquired temperament... It is in this way that after having planted, so to speak, its roots in the organs of internal life, passion can end up by subjugating intelligence and leading thought into the circle of the same images. Everything would seem therefore to return into the fatal laws of the organism... But intelligence and will are not yet necessarily slaves, for as long as consciousness has a share in these phenomena. The activity of the will in its principle[24] could still perhaps, by a more energetic determination, interrupt its charm.

---

[23] Who has not felt, for example, the pleasure inspired by the interesting and instructive conversation of friends to whom one is tied by relations of taste and occupation, in the moments, above all, when one satisfies with them a natural need, such as eating or walking, etc? Organic well-being exalts all the more the feelings of the soul and the ideas of the mind, and brings forth a multitude of moments of clarity, of lively and agreeable conceptions ...

[24] How much is this wise maxim true: *principiis obsta*! [Ovid, *Remedia amoris*, v. 91; *The Art of Love and Other Poems,* ed. G. P. Goold (Cambridge, MA: Harvard University Press, 2014), p. 185: 'resist beginnings']. Almost the whole of morality is enclosed in these two words.

4. There is, in the end, a sort of purely moral passion, grounded on a sort of instinct proper to the moral being that is sociable by its very nature, perhaps a quite unreflective instinct in its principle but which, allying itself to the progress of intelligence, is extended, modified, and developed with it, but cannot be replaced, imitated, or even conceived by it. It is here that our moral ideas adopt that affective form, this tinge of sentiment that characterizes them. It is here also that resides the indivisible tie that interposes itself between the naked elements of these ideas, and makes them communicate both to the intuition of the mind and to the sensibility of the heart. Of course, one does not know the nature of these ideas in order to submit them to a cold analysis that would separate and count their elements, and this just as the chemist who applies his reactives to the dissolution of the brute or organic composites has no grasp of the very force of organization or aggregation that had unified these parts in the natural composite.

The moral sense, which is the source of the passions and the sentiments or ideas of which we are speaking, can be characterized in particular as sympathetic. It is the moral sense that, beyond all the artificial causes capable of perverting it, constantly attracts man to man, binds them together by chain of need and pleasure, returns all their common pleasures and their mutual, sacred happiness. It is this that gives rise to all the sweet, expansive passions, all the great and generous sentiments, these vast and sublime ideas that possess the means of public and individual felicity, assure the well-being of the individual, the amelioration and the progress of the species...

Here also is to be found the complete sanction of the *laws of nature*, the sweet and imperious sentiment of *duty*, the pure and celestial pleasure which is always attached to its accomplishment, and the unfailing pain that follows or accompanies its infraction...

But such beautiful and extensive subjects cannot be treated as they should be within a particular question in which they enter only secondarily and as accessories...I end here from respect as much as by necessity...It is enough to recognize the characteristics of *feeling* properly so called – and that it should not be confused with *sensation*, dependent on material objects, nor with any immediate impression of a passive and spontaneous affectability. One should recognize the characteristics of this higher feeling in its inalterability by habit, which ceaselessly withers and changes all our immediate affection, in its constant relations with a reflective activity that gives birth to it, copies it and reproduces it in consciousness, in the particular relations that it bears to the diverse intellectual ideas, and above all with the system of moral ideas, in the

Of the Relations of Apperception, Intuition and Feeling with Notions and Ideas 163

attraction, the charm and the elevation that it communicates to all the products of the intelligence, and finally in the characteristics of fixity and permanence that it assures for the memories of the past that it brings back to life...

* * *

If I could return to the long chain of ideas and facts of which this doubtless over-long essay is composed, I would present a summary that, if it was exact, would contribute to lengthening the volume. This summary, even done well, would not be of much use to me, since I could substitute it for the work as a whole, which, being reduced to its simplest expression, would be more valuable, perhaps, or at least in a more suitable form for an academic essay. I have, however, neither the time nor the strength to retrace my steps, and, after having reached a series of final *equations*, I will have to leave all the terms that I have developed, without being able to make the *reduction* necessary to present clearly, as a result, the solution to the problem.

To conclude, therefore, too quickly perhaps, and, in summarizing roughly what I have written and in a manner that will be vague for those who have not read all the detail that preceded it, I say:

1. there is an *internal immediate apperception that consists neither in repeated observations nor in abstractions from the rules of the faculty of sensing and thinking*, but rather in the primitive fact of our egoity, bound to the free production of the effort that determines the most simple voluntary movement as much as the most elevated intellectual act.
2. *apperception is different to intuition*, as a cause is different to its effect, or as the act itself, immediately apperceived in its free determination, is distinct from its *result*, mediately perceived, or represented outside of the subject or without any consciousness of productive force.
3. finally, the *difference that separates intuition from sensation and from feeling* can be expressed by a sort of metaphysical proportion: what *apperception* is to *intuition, feeling* is to *sensation*.

All the distinctions and details comprised in the terms of the statement of the proposed question are not therefore purely arbitrary or conventional; they are not even taken uniquely in the *analogy of language*, but, above all, in the analogy of the primitive facts of our existence. All are related to the fundamental and real difference that separates, in our inner sense, two opposed states of our mixed being: the one in which it apprehends itself or immediately apperceives itself as *cause* of what it does, and the one in which it is and immediately feels itself a passive effect, dependent as well as modified, by some foreign cause that modifies it...

Notes

Introduction

*   'The essay on "immediate apperception"' and 'Maine de Biran and his main philosophical interlocutors' are by Alessandra Aloisi; 'Maine de Biran's life and works' and 'Maine de Biran's legacy' are by Marco Piazza.

i   See V. Cousin, *Cours de Philosophie. Introduction à l'histoire de la philosophie* (Paris: Pichon et Didier, 1828), pp. 25–6.

ii   H. Bergson, 'Compte rendu des *Principes de métaphysique et de psychologie* de Paul Janet', *Revue philosophique*, 44(2), nov. 1897, pp. 526–51, p. 550. In a *Tableau récapitulatif* of French philosophy, Bergson does not hesitate to define Maine de Biran as the 'greatest metaphysician after [...] Descartes and Malebranche', and asks 'if the path opened by this philosopher is not the one on which metaphysics must proceed definitively' (H. Bergson, 'La philosophie française', *La Revue de Paris*, livraison du 15 mai 1915, pp. 236–56).

iii   F. Ravaisson, *La philosophie en France au XIXe siècle. 1867, suivie du Rapport sur le prix Victor Cousin. (Le scepticisme dans l'antiquité).* 1884 (Paris: Hachette, 1885), pp. 17, 275.

iv   See M. Henry, *Philosophie et phénomenologie du corps. Essai sur l'ontologie biranienne* (Paris: PUF, 1965), *Philosophy and Phenomenology of the Body*, trans. G. Etzkorn (The Hague: Martinus Nijhoff, 1975); P. Ricoeur, *Soi-même comme un autre* (Paris, Seuil, 1990), pp. 371–2, *Oneself as Another*, trans. K. Blamey (Chicago, IL, and London: University of Chicago Press, 1992), pp. 320–1. Gilbert Romeyer-Dherbey goes in the same direction with his *Maine de Biran ou le penseur de l'immanence radicale* (Paris: Seghers, 1974).

v   On this subject, see M. Piazza, 'Fra camere e torri, in vista di se stessi. Maine de Biran, Xavier de Maistre e Henri Beyle', in M. Bettetini and S. Poggi (eds.), *I viaggi dei filosofi* (Milan: Raffaello Cortina, 2010), pp. 159–76.

vi   The most recent organic analysis of the Biranian philosophy of individuality is contained in Anne Devarieux, *Maine de Biran. L'individualité persévérante* (Grenoble: Editions Jérôme Millon, 2004) (on *effort*, see pp. 130–50).

vii   J. Gérard, *La philosophie de Maine de Biran. Essai suivi de fragments inédits* (Paris: Librairie Germer Baillière, 1876), p. 73.

viii   Maine de Biran published only three texts in his lifetime: *Influence de l'habitude sur la faculté de penser* (Paris: Heinrichs, an XI-1802), *The Influence of Habit on* the *Faculty of Thinking*, trans. M. Donaldson Bohem (Baltimore: Williams & Wilkins, 1929; new ed.: Westport, Conn.: Greenwood Press, 1970); the *Examen des leçons de philosophie de M. Laromiguière* (Paris: Fournier, 1817), 120, pp. In-8 °, anonymous; and the short *Exposition de la doctrine philosophique de Leibniz* (Paris: Michaud, 1819), published simultaneously within the *Leibniz* entry in the *Biographie universelle ancienne et moderne* by Michaud, t. XXIII, pp. 603–26. Among these three texts, the only one of a certain amplitude, by subject matter as well as by number of pages, is the essay on habit, which Maine de Biran had to publish as a result of winning the competition.

ix   H. Gouhier, *Les Conversions de Maine de Biran* (Paris: Vrin, 1947, published 1948), p. 22.

x   See Maine de Biran, *Correspondance avec Ampère*, in *Œuvres*, t. XIII/1, A. Robinet and N. Bruyère (eds.) (Paris: Vrin, 1993) and *Correspondance philosophique (1766–1804)*, in *Œuvres*, t. XIII/2, A. Robinet and N. Bruyère (eds.) (Paris: Vrin, 1996).

xi   In addition to the essay on the *Influence de l'habitude sur la faculté de penser*, awarded by the 'Classe des Sciences morales et politiques' of the Institut de France in 1802 and to the essay *De l'aperception immédiate*, the first English translation of which is given here, see also the essay *Sur la décomposition de la pensée*, awarded by the Section of History and Ancient Literature of the same Institut in 1805, and the essay on the *Rapports du physique et du moral de l'homme*, awarded by the Academy of Copenhagen in 1811. The number of essays presented at the 'Société médicale de Bergerac', which was founded Maine de Biran together with a group of doctors, surgeons and health officials, and of which he was elected president, is also relevant: cf. Maine de Biran, *Œuvres*, t. V.

xii   See Maine de Biran, *Œuvres*, t. X/2, p. 15.

xiii   The text was first published by Victor Cousin in the third volume of his edition of Maine de Biran's *Œuvres philosophiques* (Paris: Ladrange, 1841). Three critical editions of this work are available: one by José Echeverria (Paris: Vrin, 1963), one by Ives Radrizzani (as volume V of the *Œuvres* of Maine de Biran, edited by F. Azouvi: Paris: Vrin, 1995), and one by Anne Devarieux (Paris: Le Livre de Poche, 2005).

xiv   See the section below, on Biran's main philosophical interlocutors.

xv   Maine de Biran, *Of Immediate Apperception*, p. 66. Page numbers refer to the present English edition.

xvi   See E. Bonnot de Condillac, *Traité des sensations*, part I, chap. I, § 2, in *Oeuvres philosophiques de Condillac*, G. Le Roy (ed.), *Corpus général des philosophes français*, Paris, 1947–1951, t. I, p. 224a, *Treatise on the Sensations*,

Notes

167

trans. G. Carr (Los Angeles: University of Southern California School of Philosophy, 1930), p. 3.

xvii   See X. Bichat, *Recherches physiologiques sur la vie et la mort* (Paris: Brosson, Gabon et Cie, 1799), *Physiological Researches on Life and Death*, trans. F. Gold (London: Longman, 1815), part I, ch. IX, § 2, p. 135.

xviii See M. Piazza, 'La morale sensitiva e il journal d'une oeuvre. Maine de Biran e il suo *Journal*', *Intersezioni*, 19/1999, pp. 269–81, and *Il governo di sé. Tempo, corpo e scrittura in Maine de Biran.*

xix   See Maine de Biran, 'Fragments sur les fondements de la morale et de la religion', in *Œuvres*, t. X/1, *Dernière philosophie: morale et religion*, M. de Launay (ed.) (Paris: Vrin, 1987), pp. 107–28.

xx   See Gouhier, *Les conversions de Maine de Biran*, pp. 108–82.

xxi   See Maine de Biran, *Correspondance philosophique (1766–1804)*.

xxii   See p. 45. On the presence of Locke in the thought of Maine de Biran, see L. Even, *Maine de Biran critique de Locke* (Louvain-La-Neuve: Éditions de l'Institut Supérieur de Philosophie, 1983).

xxiii See pp. 45–46.

xxiv   See pp. 46–47.

xxv   See pp. 47–48.

xxvi   See p. 52.

xxvii See pp. 53–54.

xxviii See p. 53.

xxix   See p. 54.

xxx   See p. 55.

xxxi   See F. Azouvi and D. Bourel, *De Königsberg à Paris. La réception de Kant en France (1788–1804)* (Paris: Vrin, 1991); L. Fedi, *Kant, une passion française 1795–1940* (Hildesheim: Olms, 2018).

xxxii 1740–1814. Often referred to as 'Ancillon père' to distinguish him from his son, Johann Peter Friedrich (Jean Pierre Frédéric) Ancillon (1767–1837), in turn referred to by some as 'Ancillon fils', also a member of the Berlin Academy.

xxxiii See L. F. Ancillon, *Mémoire sur les fondements de la métaphysique*, in *Mémoires de l'Académie royale des science set des belles-lettres depuis l'avénement de Fréderic Guillaume II au trône, 1799–1800, Classe de philosophie speculative* (Berlin: Decker, 1803), pp. 95–148; Azouvi, Bourel, *De Königsberg à Paris*, pp. 41–53 (where excerpts from Ancillon père's essay are reported).

xxxiv See N. E. Truman, *Maine de Biran's Philosophy of Will* (New York: The Macmillan Company; London: Macmillan, 1904 p. 17. See also: M. Piazza and D. Vincenti, 'The Self-Apperception and the Knower as Agent: An Introduction to Maine de Biran's *Notes* about Kant', *Philosophical Inquiries*, 4(1), 2016, pp.

103–14. Here (pp. 117–34), the reader can also find an English translation of Biran's *Note on Kant's Antinomies* and *Notes on Kant's Philosophy*, both included in Maine de Biran, *Oeuvres*, t. XI/2, *Commentaires et marginalia: dix-huitième siècle*, ed. B. Baertschi (Paris: Vrin, 1993), pp. 127–45 (endnotes pp. 312–18).

xxxv   See M. Vallois, *La formation de l'influence kantienne en France* (Paris: Alcan [1924]), p. 245.

xxxvi   See p. 107.

xxxvii   See Azouvi, *Maine de Biran*, pp. 249–50.

xxxviii   See Truman, *Maine de Biran's Philosophy of Will*, p. 17.

xxxix   Truman, *Maine de Biran's Philosophy of Will*.

xl   L. S. Stebbing, *Pragmatism and French Voluntarism. With especial reference to the Notion of Truth in the Development of French Philosophy from Maine de Biran to Professor Bergson* (Cambridge: Cambridge University Press, 1914).

xli   A. Kuehtmann, *Maine de Biran. Ein Beitrag zur Geschichte der Metaphysik und der Psychologie des Willens* (Bremen: M. Nössler, 1901); A. Lang, *Maine de Biran und die neuere Philosophie. Ein Beitrag zur Geschichte des Kausalproblems* (Köln a. Rh.: J. P. Bachem [1901]).

xlii   G. Amendola, *Maine de Biran. Quattro lezioni tenute alla Biblioteca filosofica di Firenze nei giorni 14, 17, 21 e 24 gennaio 1911* (Florence: La rinascita del libro, 1911).

xliii   L. Ventura, *La teoria della conoscenza in Maine de Biran* (Milan-Rome-Naples: Società Editrice Dante Alighieri, 1915).

xliv   Maine de Biran, *Œuvres*, ed. F. Azouvi, 13 vols (Paris: Vrin, 1984–2001).

xlv   See F. Azouvi, *Maine de Biran. La science de l'homme* (Paris: Vrin, 1995); A. Antoine, *Maine de Biran. Sujet et politique* (Paris: PUF, 1999); Anne Devarieux, *Maine de Biran*.

xlvi   Gouhier, *Les Conversions de Maine de Biran*.

xlvii   A. Huxley, 'Variations on a Philosopher', in *Themes and Variations* (London: Chatto & Windus, 1950), pp. 1–152.

xlviii   Maine de Biran, *Journal, édition intégrale publiée par H. Gouhier*, 3 vols (Neuchâtel: Éditions de la Baconnière, 1954–1957).

xlix   See M. Piazza, *Il governo di sé. Tempo, corpo e scrittura in Maine de Biran* (Milan: Unicopli, 2001).

l   See P. Vermeren, *Victor Cousin. Le jeu de la philosophie et de l'état* (Paris: L'Harmattan, 1995), pp. 39, 48.

li   See Vermeren, *Victor Cousin*, pp. 208–9; V. Cousin, 'Préface de l'éditeur', in *Nouvelles considérations sur les rapports du physique et du moral de l'homme. Ouvrage posthume de M. Maine de Biran*, publié par M. Cousin (Paris: Ladrange, 1834), pp. I–XLII.

Notes

lii   See Vermeren, *Victor Cousin*, p. 47.

liii   See Vermeren, *Victor Cousin*, p. 208.

liv   F. Ravaisson, *De l'Habitude* (Paris: Fourinier, 1838); *Of Habit*, preface C. Malabou, eds. C. Carlisle and M. Sinclair (London: Continuum, 2008).

lv   F. Ravaisson, 'Philosophie contemporaine – Fragments de philosophie par M. Hamilton', *Revue des Deux Mondes*, t. 24, 1840, pp. 396–427, particularly pp. 416, 420; 'Contemporary Philosophy', trans. J. Dunham in *Selected Essays*, ed. M. Sinclair (London: Bloomsbury, 2016), pp. 59–83, particularly pp. 73, 76.

lvi   See F. Ravaisson, 'Philosophie contemporaine – Fragments de philosophie par M. Hamilton', p. 422, 'Contemporary Philosophy', p. 78.

lvii   F. Ravaisson, *La philosophie en France au dix-neuvième siècle, 1867, suivi de Rapport sur le Prix Victor Cousin (Le scepticisme dans l'antiquité), 1894* (Paris: Hachette, 1895), p. 178.

lviii   H. Bergson, 'Cours du Collège de France, «Les théories de la volonté»', in *Mélanges* (Paris: PUF, 1972), p. 688.

lix   See H. Bergson, review of 'Principes de métaphysique et de psychologie. Par Paul Janet', *Revue philosophique de la France et de l'Étranger*, nov. 1897, pp. 525–51, p. 550.

lx   See H. Gouhier, 'Maine de Biran et Bergson' (1948), in *Études sur l'histoire des idées en France depuis le XVIIe siècle* (Paris: Vrin, 1980), pp. 97–125, p. 120.

lxi   See Anne Devarieux, 'Henri Bergson ou la « seconde vie » de l'effort biranien', in S. Abiko, H. Fujita and Y. Sugimura (eds.), *Considérations inactuelles. Bergson et la philosophie française du XIXe siècle* (Hildesheim: Georg Olms Verlag AG, 2017), pp. 21–44, p. 29.

lxii   See L. Lavelle, *Le moi et son destin* (Paris: Aubier, 1936), p. 15; *Les puissances du moi* (Paris: Flammarion, 1948), p. 179. On Lavelle as Maine de Biran's interpreter, see Anne Devarieux, 'Puissance(s) du moi: Louis Lavelle et Maine de Biran', *Laval théologique et philosophique*, 69(1), 2013, pp. 35–56.

lxiii   See L. Lavelle, *L'erreur de Narcisse* (Paris: Table ronde, 2003), p. 39.

lxiv   L. Lavelle, *De l'Acte* (Paris: Aubier, 1992), p. 20.

lxv   See Maine de Biran, *Essai sur les fondements de la psychologie*, in *Œuvres*, tt. VII/1-2, F.C.T. Moore (ed.) (Paris: Vrin, 2001), t. VII/1, p. 39.

lxvi   M. Henry, 'Phénoménologie non-intentionnelle: une tâche de la phénoménologie à venir', in D. Janicaud (ed.), *L'intentionnalité en question. Entre phénoménologie et sciences cognitives* (Paris: Vrin, 1995), pp. 383–97, reprinted in M. Henry, *Phénoménologie de la vie. Tome I: De la phénoménologie* (Paris: PUF, 2003), pp. 105–21, p. 105; 'Qu'est-ce que cela que nous appelons la vie?', *Philosophiques*, 5(1), 1978, pp. 133–50, reprinted in *Phénoménologie de la vie. Tome I: De la phénoménologie*, pp. 39–57, p. 51.

Notes

lxvii See Devarieux, *Puissance(s) du moi: Louis Lavelle et Maine de Biran*, pp. 55–6.

lxviii Henry, *Philosophie et phénoménologie du corps*, p. 12, trans., p. 8.

lxix See K. Mrówka, 'La philosophie biranienne du corps propre dans les intérpretations contemporaines', *Organon*, 33, 2004, pp. 83–91, p. 84.

lxx François Azouvi reconstructed how Maine de Biran derived the expression *'le corps propre'* ('one's own body') from Lelarge de Lignac in order to understand the inner space perceived by the ego in internal apperception: see F. Azouvi, 'Genèse du corps propre chez Malebranche, Condillac, Lelarge de Lignac et Maine de Biran', *Archives de Philosophie*, 45(1), 1982, pp. 85–107, p. 97. A concise definition is contained in the annotations on Lignac drawn up by Maine de Biran in 1815: see Maine de Biran, 'Notes sur quelques passages de l'Abbé de Lignac', in *Œuvres*, t. XI/2, *Commentaires et marginalia: dix-huitième siècle*, B. Baertschi (ed.) (Paris: Vrin, 1993), pp. 59–81, p. 73. In the essay *De l'aperception immediate*, the idea of the 'interior space of one's own body' appears for the first time in the work of Biran. This demonstrates the familiarity of Maine de Biran with the technical significance attributed to this expression well before he wrote the commentary on the work of Lignac, as Azouvi recognizes ('Genèse du corps propre chez Malebranche, Condillac, Lelarge de Lignac et Maine de Biran', p. 98).

lxxi See Henry, *Philosophie et phénoménologie du corps*, p. 84, trans., p. 61.

lxxii Henry, *Philosophie et phénoménologie du corps*, p. 174, trans. p. 126.

lxxiii Henry, *Philosophie et phénoménologie du corps*, p. 176, trans. p. 127.

lxxiv Bruaire, *Philosophie du corps* (Paris: Seuil, 1968), p. 149.

lxxv Bruaire, *Philosophie du corps*, p. 145.

lxxvi Bruaire, *Philosophie du corps*, p. 145.

lxxvii Bruaire, *Philosophie du corps*, p. 153 (italics in the original).

lxxviii Bruaire, *Philosophie du corps*, pp. 153–4.

lxxix M. Merleau-Ponty, *L'union de l'âme et du corps chez Malebranche, Biran et Bergson*. Notes recueillies et rédigées par Jean Deprun. Nouvelle éditon revue et augmentée d'un fragment inédit (Paris: Vrin, 1978), pp. 47–8, trans. P. B. Milan, *The Incarnate Subject. Malebranche, Biran, and Bergson on the Union of the Body and Soul* (Amherst, NY: Humanity Books, 2001), p. 62.

lxxx Merleau-Ponty, *L'union de l'âme et du corps*, p. 48, trans. p. 62.

lxxxi Merleau-Ponty, *L'union de l'âme et du corps*, pp. 50–1, trans. p. 64.

lxxxii Merleau-Ponty, *L'union de l'âme et du corps*, p. 50, trans. p. 64.

lxxxiii Merleau-Ponty, *L'union de l'âme et du corps*, pp. 50–1, trans. p. 64.

lxxxiv Merleau-Ponty, *L'union de l'âme et du corps*, p. 51, trans. p. 65.

lxxxv Merleau-Ponty, *L'union de l'âme et du corps*, p. 66, trans. p. 76.

lxxxvi Merleau-Ponty, *L'union de l'âme et du corps*, p. 75, trans. p. 83.

lxxxvii Merleau-Ponty, *L'union de l'âme et du corps*, p. 56, trans. p. 68.

lxxxviii B. Baertschi, *L'Ontologie de Maine de Biran* (Fribourg: Editions universitaires, 1982), p. 1.

lxxxix Baertschi, *L'Ontologie*, pp. 1–2.

xc Baertschi, *L'Ontologie*, pp. 4–5.

xci Baertschi, *L'Ontologie*, p. 211.

xcii Baertschi, *L'Ontologie*, pp. 198, 88.

xciii Baertschi, *L'Ontologie*, p. 433; the quote is taken from Henry, *Philosophie et phénoménologie du corps*, p. 12; trans. p. 8.

xciv Baertschi, *L'Ontologie*, p. 433.

Of Immediate Apperception

i Ovid, *Tristia*, book I, poem III, v. 12.

ii H. Boerhaave, *Praelectiones academicae de morbis nervorum* (Lugduni Batavorum: van der Eyck & Pecker, 1761).

iii Hippocrates, *De alimento*, liber XXIII.

Second Part

i Approximate quotation from Montaigne, *Essais*, trans. *The Essays of Montaigne*, by E. J. Trechmann, New York/London: Oxford University Press, 1946, book I, chapter XXI.

ii X. Bichat, *Recherches physiologiques sur la vie et la mort* (Paris: Brosson, Gabon et Cie, 1799), trans. *Physiological Researches on Life and Death*, ed. F. Gold (London: Longman, 1815), part I, ch. IX, § 2, p. 135.

iii G. E. Stahl, *Theoria medica vera*, Halae: literis Orphanotrophei, 1708, *Physiologia*, section V, *De sensu*, t. I, p. 283. ['It keeps an active watch'].

iv Buffon, *Histoire naturelle des animaux*, in *Œuvres philosophiques de Buffon*, ed. Piveteau (Paris: PUF, 1954), pp. 337b–338a, trans. *Buffon's Natural History*, t. 5 (London, 1797), pp. 55–6.

v J. Locke, *An Essay Concerning Human Understanding*, ed. R. Woolhouse (London: Penguin, 1997), Book II, cap. XXVII, § 9.

vi Enormôn (ἐνορμῶν) is attested in Hippocrates' *Epidemics* (6.8.7). The Greek word comes from ἐνορμ-άω, meaning 'to rush in', and is generally rendered in Latin as *impetum faciens*, which conveys a similar sense of motion. We might translate *enormôn* and *impetum faciens* as 'life force' or 'vital impulse'.

vii Lucretius, *De rerum natura*, trans. A. Stallings, *The Nature of Things* (London: Penguin, 2007), book II, v. 254.

viii	J.-B. Mérian, 'Seconde dissertation ontologique sur l'action, la puissance et la liberté', pp. 486–97.
ix	See Locke, Essay, Book II, chap. XXI, § 30.
x	See E. B. de Condillac, *Essai sur l'origine des connaissances humanines*, Part I, Section I, chapter I, §1, in *Oeuvres philosophiques de Condillac*, t. I, p. 6a, trans. *Essay on the Origin of Human Knowledge*, H. Aarsleff (ed.) (Cambridge: Cambridge University Press, 2001), p. 11.
xi	See D. Hume, *An Enquiry Concerning Human Understanding*, T.L. Beauchamp (ed.) (Oxford: Oxford University Press, 2014), section VII, part I.

Second Section

i	G. E. Stahl, *Theoria medica vera, Physiologia*, section V, De sensu, t. I, p. 284.
ii	Porphyry, *Sententiae ad intelligibilia ducentes* (Leipzig: Teubner, 1975), 15, p. 7: 'Memory is not the keeper of images, but the faculty capable of bringing forth new designs from things previously conceived by the mind.'
iii	See B. Franklin, *Experiments and Observations on Electricity made at Philadelphia in America* (London, 1751).

Index

Aloisi, A., 165
Amendola, G., 14, 168
Ampère, A.-M., 3, 15
Anaxagoras, 85, 90
Ancillon, J.P.F., 167
Ancillon, L.F., 13, 41, 167
Archimedes, 154
Aristotle, 47, 50, 54
Azouvi, F., 14, 167, 168, 170

Bacon, F., 27, 28, 29, 32, 42, 62, 69
Baertschi, B., 19, 20, 170, 171
Barrow, I., 155
Barthez, J., 77
Bergson, H., 1, 16, 17, 18, 20, 165, 169
Berkeley, G., 126
Bichat, X., 6, 92, 97, 167, 171
Boerhaave, H., 61, 171
Bonaparte, N., 2
Bonnaterre, P.J., 135
Bonnet, Ch., 88, 149
Bourel, D., 167
Bouterwek, F., 94
Bruaire, C., 18, 170
Buffon, G.-L. Leclerc, Comte de, 77, 119, 148, 171
Butini, J.A., 88

Cabanis, P.J.G., 10, 42, 94
Cavalieri, B.F., 155
Condillac, É. Bonnot de, 1, 2, 4, 5, 6, 9, 10, 11, 14, 15, 16, 28, 29, 33, 35, 36, 39, 44, 51, 55, 60, 64, 65, 71, 78, 80, 88, 89, 104, 110, 111, 112, 113, 126, 132, 146, 148, 149, 154, 159, 166, 172
Corneille, P., 154
Cousin, V., 1, 15, 16, 165, 166, 168
Cureau de La Chambre, M., 151
Cuvier, F., 15
Cuvier, G., 15

Descartes, R., 4, 11, 53, 54, 86, 98, 105, 106, 159, 165
Destutt de Tracy, A.-L.-C., 3, 9, 10, 14, 36, 59, 69, 89, 94, 122, 145, 149
Devarieux, A., 17, 20, 165, 166, 168, 169
Dromelet, C., 20

Echeverria, J., 166
Elisabeth of Bohemia, 159
Engel, J.J., 106
Euclid, 56
Even, L., 167

Fedi, L., 167
Fichte, J.G., 94
Franklin, B., 153, 172

Gérando, J.-M. de, 15, 85, 94
Gérard, J., 3, 165
Gouhier, H., 3, 8, 14, 166, 167, 168, 169
Grealis, C., 20

Hartley, D., 149
Henry, M., 1, 17, 19, 20, 165, 169, 170, 171
Hippocrates, 61, 171
Hobbes, Th., 21, 146
Hume, D., 7, 103, 104, 105, 126, 172
Huxley, A., 14, 168

Kant, I., 4, 12, 13, 37, 38, 51, 54, 80, 113
Kepler, J., 153, 154, 155
Kuehtmann, A., 14, 168

Lang, A., 14, 168
Laromiguière, P., 15
Lavelle, L., 17, 169
Lavoisier, A.-L. de, 28
Leibniz, G.W., 4, 11, 12, 15, 45, 50, 52, 53, 54, 55, 56, 61, 86, 91, 107, 110, 113, 119, 130, 155, 159
Lelarge de Lignac, J.-A., 170
L'Épée, Ch.-M. de, 138

Leroux, P., 15
Locke, J., V, 4, 11, 29, 44, 45, 46, 47, 49, 50,
    51, 53, 54, 71, 80, 89, 90, 91, 92, 98, 110,
    111, 122, 146, 159, 167, 171, 172
Louis XIII, 151
Louis XVI, 2
Louis XVIII, 2
Lucretius, 133, 171
Lyonnet, P., 148

Malebranche, N. de, 1, 54, 106, 109, 110,
    111, 165
Mérian, J.-B., 90, 134, 171
Merleau-Ponty, M., 17, 18, 170
Montaigne, M. de, 73, 171
Mrówka, K., 170

Newton, I., 153, 154, 155

Ovid, 161, 171

Piazza, M., 165, 167, 168
Pinel, Ph., 78
Plato, 54
Porphyry, 148, 172
Prévost, P., 39

Pythagoras, 154

Radrizzani, I., 20, 166
Ravaisson, F., 1, 16, 17, 18, 165, 169
Reid, Th., 102
Rey Régis, J.-J. (Cazillac), 108
Ricoeur, P., 1, 165
Romeyer-Dherbey, G., 165
Rousseau, J.-J., 6, 75
Royer-Collard, P.-P. 15

Schelling, F.W.J., 4, 94
Smith, A., 102
Stahl, G.E., 87, 98, 124, 171, 172
Stebbing, S., 14, 168
Stewart, D., 151
Suabedissen, D.T.A., 4

Truman, N.E., 14, 167, 168

Vallois, M., 168
Vancourt, R., 19
Ventura, L., 14, 168
Vermeren, P., 168
Vida, M.G., 74
Vincenti, D., 167

CPSIA information can be obtained
at www.ICGtesting.com
Printed in the USA
LVHW081536101221
705865LV00017B/1829